Solutions

Intermediate Student's Book

English Language Academy
9, Tower lane, Sliema SLM 1611, Malta
Telephone: +356 2134 6264
Fax: +356 2133 9656
E-mail: info@elamalta.com
http://www.elamalta.com

OXFORD
UNIVERSITY PRESS

m Falla   Paul A Davies

UNIT	A VOCABULARY AND LISTENING	B GRAMMAR	C CULTURE
1 Caught on Camera	p4 Fashion Describing clothes (*spotty, tight, lacy,* etc.); Clothes (*fleece, leggings, v-neck,* etc.); Compound adjectives (*short-sleeved,* etc.) Grammar: order of adjectives 🎧 Radio fashion commentary	p5 Present tense contrast Dynamic and state verbs (*feel, look,* etc.)	p6 Big Brother Looking out for you? 🎧 Opinions on CCTV cameras
	Get Ready for your Exam 1 p12 • **Listening** Multiple-choice statements • **Speaking** Picture comparison • **Use of English** Multiple-choice gapfill • **Reading** Multiple matching • **Writing** An informal letter		
2 Looking back	p14 How did you feel? Feelings (*afraid, proud, upset,* etc.) Noun formation from verbs and adjectives (*happy, happiness,* etc.) 🎧 Talking about feelings	p15 Past tense contrast	p16 Remembering the past Vocabulary: words about war 🎧 Remembrance Day Project: anniversary announcement
	• Language Review Units 1–2 p22 • Skills Round-up Units 1–2 p23		
3 A good job	p24 The world of work Describing activites at work, hours and pay Describing work (*stressful, menial, rewarding,* etc.) Agent nouns: *-er, -or, -ist, -ant, -ian;* Useful phrases with *work* 🎧 Radio job advertisements	p25 Defining relative clauses *who, whose, where, which* and *that*	p26 Education for life? University in the UK Vocabulary: phrasal verbs: separable 🎧 A university education
	Get Ready for your Exam 2 p32 • **Reading** Missing sentences • **Use of English** Cloze gapfill • **Speaking** Situational role-play • **Listening** Matching statements to speakers • **Speaking** Picture comparison		
4 Body and mind	p34 The human body Parts of the body (*chin, hip, waist,* etc.) 🎧 Idioms with parts of the body (*pulling my leg,* etc.) Inside the body (*bone, lungs, vein,* etc.)	p35 Past simple and present perfect contrast Time expressions (*yesterday, this morning, yet,* etc.)	p36 Public health? A healthy appetite? Vocabulary: food and nutrition (*calories, fibre, vitamins,* etc.) 🎧 Health issues Vocabulary: legal collocations (*pass a law,* etc.) Pronunciation: compound nouns
	• Language Review Units 3–4 p42 • Skills Round-up Units 1–4 p43		
5 Tomorrow's world	p44 Computing Computing (*app, username, network,* etc.) Grammar: zero conditional 🎧 In a computer shop Pronunciation: abbreviations Noun prefixes (*auto-, ex-,* etc.)	p45 Speculating and predicting *could, may, might, will* First conditional	p46 Time capsules 🎧 Time capsules in New York Project: Time capsule
	Get Ready for your Exam 3 p52 • **Reading** True/False statements • **Use of English** Word formation gapfill • **Speaking** Debate • **Listening** Matching • **Writing** An announcement		
6 Mystery	p54 Crime at the manor Compound nouns 🎧 Interview with a police officer Vocabulary: Easily confused words	p55 Reported speech (statements) *say* and *tell*	p56 Crime writers 🎧 A crime story
	• Language Review Units 5–6 p62 • Skills Round-up Units 1–6 p63		
7 Real relationships	p64 Relationships Dating and relationships 🎧 Talking about couples; Time expressions (*after that …, the same day …* etc.); Three-part phrasal verbs	p65 Comparison Comparative and superlative adverbs *Less* and *least* Superlatives and the present perfect Comparatives, clauses and simple nouns Double comparatives	p66 Love poems Love's secret One Perfect Rose 🎧 The life of William Blake Vocabulary: idioms with *heart* and *head*
	Get Ready for your Exam 4 p72 • **Reading** Multiple-choice • **Speaking** Picture-based discussion • **Use of English** Cloze gapfill • **Listening** True/False • **Speaking** Picture description		
8 Globetrotters	p74 Getting from A to B Useful adjectives (*cheap, slow,* etc.) Travel compound nouns (*buffet car, hard shoulder,* etc.) Pronunciation: word stress 🎧 Travel locations	p75 The passive	p76 Explorers A British Tradition Vocabulary: expedition adjectives (*gruelling, intrepid,* etc.) Phrasal verbs: *set off, look up to,* etc. 🎧 Captain Scott's last expedition
	• Language Review Units 7–8 p82 • Skills Round-up Units 1–8 p83		
9 Money, money, money!	p84 Money and payment Money and payment (*bargains, till,* etc.) 🎧 Talking about shopping; Prepositions: *shop for, sold out,* etc. Banking (*PIN number, direct debit,* etc.)	p85 *have something done* Reflexive pronouns	p86 Advertising Product placement Vocabulary: advertising (*brand, slogan,* etc.) 🎧 Opinions on advertising
	Get Ready for your Exam 5 p92 • **Listening** Short-answer questions • **Use of English** Multiple-choice gapfill • **Speaking** Situational role-play • **Reading** Multiple matching • **Writing** A formal letter		
10 Be creative	p94 Performers Musical performers (*busker, string quartet,* etc.) Describing music (*beat, solo,* etc.) Artists and artistic activities 🎧 Musical performances	p95 Participle clauses	p96 Music festivals Vocabulary: compound nouns 🎧 Talking about festivals
	• Language Review Units 9–10 p102 • Skills Round-up Units 9–10 p103		

GET READY FOR B2 EXAMS 1&2 p104 GRAMMAR BUILDER AND REFERENCE p108 VOCABULARY BUILDER p127
🎧 Listening (1.01 = disk 1, track 1 / 2.01 = disk 2, track 1)

D GRAMMAR	**E** READING	**F** SPEAKING	**G** WRITING
p7 Verb patterns Verb + infinitive or *-ing* form Verbs that change their meaning (*hate*, *hate to*, etc.)	p8 Eyeborg Hearing colours Vocabulary: adjective prefixes: *un-, dis-, in-, im-, il-* and *ir-*	p10 Photo description 🎧 Talking about a photo Vocabulary: expressions with *look* (*look like*, *look as if*, etc.)	p11 An informal letter Vocabulary: informal phrases in letters
p17 *used to* Pronunciation: *used to*	p18 Amnesia Identity crisis 🎧 Song: Ugly	p20 Narrating events Grammar: Exclamatory sentences (*How interesting!*, etc.) Vocabulary: phrases for structuring a story *-ed/-ing* adjectives	p21 Narrative Narrative time expressions (*last summer...* etc.) Phrasal verbs (*get on*, *take off*, etc.)
p27 Non-defining relative clauses	p28 Reversing roles A man's world?; Woman's work? Vocabulary: jobs and noun gender	p30 A job interview Grammar and pronunciation: Question tags Vocabulary: qualities needed for jobs 🎧 Job interviews	p31 A job application Vocabulary: forms of address in formal letters
p37 Present perfect continuous Present perfect simple or present perfect continuous?	p38 All in the mind Mind over matter? Vocabulary: homonyms (*mind*, *trip*, etc.) Grammar: clauses expressing purpose	p40 At the doctor's Vocabulary: symptoms (*dizzy*, *swollen*, etc.) Giving advice (*If I were you ..., In your position, I would ...*, etc..) 🎧 Seeing the doctor Pronunciation: giving advice	p41 An announcement Grammar: rhetorical questions
p47 Future perfect and future continuous	p48 Visions of the future Fifty years on Vocabulary: verb + noun collocations	p50 Talking about plans Grammar: *will, going to, may/might* and present continuous Vocabulary: making, accepting and declining suggestions (*Shall we...?* etc.) 🎧 Weekend plans	p51 An informal email Grammar: verbs followed by infinitives and clauses Conjunctions/future time clauses (*when, as soon as, until*, etc.)
p57 Reported speech (questions)	p58 Who was he? Kaspar Hauser Vocabulary: phrasal verbs: inseparable	p60 Speculating about events Grammar: *must have, could have, might have, can't have* Vocabulary: reacting to speculations (*No way!, I doubt it*, etc.) 🎧 Speculating about news reports Pronunciation: speculating about events	p61 A formal letter: asking for information Grammar: indirect questions, verbs with two objects
p67 Talking about imaginary situations Second conditional *I wish, If only, I'd rather*	p68 Love on the Internet Can science help you to find love? Vocabulary: noun + preposition combinations 🎧 Song: This ain't a love song	p70 Stimulus description Vocabulary: adjectives to describe venues (*crowded, romantic*, etc.) Expressing contrast (*however, whereas*) Pronunciation: expressing contrast	p71 For and against essay Vocabulary: presenting arguments
p77 Indefinite pronouns: *some-, any-, no-, every-*	p78 A year away Travelling with friends Vocabulary and pronunciation: acronyms	p80 Travel problems Vocabulary: tourism (*campsite, cruise, villa*, etc.) Making a complaint; Pronunciation: complaining 🎧 Holiday complaints	p81 Description of a place Vocabulary: adjectives describing places (*breathtaking, isolated*, etc.) Grammar: introductory *it*
p87 Third conditional Pronunciation: *have*	p88 A charmed life The World's Luckiest Man Vocabulary and pronunciation: preposition + noun phrases 🎧 Song: Doesn't mean anything	p90 Photo description Vocabulary: speculating (*I can't be sure, but ..., It could be that ...*) Vocabulary: giving information and opinions	p91 Opinion essay Structuring an essay Vocabulary: linking words
p97 Determiners: *all, each, very, every, few, little*, etc. Determiner + *of*	p98 Beautiful minds Alonzo Clemons and Richard Wawro Vocabulary: artistic verbs and nouns (*sculpt/sculptor*, etc.)	p100 Stimulus description Grammar: *so* and *such* Pronunciation: giving an opinion Vocabulary: expressing a strong opinion	p101 Book review Nominal subject clauses Vocabulary: describing books and stories

THIS UNIT INCLUDES
Vocabulary ■ describing clothes ■ compound adjectives ■ adjective prefixes
Grammar ■ order of adjectives ■ present tense contrast ■ dynamic and state verbs
■ verb patterns
Speaking ■ discussing the issue of surveillance ■ discussing a disability
■ describing a photograph
Writing ■ an informal letter

1A   VOCABULARY AND LISTENING Fashion

I can describe clothes.

1 **VOCABULARY** Check the meaning of the words in the box. Then make a list of the clothes you can see in the photos, adding one adjective from the box to each.

a shiny dress, a woolly scarf

Describing clothes

Patterns: checked flowery plain spotty stripy
Shape: baggy long loose short tight
Texture: fluffy furry lacy shiny smooth sparkly woolly
Materials: cotton fur leather nylon velvet wool
Other: full-length high-heeled long-sleeved matching short-sleeved

2 **VOCABULARY** The people in the photos were described on a website as Hollywood's worst-dressed celebrities. Do you agree? Give reasons using the adjectives below.

Describing fashion awful beautiful cool cute
elegant gaudy great old-fashioned scruffy smart
stylish trendy

>>> **VOCABULARY BUILDER 1.1: PAGE 127** <<<

3 🎧 1.02 Listen to the radio show. Which two celebrities in the photos are described?

4 🎧 1.02 **PRONUNCIATION** Complete these phrases from the radio show using words from exercise 1. Then listen again, repeat and check.

1 a beautiful, _____, white dress
2 a small, _____ clutch bag
3 a grey, _____ T-shirt
4 very casual _____ dark-blue jeans
5 a smooth, red, _____ jacket
6 a long, brown, _____ scarf
7 shiny, _____ trousersuit
8 _____, black, high-heeled shoes

5 What order do the adjectives in exercise 4 appear in? Complete the rule in the *Learn this!* box with *colour*, *material* and *shape*.

LEARN THIS!

Order of adjectives
When we have more than one adjective before a noun, they usually come in this order:
1 opinion   3 texture
2 size, length or   4 pattern or _____
_____   5

>>> **GRAMMAR BUILDER 1.1: PAGE 108** <<<

6 **SPEAKING** Describe the other two outfits in exercise 1.

He's wearing baggy blue jeans ...

7 **SPEAKING** Ask and answer these questions with a partner. Give reasons for your answers.

1 Do you like buying clothes?
2 Are you interested in fashion?
3 Do you wear fashionable clothes? Why? / Why not?

>>> **VOCABULARY BUILDER 1.2: PAGE 127** <<<

1 SPEAKING Look at the picture of Zoe. What is she doing?

Max	Hey, Zoe. You're always using the computer when I need it! It's so annoying!
Zoe	I'm chatting with Ella.
Ella	Hi, Max. What are you up to?
Max	Oh, hi, Ella. I'm doing my science homework, but I need to look something up on the Internet.
Zoe	Ask Ella. She always comes top of the class in science.
Max	OK, what about this? At what temperature does oxygen change from a gas to a liquid?
Ella	Minus 183° C.
Max	Wow! Thanks, Ella.
Zoe	Hey, Ella, do you fancy seeing *Inception* at the cinema tonight?
Ella	OK. What time does it start?
Zoe	Seven. I'm meeting Jo at 6.45 outside the cinema.
Max	Cool. I love science fiction films. Can I come?
Zoe	No, you can't!

2 🎧 1.03 Read and listen to the dialogue. Underline the examples of the present simple and present continuous forms in the text.

3 Study the examples in the dialogue. Then write *simple* or *continuous* for each use in the chart below. Which two uses refer to the future?

We use the present ...
1 _____ for habits and routines.
2 _____ for something happening now or about now.
3 _____ for describing annoying behaviour (with *always*).
4 _____ for a permanent situation or fact.
5 _____ for arrangements in the future.
6 _____ for timetables and schedules (e.g. cinema programmes).

4 Read the *Learn this!* box and find two examples of state verbs in the dialogue in exercise 1.

> **LEARN THIS!**
>
> **Dynamic and state verbs**
> Dynamic verbs describe actions and can be used in the simple or continuous forms. State verbs describe states or situations, and are not usually used in continuous tenses. Common state verbs include:
> *believe belong forget hate know like love mean need prefer remember understand want*

⟫⟫ GRAMMAR BUILDER 1.2: PAGE 108 ⟪⟪

5 🎧 1.04 Complete the dialogue with the present simple or present continuous form of the verbs in brackets. Listen and check.

Ella	Who ¹_____ (you / phone)?
Zoe	Jo. The film ²_____ (start) in five minutes. She ³_____ (never / arrive) on time. ... Hi, Jo. ⁴_____ (you / come) to see the film? ... OK. She ⁵_____ (just / get off) the bus. She'll be here in a minute.
Ella	Great. What ⁶_____ (you / do) after the film?
Zoe	We ⁷_____ (go) for a pizza. ⁸_____ (you / want) to join us?
Ella	Yes, I ⁹_____ (love) pizza. But the last bus home ¹⁰_____ (leave) at 10.30. I mustn't miss it.
Max	Hi, Zoe. Hi, Ella.
Zoe	What ¹¹_____ (you / do) here, Max?
Max	I'm going to see the film. I ¹²_____ (wait) for Sam. Shall we all sit together?
Zoe	No way!

⟫⟫ GRAMMAR BUILDER 1.3: PAGE 109 ⟪⟪

6 For each verb below write two sentences, one in the present simple and one in the present continuous. Remember that the present continuous can refer to current actions or future arrangements.

go have play speak study wear

My dad goes to work by bus. Tomorrow he's going to work by car.

7 SPEAKING Tell your partner:
1 two things you do every weekend and two things you don't do.
2 two things that are happening in the classroom now.
3 two things you're doing this evening and two things you aren't doing.
4 two facts about yourself or your friends.
5 two things that people are always doing which annoy you.

1 SPEAKING **Look at the photo and answer these questions.**

1 What do Closed-Circuit Television (CCTV) cameras record?
2 Where do you usually find CCTV cameras?

2 🎧 **1.05 Read the text. What sort of text is it?**
a an opinion article   b a narrative   c a description

LOOKING OUT FOR YOU?

Today, there are more than four million CCTV cameras in Britain. That's one camera for every fifteen people. The cameras are there to film dangerous or illegal behaviour. But they don't just watch criminals – they watch almost all of us, almost all of the time. Every time we use a cashpoint machine, travel on public transport or go into a shop, a camera records our actions. Shops say that this technology helps to catch shoplifters – but only by treating everybody as a potential criminal.

Cameras are not the only way of monitoring our actions. Every time you use your mobile phone, the phone company knows the number of the phone you are calling and how long the call lasts. It is even possible to work out your location. The police often use this information when they're investigating serious crimes.

And what about satellites? Are they watching us from space? How much can they see? Anybody with a computer can download 'Google Earth' and get satellite photos of the entire world. Perhaps governments are using even more powerful satellites to watch their citizens.

Even when you are at home, you are not necessarily safe from surveillance. When you use your computer to visit websites, you are probably sending and receiving 'cookies' without realising it. Cookies transfer information from your computer to the website and, in theory, could record which websites you visit. Some cookies, called 'zombie cookies', are very difficult to remove from your computer. Modern technology is making it easier and easier to stay in contact, but it is also making it nearly impossible for us to hide.

3 **Choose the correct answers.**

1 CCTV cameras record the actions of
a one in fifteen people in the UK.
b four million people in the UK.
c all criminals in the UK.
d nearly everybody in the UK.

2 When you use a mobile phone, the company knows
a the name of the person you are speaking to.
b what you are saying.
c how long you have had the phone.
d where you are.

3 The author of the text thinks that governments
a might use 'Google Earth' to help solve crimes.
b might be watching all of us from space.
c might record all of our phone calls.
d might record all of the websites we visit.

4 When you surf the Internet, cookies
a record every letter that you type.
b record your passwords and emails.
c send information to your computer.
d send information to websites.

4 🎧 **1.06 Listen to Martin and Sophie discussing the use of CCTV cameras. Answer the questions.**

1 Who is in favour of CCTV cameras and who is against them?
2 Does either of them change their mind?

5 🎧 **1.06** VOCABULARY **Use the words below to complete the opinions expressed by the speakers. Then listen again and check.**

<u>Crime</u> criminals guilty information police police state safety surveillance technology

1 _____ deters people from committing crime.
2 Personal privacy is more important than catching _____.
3 Public _____ is more important than personal privacy.
4 Surveillance makes everybody feel _____.
5 It's the first step towards a _____.
6 The police might misuse the _____.
7 We rely too much on _____ to solve social problems.
8 More surveillance means the _____ can catch more criminals.

6 Put the sentences in exercise 5 into two groups: *Arguments for CCTV cameras* and *Arguments against CCTV cameras*. In your opinion, which is the strongest argument in each group?

7 SPEAKING **Discuss these questions. Use the arguments in exercise 5 and the phrases below to help you.**

1 Are there a lot of CCTV cameras in your town? Where are they? Why are they there?
2 Do you think CCTV cameras are a good thing or a bad thing? Why? / Why not?

<u>Expressing opinions</u>
I think / don't think ...   In my opinion / view, ...
You can't deny that ...   There's no doubt that ...

1D GRAMMAR Verb patterns
I can identify and use verb patterns.

1 SPEAKING Look at the photo. What do you think the woman's job is?

You can't avoid seeing images of supermodels wherever you go. Their faces are everywhere: on the TV, in magazines and on billboards. They all want to work for big names, like L'Oréal or Gucci, so they spend hours working out in the gym and looking after their appearance. They seem not to mind the attention … but what's it actually like being in the public eye all the time?

2 Read the text about supermodels. Find these verbs. Are they followed by an infinitive or an *-ing* form?

1 avoid _____   3 spend (time) _____
2 want _____   4 seem _____

3 🎧 1.07 Listen to a supermodel talking about her life. Are these sentences true or false?

1 She leads a normal life.
2 She doesn't go out much.
3 A friend of hers had problems with photographers.

4 🎧 1.07 Listen again. Complete the sentences with the correct form of the verbs in brackets.

1 I don't expect _____ a perfectly normal life. (lead)
2 Some models hardly go out and they avoid _____ to clubs and restaurants. (go)
3 They never agree _____ for photos for the paparazzi. (pose)
4 I manage _____ my private life separate from my public life. (keep)
5 I can't imagine _____ any privacy at all – that would be awful. (not have)
6 He couldn't face _____ the villa. (leave)
7 So he ended up _____ in the villa for most of the holiday. (stay)

5 Add the verbs in exercises 2 and 4 to the chart below.

verb + infinitive	verb + *-ing* form
decide, happen, mean promise, …	fancy, feel like, can't help suggest, …

⟫⟫ GRAMMAR BUILDER 1.4: PAGE 110 ⟪⟪

6 Complete the second sentence so that it has the same meaning as the first. Use the verbs in brackets and an infinitive or *-ing* form.

1 Sara thinks that she'll be a model when she's older. (expect)
   Sara _____ a model when she's older.
2 My mum hates to see very thin models. (can't stand)
   My mum _____ very thin models.
3 I really like reading fashion magazines. (enjoy)
   I _____ fashion magazines.
4 He says he won't eat food that is bad for him. (refuse)
   He _____ food that is bad for him.
5 Vivienne didn't manage to keep her contract with Max Factor. (fail)
   Vivienne _____ her contract with Max Factor.
6 Pete's always looking in the mirror. It's so annoying! (keep)
   Pete _____ in the mirror. It's so annoying!
7 I really don't want to watch another fashion show. (can't face)
   I really _____ another fashion show.

LEARN THIS!

Verbs that change their meaning
Some verbs can be followed by an infinitive or an *-ing* form, without much difference in meaning:
I love to take photos. / I love taking photos.
It started to rain. / It started raining.
Some verbs change meaning depending on whether they are followed by an infinitive or an *-ing* form:
forget   go on   remember   stop   try

7 Read the *Learn this!* box. Then translate these sentences. How does the meaning of the verbs change?

1 Don't forget to watch the match on Saturday.
2 I'll never forget watching the World Cup Final.
3 He stopped to buy some bread.
4 He stopped buying bread.
5 I tried windsurfing, but I didn't like it.
6 I tried to windsurf, but I couldn't even stand up on the board.

⟫⟫ GRAMMAR BUILDER 1.5: PAGE 110 ⟪⟪

8 SPEAKING Work in pairs. Tell your partner about something that you:

1 forgot to do.
2 will never forget doing.
3 never remember to do.
4 tried to do, but couldn't.
5 tried doing, but didn't enjoy.

HEARING COLOURS

A Imagine being totally colour-blind, living in a world of greys, being unable to see the difference between red and blue or yellow and pale green. That's what life is like for Neil Harbisson. He was born with an irreversible condition called achromatopsia, or total colour blindness. That would make life difficult for anyone, but Neil is an artist – and the incredible thing is, he paints in colour.

B When Neil was an art student, he only painted in black, white and grey because that is all he saw. He was very dissatisfied with his paintings. But one day, a young scientist called Adam Montandon visited the college to give a lecture. The two met and when Neil explained his problem, Adam decided to try to find a way to allow Neil to 'see' colours using sound.

C Neil thought it was an impossible task, but Adam made a special device that let him 'hear' six colours. This is how it worked: light travels in waves, and different colours of light have different wavelengths. Red light has a long wavelength and violet light has a short wavelength. Adam used this fact to

1 **SPEAKING** Look at the photo. What can you see? What is happening? Do you like the painting?

2 🎧 1.08 Read the text. Choose the best summary.

1 Neil Harbisson used to be colour-blind, but a special device now means he can see colours through sound, although he still usually paints in black and white.

2 Colour-blind since birth, Neil Harbisson can now paint in colour. But he isn't very happy with his paintings and thinks the device he wears is uncomfortable and noisy.

3 Neil Harbisson used to paint in black and white, but now paints in colour. He is colour-blind and wears a special device that makes sounds corresponding to the colour he is looking at.

3 Read the text again. Match the headings (1–7) with the paragraphs (A–F). There is one heading that you do not need.

1 A lucky meeting
2 A more complex device
3 The device is too noisy
4 How Neil's life has changed
5 Colour-blind since birth
6 Some unexpected problems
7 How the device works

4 Answer the questions.

1 Is Neil completely colour-blind?
2 How did Neil meet Adam Montandon?
3 What type of sound does the device make when the camera sees (a) red light? (b) violet light?
4 How does the Eyeborg that Neil wears now differ from the first device that Adam made for him?
5 What else does Neil have to carry with him, apart from the camera?
6 How does the fact that Neil played the piano as a child help him to use the Eyeborg?
7 What problems has the Eyeborg caused Neil?

5 **VOCABULARY** Read the information in the *Learn this!* box and find five more adjectives with prefixes in the text.

LEARN THIS!

Adjective prefixes
We use the prefixes *un-*, *dis-* and *in-* to give an adjective the opposite meaning.
uncomfortable   dissatisfied   incredible
Before *m* and *p*, *in-* usually changes to *im-*: *impossible*
Before *r*, *in-* usually changes to *ir-*: *irresponsible*
Before *l*, *in-* usually changes to *il-*: *illogical*

▶▶▶ **VOCABULARY BUILDER 1.3: PAGE 127** ◀◀◀

6 **SPEAKING** Discuss this question in pairs or small groups. Brainstorm ideas first.

What problems does a person who is totally colour-blind face in everyday life?

7 **SPEAKING** Present your three best ideas to the class.

create a camera that measures the wavelength of the light that enters it and then makes a sound that corresponds to the colour of the light. So, if the camera sees red, it makes a low sound, if it sees violet, it makes a high sound.

low sound → high sound

D Adam has now developed a much more sophisticated device, called the Eyeborg, that allows Neil to see 360 different colours. Neil wears a camera on his head, which is attached to a laptop computer in a backpack. The computer analyses the colour and sends a sound to Neil's wireless headset. It was a bit uncomfortable at first, but Neil soon got used to it.

E The Eyeborg has made a huge difference to Neil's art. He now uses a wide range of colours. If he wants to paint something, he points his camera at it and memorises the sound. Then he starts mixing colours, pointing his camera at the paint, and stops mixing when he hears the same sound again. Neil has had to memorise a lot of sounds, but he played the piano as a child and this has helped him a great deal.

F 'I've got used to all the sounds,' he says. 'It's noisy, but probably not much noisier than a busy city street.' However, it has created some unusual problems. People sometimes think that he is videoing them and they don't like that. Security guards occasionally ask him to leave shops! But Neil is now inseparable from his Eyeborg and wears it all the time.

1 Look at the photo and identify the people and things below.

a camera flash   a celebrity   a notebook
a paparazzi photographer   a reporter   a sign

2 🎧 1.09 Listen to a student talking about the photo. Which of the following does he include in his description?

a actions   b experiences   c people   d location

3 Complete the phrases the student used for identifying people and things in the photo. Use the prepositions below.

in   in   in   on   to   with

1 a sign ___ the background
2 the man ___ the grey suit
3 the people ___ the right of the man
4 ___ the top right-hand corner of the photo
5 the woman ___ long blonde hair
6 the people ___ the left

LEARN THIS!

Expressions with *look*
look (a bit / just) like + noun / person
look + adjective
look as though / as if / like + clause

4 Read the *Learn this!* box. Then complete the sentences with the correct form of the expressions with *look*.

1 It _____ it says 'Theatre'.
2 The woman in the sunglasses _____ a pop singer or film star.
3 He _____ very excited.
4 They _____ paparazzi.
5 It _____ she's signing her autograph.

5 🎧 1.09 Listen again and check your answers to exercises 3 and 4.

6 Read the exam strategy. Complete the phrases with the verbs below.

say   see   suppose   think about   thought about

EXAM STRATEGY

After you have described the picture, the examiner will ask you some questions. When you answer these questions from the examiner, do not give single-sentence answers. In order to create time to think, you can use these phrases:

Let me _____ , ...
Let me _____ that for a moment.
Well, um, I _____ ...
I've never really _____ that.
It's difficult to _____ really.

7 🎧 1.10 Listen to the next part of the exam. How many questions does the examiner ask? Which phrases from the exam strategy does the student use?

8 SPEAKING Work in pairs.

Student A: make notes about the photo below.
Student B: make notes about the photo on page 7.

Then describe your photo to your partner, using phrases from exercise 3 and the *Learn this!* box.

9 SPEAKING Work in pairs. Take turns to ask your partner the questions below. When you answer the questions, use phrases from the exam strategy if you need time to think.

Questions for Student A to answer:
1 Why do you think the photographers are taking photos?
2 Do you think there's too much sport on television and in the newspapers? Why do you think that?

Questions for Student B to answer:
1 Do you think this woman enjoys her job? Why? / Why not?
2 How difficult do you think it is being in the public eye all the time?

Dear Mary,

I'm Johana Paulerová. I'm 17 years old and I'm from Ostrava. My dad is a shop manager and my mum is a nurse. I've got two brothers. They are called Jan and Robert.

I like reading and watching films. I also like spending time with my friends. We often go shopping together, or to a café or the cinema.

I go to Gymnázium Písek. There are 500 students in the school, and 25 in my class. I'm studying for my Maturita exam. I study five subjects.

What time does your plane arrive in Ostrava? Please let me know. See you soon. Regards Johana

Hi Luke

My name is Pablo Perez and I'm 17 years old. I live in a village quite close to Mendoza with my mum, dad, and older sister. I've got loads of hobbies and interests. I love football (playing and watching) and I go swimming a lot. I'm into computer games and I like listening to music. My favourite band is the Black Eyed Peas. I go to Instituto Parroquial Don Francisco de Merlo. I'm studying for my exams, including English, of course! My best subject is maths, and my worst is probably history. There are 22 students in my class – ten girls and twelve boys. Drop me a line and let me know what time your plane gets in. We can pick you up from the airport. I'm really looking forward to meeting you. Best wishes

Pablo

1 **SPEAKING** Look at the photo with the second letter. Describe Pablo's family (appearance, age, clothes, etc.).

2 Read the letters quickly. Answer these questions.

1 Who are Johana and Pablo writing to?
2 Why are they writing? Choose two of the reasons below.

to ask for information   to ask for news   to give news
to introduce themselves

3 Read the exam task and the exam strategy. How well do Johana and Pablo follow the instructions in the task?

A British exchange student is coming to stay at your house for a week. Write a letter (120–150 words) to him / her.
• Introduce yourself and give some information about your family.
• Give some information about your hobbies.
• Give some information about your school.
• Ask about his / her plane times and offer to meet him / her at the airport.

EXAM STRATEGY

Read the question very carefully and make sure you include all the information that is required and that your letter is the correct length. When you have finished, read the question again and double-check your work.

4 **VOCABULARY** Find words and expressions in Pablo's letter with similar meanings to the words and expressions below.

1 near to   3 I like   5 arrives
2 a lot of   4 write to me   6 collect you from

5 What differences are there between Johana and Pablo's letters? Think about: use of paragraphs, sentence structure and variety of vocabulary.

6 Choose the most appropriate options for an informal letter. There may be more than one possible answer.

1 Start the letter with: **Hi Mike** / **Dear Mike** / **Dear Sir**.
2 Finish the letter with: **Write soon** / **Awaiting your reply** / **I look forward to hearing from you** / **Bye**.
3 Before you sign your name write: **Best wishes** / **Yours faithfully** / **All the best** / **Regards**.
4 You should use **full forms (I am)** / **contracted forms (I'm)**.
5 You **can use** / **shouldn't use** informal and colloquial language (e.g. *mates* rather than *friends*).

7 You are going to spend a week at the home of a British exchange student. Write a letter (120–150 words) to him / her.

• Introduce yourself and give some information about your family.
• Give some information about your hobbies.
• Ask about the town you are going to stay in (size, things to do, etc.).
• Tell him / her about your travel arrangements and ask who will meet you at the airport.

CHECK YOUR WORK

Have you:

☐ included the information in the task in exercise 7?
☐ written the correct number of words?
☐ checked your spelling and grammar?

Listening

1 **Get ready to LISTEN** Work in pairs. Ask and answer the questions.

1 Do you judge people by their appearance? Why? / Why not?
2 Are first impressions important? Why? / Why not?

2 🎧 1.11 Do the exam task.

LISTENING exam task

Listen and choose the correct answers: A, B or C.

1 If you are unhappy with your appearance,
  A you'll make other people unhappy too.
  B it will affect your behaviour.
  C other people won't appreciate you.
2 If you accept things about yourself that you cannot change,
  A you will feel more confident.
  B you will find it is easier to hide these things.
  C you will feel proud.
3 The speaker advises us to
  A throw away old clothes even if they look good.
  B throw away clothes that don't suit us.
  C pay for some good advice.
4 The speaker advises us to
  A get a new pair of jeans.
  B become body-builders.
  C exercise because it will make us feel better.
5 On the whole, the speaker's attitude is
  A helpful.
  B critical.
  C neutral.

Speaking

3 **Get ready to SPEAK** Describe photo A below. Say:
• where the women are and what they are doing
• how they are feeling and why.

4 Do the exam task.

SPEAKING exam task

Compare and contrast the two photos in exercise 3. Answer the questions.

1 Who is buying clothes 'off the peg'? Who is having clothes specially made?
2 What are the advantages and disadvantages of having clothes specially made for you?
3 Which shopping experience would you find more enjoyable? Why?
4 Do you prefer shopping alone, or with someone else? Why?

Use of English

5 Do the exam task.

USE OF ENGLISH exam task

Choose the best word(s) (A–D) to complete each gap.

Self-cooling clothes may seem [1]_____ the stuff of science fiction, but one Japanese company [2]_____ created such products by [3]_____ fans to shirts and jackets. Shirts and jackets [4]_____ by Kuchou-fuku keep the wearer comfortable [5]_____ in sweltering heat. And they're also environmentally friendly as they use just one-fiftieth [6]_____ the energy of small air-conditioner units which cool entire rooms. The company has sold about 5,500 of the garments [7]_____ they went on sale three years ago, mostly to factory workers. But [8]_____ cool the clothes are, they seem unlikely [9]_____ very popular. The fans fill the shirts with air, making the wearers look a bit fat. 'My daughter won't wear them because the shape is no good,' admitted Hiroshi Ichigaya, [10]_____ works for the company that produces the clothes.

	A	B	C	D
1	similar	like	as	to
2	will have	has	have	having
3	add	to add	adding	added
4	make	making	makes	made
5	although	even	however	despite
6	of	to	than	for
7	when	while	for	since
8	whatever	however	how	although
9	to become	become	becoming	became
10	which	that	who	whose

Reading

6 **Get ready to READ** Match 1–7 with A–G to make expressions describing some interesting activities. Then answer the questions below.

1 fly	A stunts
2 walk	B music
3 row	C a boat
4 design	D the tightrope
5 do	E with three objects
6 juggle	F metal jewellery
7 play	G a kite

1 Which is a sporting activity?
2 Which activities require creative skills?
3 Which activity can't be done if there's no wind?

7 Do the exam task.

READING exam task

Read the texts. Match the texts (A–E) with the statements (1–7). Each text can be used more than once. Write the line number where you find evidence for the statement.

THE MAGIC GARDEN
Teenage summer festival 12–17 June

A Come and share all the fun of the circus! You will learn how to juggle with 2, 3 and 4 objects. You can practise walking the tightrope. Don't worry, it isn't dangerous! Learn clown tricks and dress up like a clown – amaze and amuse your friends! Monday, Tuesday and Thursday 1–5 p.m. Sessions take place in the main tent next to the lake. **5**

B Be creative and original! Jewellery making for everyone. Design your own necklaces and bracelets. Learn how to work with leather, metal, stones, feathers and bone. Make beautiful gifts for yourself and others. Every morning from 10 a.m. till **10** 12 noon. You will need two or three mornings to make a great piece of jewellery. Craft tent beside Gate 2.

C Come fly with us! We have amazing kites available, all shapes and sizes, all colours, big and small. Learn how to fly them and do stunts and tricks. Try our enormous sit-on kite and fly **15** yourself! Every afternoon from 2 p.m. when it's windy. Come to the hill behind the food tents.

D Come and listen to our fantastic live bands – Black Stripes, Snakebite and Fallacy! And introducing The Rainmakers. Join them for a live performance. Open microphone spot – **20** make some music yourself. Bring along an instrument, if you have one, or just sing. You might even become famous! All day, every day. Come to stages 1, 2 and 3.

E Messing about on the water! Join in the rowing race, once across the lake. Great prizes to be won! Learn how to row – **25** lessons for all ages. Anytime. If rainy, put on raincoats. Lessons every morning. Races at 2 p.m. Come to the pier on the lake.

	Text	Line no.
1 This event depends on the weather.		
2 This event teaches you how to make people laugh.		
3 This event gives you the chance to be on stage.		
4 This event is only on some afternoons.		
5 This event doesn't involve lessons in anything.		
6 This event includes a competition.		
7 This event teaches you how to produce something.		

Writing

8 Do the exam task.

WRITING exam task

You have recently moved, and changed school. Write a letter to a British penfriend in which you:

- Give some information about your new school and your new class
- Describe who you have met and how you have been welcomed into your new school
- Describe a new friend you have made
- Describe the friend's appearance and his / her interests
- Say what you like about him / her and how you spend your free time together.

THIS UNIT INCLUDES

Vocabulary ▪ adjectives for feelings ▪ noun formation ▪ adjective + preposition collocation
Grammar ▪ Contrast: past simple, past continuous and past perfect ▪ *used to*
Speaking ▪ talking about a special memory
Writing ▪ a narrative

2A   VOCABULARY AND LISTENING   How did you feel?

I can describe how I feel.

1 **VOCABULARY** Look at the photos. How do you think these people are feeling? Use the adjectives below. Why do you think they are feeling like that?

<u>Feelings</u> afraid amused ashamed confused delighted depressed disappointed embarrassed fed up guilty homesick irritated jealous nervous pleased proud relieved satisfied shocked upset

> I think the boy in photo 1 looks … . Maybe he …

2 🎧 1.12 Listen to eight short extracts. How is each person feeling? Choose the correct adjective.

1 afraid / depressed
2 amused / irritated
3 delighted / jealous
4 fed up / nervous
5 homesick / relieved
6 disappointed / embarrassed
7 confused / upset
8 guilty / shocked

LEARN THIS!
Adjectives to describe feelings are often used in this structure: *adjective + preposition + noun (or pronoun)*.
Different adjectives take different prepositions:
I'm bored with this weather.
Are you scared of spiders?
In a *Wh-* question, the preposition often goes at the end:
What are you angry about?
Who is she scared of?

3 Read the *Learn this!* box. Add the adjectives in the examples to the chart below.

about	with	of
confused	pleased	jealous
guilty	fed up	proud
depressed	satisfied	afraid
relieved	irritated	ashamed
1_____	2_____	3_____

4 🎧 1.13 Complete the questions with the correct prepositions. Then listen to five people talking about events in their life and answer the questions.

1 Who was Milly afraid _____ ? Why?
2 What was Sam relieved _____ ? How did he react?
3 Who was Alex proud _____ ? Why?
4 What was Sophie fed up _____ ? What did she do about it?
5 Who was Tom jealous _____ ? Why?

5 Look at the adjectives below and make notes about the last time you felt like this.

1 nervous   3 delighted   5 shocked   7 homesick
2 irritated   4 afraid   6 confused   8 disappointed

I   *nervous – had an important exam*

6 **SPEAKING** Work in pairs. Ask and answer questions using the adjectives in exercise 5.

> When did you last feel nervous?

> About a month ago. I had a piano exam and I was really nervous about it.

⟫⟫⟫ **VOCABULARY BUILDER 2.1: PAGE 127** ⟪⟪⟪

1 Read Kyle's description of a memorable experience. What positive and negative effects did the weather have?

When I was fifteen, I went to a music festival with my brother and his friends. We arrived on Friday evening, looked at the programme and decided to go to the Main Stage to hear Metallica. As we were walking across the park, there was a flash of lightning. A storm was coming, although it wasn't raining yet. When we reached the Main Stage, Metallica had started playing.

We were all really impressed with the band. I'd watched a few of their songs on YouTube, but I hadn't seen them live. Their show was amazing! By this time, it was raining hard, but we didn't mind. In fact, it made the atmosphere more dramatic. Thousands of people were cheering and dancing in the rain! Then suddenly, the music stopped. The water had damaged the sound equipment!

2 Look at the verbs in red in the text. What tense are they, past simple, past continuous or past perfect? Find an affirmative and a negative example of each tense.

3 Read and complete the *Learn this!* box with the names of the tenses. Find examples of each rule in the text.

LEARN THIS!

Past tenses
When we're narrating events in the past:
1 we can use the _____ to set the scene.
The sun was shining and birds were singing.
2 we use the _____ for actions or events that happened one after another.
She stood up, opened the door and left.
3 we use the _____ for an action or event that interrupted a background event; we use the _____ for the background event.
While we were having lunch, my phone rang.
4 we use the _____ to talk about an event that happened before another event in the past.
I couldn't find Suzie because she had gone home.

>>> GRAMMAR BUILDER 2.1 (Ex 1): PAGE 111 <<<

4 SPEAKING Work in pairs. Discuss the difference in meaning between these sentences.
1 When we got to the main stage, Muse played my favourite song.
2 When we got to the main stage, Muse were playing my favourite song.
3 When we got to the main stage, Muse had played my favourite song.

5 🎧 1.14 Complete Julie's account of a memorable event. Use the past simple, the past continuous and the past perfect form of the verbs in brackets. Then listen and check.

When I was about twelve, I ¹_____ (go) to the Notting Hill Carnival in London with my dad. We ²_____ (travel) there by underground. At about midday, we ³_____ (get off) the train, ⁴_____ (walk) up the steps and ⁵_____ (come) out of the station. I was really shocked – I ⁶_____ (never / see) so many people in one place! A band ⁷_____ (play) reggae music and people ⁸_____ (dance) in the street. As I ⁹_____ (walk) along the street with my dad, I ¹⁰_____ (stop) to watch the band for a few minutes. But when I ¹¹_____ (turn) around, my dad ¹²_____ (go)! I was really scared. Fortunately, my dad ¹³_____ (write) his mobile number on a piece of paper. I ¹⁴_____ (walk) into a shop and ¹⁵_____ (ask) the shop assistant to phone the number. When my dad ¹⁶_____ (answer) and ¹⁷_____ (hear) my voice, he was really shocked. He ¹⁸_____ (not notice) that I wasn't with him!

6 Complete these questions about Julie's story using the past simple, past continuous or past perfect.
1 How _____ (Julie / travel) to the Notting Hill Carnival?
2 How _____ (Julie / feel) when she came out of the station?
3 What kind of music _____ (the band / play)?
4 What _____ (her dad / write) on a piece of paper?
5 Who _____ (Julie / ask) for help?
6 Why _____ (her dad / be) shocked when she phoned him?

7 In pairs, ask and answer the questions in exercise 6.

8 SPEAKING Tell your partner about a memorable occasion when you had a shock. Use these prompts to help you.
• *It happened at …*
• *It was …ing   Everyone was …ing*
• *Suddenly, I realised that …*
• *In the end, …*

>>> GRAMMAR BUILDER 2.1 (Ex 2-3): PAGE 111 <<<

2C CULTURE Remembering the past

I can discuss the significance of important days.

1 SPEAKING Look at the photo. Where is this monument? What does it commemorate?

2 VOCABULARY Work in pairs. Match the words below with the definitions.

battlefield casualties comrades conflicts officer poppies war

1 a person who tells soldiers what to do
2 people who fight on the same side as you
3 a place where soldiers fight
4 people injured or killed in a battle
5 a situation in which countries or groups of people fight against each other
6 periods of fighting
7 red flowers

3 🎧 1.15 Listen to the beginning of a radio programme about Remembrance Day. Complete the fact file with the correct numbers.

FACT FILE: POPPY DAY

When is it? On ¹_____ th November each year.
Why that date? It's the anniversary of the end of World War ²_____ .
What happens at 11.00 a.m.? A ³_____ minute silence.
When was the first silence? In ⁴_____ .

4 Read the exam strategy. Then carefully read the questions and options in exercise 5.

EXAM STRATEGY

When you do a multiple-choice listening task, read the questions and options carefully before you listen for the first time.

5 🎧 1.16 Listen to the complete programme. Choose the correct answers.

1 On 11th November people remember
  a soldiers who have died since 1919.
  b soldiers who have died in all major conflicts since the start of World War I.
  c soldiers who died in the two world wars.
  d soldiers who died between 1914 and 1918.

2 According to one British newspaper, the first two-minute silence in London
  a finished at exactly 11 o'clock.
  b caused vehicles to stop, but not pedestrians.
  c only involved a few people in the centre of the city.
  d took place over the entire city.

3 John McCrae was
  a a Belgian officer who died before the end of World War I.
  b a Canadian doctor and officer who wrote a poem about poppies.
  c a young soldier who survived the war, but never forgot the soldiers who had died.
  d a Canadian doctor who went back to Belgium after the war and planted poppies.

4 The tradition of selling poppies to help ex-soldiers and their families began
  a in the UK, but soon spread around the world.
  b in the UK, the USA and other countries at the same time.
  c with one woman's actions.
  d soon after World War I, but stopped later.

6 SPEAKING In pairs, look at the dates (a–c) and answer these questions.

a 1st May   b 4th July   c 14th July

1 What events do these dates commemorate? In which countries are they important?
2 Do you know any other anniversaries that are nationally important in your country or in any other country?

7 PROJECT Work in groups. Write a fact file about an important date. You can use one of the dates from exercise 6, or your own ideas. Include the following information:

• What is it?
• When is it?
• Why that date?
• What happens?
• When did it start?

2D GRAMMAR *used to*

I can talk about things that were true in the past, but aren't now.

1 🎧 1.17 Read and listen to the dialogue between friends, Daisy and Evie. How does Daisy feel at the end? Complete the sentence with an adjective and your own words.

afraid guilty nervous upset

Daisy is a bit _____ at the end because …

Evie   Hi, Daisy. What have you got there?
Daisy It's a box that my dad found in the attic. It's full of my old things.
Evie   Cool! Let me see!
Daisy This is my schoolbook from primary school.
Evie   You used to have really neat handwriting!
Daisy And look. Here's a photo of me when I was five.
Evie   Did you use to wear dresses?
Daisy Yes. All the time!
Evie   How sweet! You never wear dresses now. And look at your hair! It's blonde.
Daisy I know. I didn't use to have red hair.
Evie   You used to be pretty!
Daisy What do you mean, I *used* to be pretty?!

2 Underline all the examples of *used to* in exercise 1. How do we form the negative and interrogative?

3 Read the *Learn this!* box. Complete the examples. Then match the examples with uses (1) and (2).

LEARN THIS!

affirmative
My parents ¹_____ *live in London, but now they live in Paris.*
negative
I ²_____ *have a DVD player, but I've got one now.*
interrogative
³_____ *you* ⁴_____ *walk to school? Yes, I did. But now I cycle every day.*
used to
We use *used to* for:
1 past habits, or
2 situations that were different in the past.
The form doesn't change.

4 🎧 1.18 **PRONUNCIATION** Listen and repeat the sentences from the dialogue. Answer questions 1–3.

a Did you use to wear dresses?   c You used to be pretty!
b I didn't use to have red hair.

1 How is the 's' pronounced in *used to*: /s/ or /z/?
2 Is the 'd' silent or pronounced?
3 How is *to* pronounced: /tuː/ or /tə/?

LOOK OUT!

Be careful not to confuse the verb form *used to* with the phrase *to be* (or *get*) *used to something.*
These glasses feel strange, but I'll get used to them.
She hates losing. She isn't used to it!

⟫⟫ **GRAMMAR BUILDER 2.2: PAGE 111** ⟪⟪

5 Complete the sentences with the affirmative, negative or interrogative form of *used to* and the verbs below.

be get have ~~like~~ play read speak study work

1 My brother didn't <u>use to like</u> school, but he loves it now.
2 My dad _____ tennis, but now he spends every evening at the tennis club.
3 What subjects _____ the Ancient Greeks _____ at school?
4 I _____ a games console, but it broke.
5 My sister _____ Japanese, but she learned it before she moved to Tokyo.
6 This theatre _____ a church.
7 _____ your teachers at primary school _____ angry with you?
8 My aunt _____ in a department store, but it closed.
9 I _____ books, but I'm really into detective fiction these days.

6 Have you changed a lot since you were a young child? Make notes about:

1 appearance   3 toys and games
2 likes / dislikes   4 unusual habits

7 **SPEAKING** Interview your partner about his or her childhood. Use *used to* and these prompts.

1 what / look like?
2 what things / like or hate?
3 what toys or games / play with?
4 have / any unusual habits?

> What did you use to look like?

> I used to have very short hair. I used to wear …

1 🎧 1.19 Read the text. Match each person with the condition they suffered from and the fictional character who had a similar condition.

| Emily | can't form new memories | Leonard Shelby |
| Henry | can't remember the distant past | Jason Bourne |

2 Read the sentences. Write *Emily* or *Henry*.

1 _____ had physical damage to the brain.
2 _____'s case was well-known among doctors.
3 _____ did not remember family members.
4 _____ drove a long way for no reason.
5 _____'s condition got better.
6 _____ met the same person many times, but couldn't remember her.
7 _____ could still make jokes, despite the amnesia.

3 Are these sentences true or false? If the text doesn't say, write *not known*.

1 Emily had friends in Santa Fe.
2 Emily had a husband, but no children.
3 Some doctors might think Emily wasn't telling the truth.
4 Emily's amnesia only lasted a few months.
5 Henry lost his memory because of a car crash.
6 Despite his amnesia, Henry remembered being a child.
7 Henry did not recognise Dr Corkin even after many visits.
8 There is a film which tells the story of Henry's life.

READING STRATEGY

Use the context of a word (the words which come before and after) to help work out its meaning. Try different meanings and decide which makes the most sense.

4 **VOCABULARY** Read the reading strategy. Then match these verbs from the text with the definitions (1–8) and complete the examples with the correct form of the verb.

Mental actions conclude doubt memorise realise recall recognise remind solve

1 _____ : to become aware of a fact or situation
I suddenly _____ that I was alone.
2 _____ : to deliberately store something in your memory
I don't need the script. I've _____ my lines.
3 _____ : to find the answer (to a problem or puzzle)
Sherlock Holmes used logic to _____ crimes.
4 _____ : to think something is unlikely or untrue
I've invited Naomi, but I _____ she'll come.
5 _____ : to remember
I'm sure we've met, but I can't _____ where or when.
6 _____ : to make somebody remember something
Please _____ me to send a card to my mother.
7 _____ : to know that something or someone is familiar
I _____ his face, but I can't remember his name.
8 _____ : come to a decision based on the facts
The police examined the scene and _____ that the painting had been stolen.

IDENTITY CRISIS

In the Bourne trilogy, Jason Bourne has acute amnesia. He spends three films trying to recall his own past. 'I don't know who I am,' he says. 'I don't know where I'm going, none of it.' And in a 1996 film called *Memento*, the main character, Leonard Shelby, tries to solve a murder even though he has no short-term memory – which means he cannot remember what has just happened or store any new memories. These two kinds of memory loss provide exciting plots for thrillers and mystery stories. But in real life, they are not so entertaining.

EMILY'S STORY

One day in September 2001, a 33-year-old woman from Texas, USA, got into her car and began to drive to work. She can't remember exactly what happened next, or why, but ten hours later, she was still driving. She had driven all the way from Texas to Santa Fe, about 1,000 kilometres. She didn't know anyone in Santa Fe so she checked into a motel. And then, the situation got worse.

'When I woke up the next morning, I sat up and I didn't recognise the room,' she said. 'I didn't recognise the bag that was sitting on the chair, or the clothes that were lying over the chair. I didn't recognise myself in the mirror. I didn't know my name.' When the police found Emily and took her back to her family, she didn't recognise her own children.

Emily's doctors concluded that she had a condition called 'dissociative fugue'. Patients wake up one day, lost. They have no problem remembering new information, but they've lost most of their past. There is no physical damage to the brain. For this reason, many doctors doubt these patients' stories: perhaps they are using memory loss as an excuse for starting their life again. In most cases – including Emily's – they gradually make a recovery.

5 Which of these things do you sometimes forget? What happens as a result?

- where you've put something (phone, etc.)
- the name of a singer or actor
- an important birthday
- your homework
- the name of somebody you've met (e.g. a friend of a friend)
- your own mobile number
- a word, when you're speaking in your own language

6 SPEAKING **Discuss your ideas from exercise 5 with your partner. Which of you is more forgetful?**

7 🎧 1.20 Listen and complete the song with the words below. Which are nouns and which are adjectives?

ashamed beautiful comfortable confidence
envy jealous personality strange ugly unfair

8 🎧 1.20 Listen again. What do you think the song is saying? Choose a, b or c.

a People used to say bad things about me, but I didn't believe them.
b In the past, people made me feel bad, but now I'm confident.
c People used to call me ugly, but only because they were uglier than me.

Henry's story

Henry – known for years as H.M. – is the most famous amnesiac in medical history. His brain was damaged during surgery, and as a result he suffered from a condition called anterograde amnesia. Although he could recall his childhood clearly, new experiences disappeared from his mind after a few minutes. He lived the rest of his life in the present, unable to remember what had happened five minutes earlier. 'It's like waking from a dream,' he said.

Although sufferers from anterograde amnesia cannot memorise new information, they can learn new skills. For example, patients who have guitar lessons gradually get better and better at the guitar. But every time they play, they believe that they're picking up a guitar for the first time!

Henry lived with his condition for about 50 years; his memory did not improve in that time. Suzanne Corkin, a neuroscientist, studied Henry's condition for more than 40 years, and visited him regularly. But each time she arrived, he introduced himself as if they were meeting for the first time.

One day, Dr Corkin took Henry to the Massachusetts Institute of Technology in the USA for tests. As they were walking along a corridor, she asked him if he remembered where they were. 'Of course,' he replied. 'We're at MIT!' Dr Corkin was shocked. Had his memory suddenly improved? 'How do you know that?' she asked him. Henry laughed and pointed to a student who was wearing an MIT sweatshirt. Dr Corkin realised that Henry's memory hadn't come back – but at least he had reminded her of his sense of humour.

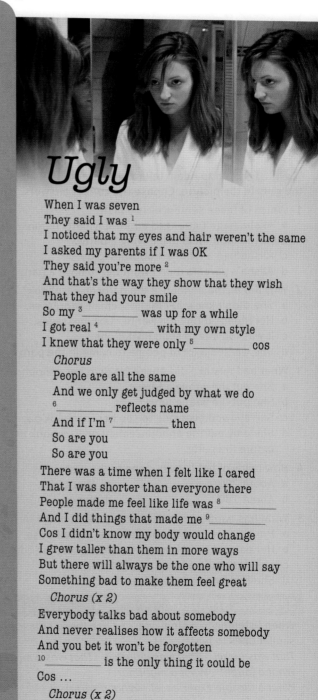

Ugly

When I was seven
They said I was ¹_____
I noticed that my eyes and hair weren't the same
I asked my parents if I was OK
They said you're more ²_____
And that's the way they show that they wish
That they had your smile
So my ³_____ was up for a while
I got real ⁴_____ with my own style
I knew that they were only ⁵_____ cos
    Chorus
    People are all the same
    And we only get judged by what we do
    ⁶_____ reflects name
    And if I'm ⁷_____ then
    So are you
    So are you

There was a time when I felt like I cared
That I was shorter than everyone there
People made me feel like life was ⁸_____
And I did things that made me ⁹_____
Cos I didn't know my body would change
I grew taller than them in more ways
But there will always be the one who will say
Something bad to make them feel great
    Chorus (x 2)

Everybody talks bad about somebody
And never realises how it affects somebody
And you bet it won't be forgotten
¹⁰_____ is the only thing it could be
Cos ...
    Chorus (x 2)

2F SPEAKING Narrating events

I can describe and react to a story.

1 Describe the picture. How do you think the people are feeling? Why? Use these words or your own ideas.

confused / confusing   excited / exciting
frightened / frightening   shocked / shocking
worried / worrying

2 🎧 1.21 **Listen to Adam telling Hailey about Alisha, one of the girls in the picture. Choose the correct answers.**

1 Which of these sentences is a fact?
  a Alisha hadn't arranged a birthday party before Friday.
  b Alisha didn't feel like having a party.
  c Alisha had a lot of schoolwork to do.
  d Alisha's parents didn't want her to have a party.

2 Why did Alisha announce the party on Facebook?
  a She didn't know her friends' email addresses.
  b Her friends didn't answer her text messages.
  c It was too late to send invitations.
  d She wanted a lot of people to come to the party.

3 What bad mistake did Alisha make in her announcement?
  a She put the wrong address.
  b She put the wrong time.
  c She allowed everyone to see her Facebook page.
  d She only put the announcement on Facebook the day before the party.

4 How many of her friends came to the party?
  a About 200.   c About 20.
  b About 180.   d None.

5 What has happened to Alisha as a result of the incident?
  a Her parents have banned parties in the house.
  b Her parents have banned her from using the computer.
  c She has made a lot of new friends.
  d She has stopped using Facebook.

SPEAKING STRATEGY

When listening to a story, you can use these phrases or similar ones to react:

That was lucky!   That was unlucky!   That was a mistake!
What a laugh!   What a nightmare!
What a terrible experience!   What a surprise!
How exciting!   How funny!   How frightening!

3 🎧 1.21 Read the speaking strategy. Listen again. Which phrases does Hailey use while Adam is telling the story?

4 🎧 1.22 **PRONUNCIATION** Listen and repeat all the phrases in the speaking strategy, copying the intonation.

⟫⟫⟫ **GRAMMAR BUILDER 2.3: PAGE 112** ⟪⟪⟪

5 🎧 1.23 Listen to Kevin telling a story about Edward. Complete the phrases that he uses to tell the story. How does Edward feel at the end of the story?

1 Guess what _____ to … the other day.
2 It _____ Saturday evening,
3 _____ , they had a great time
4 Ten minutes _____ ,
5 In the _____ ,

6 🎧 1.23 Read the *Learn this!* box and listen again. Complete the box with the phrases from exercise 5.

> **LEARN THIS!**
>
> When we tell a story, we can use the following phrases to give the story a structure:
> **Introducing the story**
> *Did you hear what happened to my friend …?*
> ¹ _____
> **Setting the scene**
> ² _____ / Christmas Day / her birthday / the first day of term, etc.
> *We were on holiday / at the cinema / in town, etc.*
> **Moving the story on**
> *So that evening / a few days later / the next day /*
> ³ _____ , …   *A while* ⁴ _____ , etc.
> **Finishing the story**
> ⁵ _____ …   *Eventually, …*

7 SPEAKING **Work in pairs. Think of a story (true or invented) about a party or special event. Use these questions to help you make notes.**

- Who is the story about? How old were they?
- When and where did it happen? What happened? Why did it happen?
- How did people react? How did they / you feel?
- What happened in the end? How do they / you feel about it now? Was it a good or bad experience?

8 Prepare a dialogue using your notes from exercise 7. Remember to include a few phrases from the speaking strategy and the *Learn this!* box.

9 SPEAKING Act out your dialogue to the class.

⟫⟫⟫ **VOCABULARY BUILDER 2.2: PAGE 128** ⟪⟪⟪

1 Read Liam's narrative. What is it about? Choose the best summary (a–c).

a a shocking experience
b a terrible holiday
c a special occasion

One day last summer, I decided to spend a day by the sea with some friends. We don't live on the coast, so we met in town at nine o'clock in the morning and got on a bus. We arrived at about ten. We found a good place, took
5 off our T-shirts and sat down on the sand. Suddenly, we heard a lot of noise. We stood up and looked around. A few people were shouting and waving near the edge of the water. At first, I thought there was a shark! But then, I realised that somebody had got into difficulty in
10 the sea. Two men went into the water and carried a girl out. She wasn't moving at all – she was unconscious. They put her down on the sand and tried to wake her up. A few minutes later, an ambulance arrived and three paramedics jumped out. They started giving the
15 girl emergency treatment. Just then the girl's mother arrived. She looked shocked and scared. Then the girl sat up and looked around. Her mother was so relieved, she broke down and started crying. In the end, the paramedics left and the girl went off with her mother.
20 She was fine. But we all felt a bit strange – especially when we were swimming in the sea! It was a day I'll never forget.

2 Read Liam's paragraph plan. Decide where the paragraph breaks should be in his narrative.

Paragraph 1: Set the scene – we go to the beach.
Paragraph 2: Lead-up – shouting. Somebody in difficulty.
Paragraph 3: Main event – girl is rescued. Paramedics and mother arrive.
Paragraph 4: The ending – the girl and her mother leave, but we feel strange.

3 Read the writing strategy about time expressions in a narrative. Which expressions are in Liam's narrative?

WRITING STRATEGY

Narrative time expressions
- We often start a narrative with a non-specific time expression:
  a few weeks ago   about a month or so ago
  one day last summer   one Sunday last year
- To show how a situation changes with time, we use:
  at first ..., (but) then ...
- To talk about an unexpected event, we use:
  Suddenly, ...
- We use these expressions to move the narrative forward in time:
  later   a few minutes later   after a while   later on
- To bring the narrative to an end, we use: *in the end ...*
  Or to emphasise that a lot of time has passed, we use:
  finally   at last

4 **VOCABULARY** Complete these phrasal verbs from Liam's narrative in exercise 1. Then choose the correct meaning for this context, a–e.

1 get _____
2 take _____
3 put _____
4 break _____
5 go _____

a become very upset
b leave
c place somebody or something on the ground
d remove (an item of clothing)
e enter (a vehicle)

⟫⟫⟫ **VOCABULARY BUILDER 2.3: PAGE 128** ⟪⟪⟪

5 Plan a narrative about an interesting experience, real or invented. Use this paragraph plan to help you.

Paragraph 1: Set the scene. Where were you? When? Who were you with?
Paragraph 2: Lead-up. What happened just before? What did you see / think?
Paragraph 3: Main event. What happened? How did you feel?
Paragraph 4: The ending. What happened in the end? How did you feel afterwards? How did people react?

6 Write a narrative using your plan from exercise 5. Write 220–250 words and try to include some time expressions.

CHECK YOUR WORK

Have you:
☐ used the plan from exercise 5?
☐ used some narrative time expressions?
☐ checked your grammar and spelling?

Unit 1

1 **Choose the correct words.**

1 I like your soft, **fluffy / scruffy** scarf. Is it fur or wool?
2 Don't wear that **checked / matching** shirt with those stripy trousers! Too many different patterns don't look good!
3 I prefer loose, **baggy / smooth** T-shirts to tight-fitting ones.
4 You can't see her shoes. She's wearing a **long-sleeved / full-length** dress.
5 This T-shirt is made of natural material. It's 100% **nylon / cotton.**

Mark: _____ /5

2 **Complete the postcard. Use the present simple or present continuous form of the verbs below.**

do   go   have   remember   stay

Hi Lucy,
We ¹_____ a lovely time here in Lanzarote. You're right.
It's a great place! I ²_____ to the beach every morning
and ³_____ there until dinner time! But today we
⁴_____ something different. ⁵_____ you _____ the
caves in the north of the island? Aren't they amazing?
See you soon
Sally

Mark: _____ /5

3 **Complete the conversation with the infinitive or -ing form of the verbs in brackets.**

Mark   Do you fancy ¹_____ (go) to the Spitz concert, Jessie?
Jessie   Not really, Mark. I really want ²_____ (watch) that new film at the cinema.
Mark   You mean *True Grit*? But you promised ³_____ (see) that film with me! You keep ⁴_____ (forget) the things you promise! I'm getting fed up with it.
Jessie   I'm really sorry, Mark! I didn't mean ⁵_____ (hurt) your feelings. Look, I'll go to the concert with you …

Mark: _____ /5

4 **Complete the sentences using the words below.**

about   like   looks   on   with

1 Let me think _____ that for a minute.
2 Can you see the boy _____ the right?
3 That film _____ a bit boring.
4 She looks _____ she's happy.
5 Do you recognise that actor _____ the earring?

Mark: _____ /5

Total: _____ /20

Unit 2

5 **Choose the best adjective to describe each person's feelings: a, b or c.**

1 I wanted to buy that coat, but it was too expensive.
   a nervous **b** confused **c** disappointed
2 I thought I'd lost my phone, but I found it in my pocket.
   a confused **b** relieved **c** embarrassed
3 I fancy the girl next door, but she fancies my friend.
   a jealous **b** afraid **c** guilty
4 My school got the best exam results in the country.
   a ashamed **b** nervous **c** proud
5 I've been abroad for two months and I really want to see my friends and family.
   a amused **b** homesick **c** shocked

Mark: _____ /5

6 **Match the sentence halves.**

1 Kurt is really pleased   **a** of heights.
2 I'm fed up   **b** of his behaviour yesterday.
3 She's scared   **c** with his new mobile phone.
4 Kevin and Megan   **d** with you! You're so rude!
   felt guilty   **e** about the lies they told.
5 He's ashamed

Mark: _____ /5

7 **Choose the correct past form to complete the sentences.**

1 'How **did you get / were you getting** to school this morning?'   'I **walked / was walking.**'
2 I **did / was doing** my homework, when the computer **broke / was breaking.**
3 When I **lived / had lived** in Rome, I **used to eat / was eating** pasta every day.
4 When we **came / had come** home, mum **already cooked / had already cooked** dinner.
5 **Did you use to love / Were you loving** roller-skating when you **were / had been** younger?

Mark: _____ /5

8 **Complete the dialogue with the phrases below.**

In the end   Guess what   it was   How exciting!
You'll never

Boy ¹_____ happened to me the other day?
Girl What?
Boy Well, ²_____ Saturday night and I was walking into town. This huge car stopped beside me …
Girl Who was it?
Boy ³_____ guess! It was the lead singer of Psycho!
Girl No!! ⁴_____ What did he say?
Boy He asked me to give him directions and then we chatted for a bit. ⁵_____ he drove away.

Mark: _____ /5

Total: _____ /20

Lead-in

1 Do you think you would make a good housemate in a shared house? Why? / Why not? Tell your partner.

Reading

2 Read the letter from Anna Porucznik, an exchange student, and choose the best ending: a, b or c. Explain your choice.

a Yours faithfully
b Yours sincerely
c Love

Dear Libby

How are you? I'm halfway through the first term at Liverpool University. My economics course is really hard, but I'm enjoying it so far.

The bad news is, I need to find a new place to live. At the moment, I've got a room in a shared house, but there are six of us and only one bathroom! Also, I lost a CD last week and I think somebody in the house took it. I noticed a few other things had disappeared too – nothing big, just a magazine or two and some socks. When I realised what was happening, I was really shocked and upset. I decided not to talk to my housemates about it because I wasn't completely sure. But I definitely don't want to live here now!

I'm sure I told you about my friend Mike. We used to work together at Golden Hills holiday camp. Now he works for an IT company in Liverpool, but I don't see him very often. We're both really busy.

That's all for now. When are you going to visit me?

Anna

3 Are these sentences true or false?

1 Anna doesn't like her course because it's too difficult.
2 Anna shares a house with five other people.
3 Anna knows that somebody in her house stole her socks.
4 Anna doesn't want to live with her housemates any longer.
5 Mike and Anna see each other quite a lot.
6 Anna would like to see Libby.

Speaking

4 Work in pairs. Take turns to be A and B.

A: You are Anna. Tell a friend what happened in your shared house and explain why you are leaving.
B: You are Anna's friend. Listen to her narrative and react using phrases from the speaking strategy on page 20.

Listening

5 🎧 1.24 Listen and answer the questions.

1 Why is Anna talking to Zara?
2 Where are they?
3 When are they planning to talk to each other again?

6 🎧 1.24 Listen again. Choose the correct answers.

1 Zara is
  a the owner of the flat.
  b one of the people who rents the flat.
  c the only person who rents the flat.
  d the person who is leaving the flat.

2 When Anna tells Zara what happened in her house, Zara says
  a she is sure one of the housemates is a thief.
  b the same thing happened to her.
  c Anna probably just lost her things.
  d she knows who took them.

3 What kind of person does Anna say she is?
  a Very clean and tidy, but not quiet.
  b Quite friendly and easy-going, but not very tidy.
  c Very tidy and quite easy-going and friendly.
  d Quiet and friendly, easy-going and quite tidy.

4 How much rent will Anna have to pay a month?
  a £900 b £500 c £400 d £150

5 What must Anna do before she moves into the flat?
  a She has to write Zara an email.
  b She has to phone Zara.
  c She has to pay a month's rent.
  d She has to sign some papers.

Writing

7 Imagine you are Anna. Write a short informal letter to your friend, Libby. Tell her about Zara and your new flat.

THIS UNIT INCLUDES

Vocabulary ▪ jobs and gender ▪ activities at work ▪ describing work ▪ expressing an opinion ▪ agreeing and disagreeing ▪ agent nouns ▪ phrasal verbs
Grammar ▪ defining relative clauses ▪ non-defining relative clauses
Speaking ▪ discussing work abroad ▪ discussing work and gender ▪ a job interview
Writing ▪ a formal letter

3A VOCABULARY AND LISTENING The world of work

I can talk about jobs and work.

1 Make a list of jobs. How many can you think of in two minutes?

2 **VOCABULARY** Read the job adverts. Use the words in red to complete the vocabulary tables.

Telesales operator
Working in our busy call centre, you will answer the phone and deal with the public. The work is challenging, but rewarding. Shift work: either 07.00–15.00 or 15.00–23.00.

Bank clerk
Well-paid job for an experienced clerk. Working mostly on your own, you will be in charge of the reception desk and serve customers. Salary negotiable.

Construction workers
Skilled and unskilled workers required: plasterers, electricians, carpenters, labourers. Work part-time or full-time (35-hour week.)

Fruit-pickers
Fruit-pickers needed for farm in Norfolk. Working in a team of ten people. You can earn up to £9.50 an hour.

3 🎧 1.25 Listen to four radio adverts for jobs. Match each advert 1–4 with a sentence a–e. There is one sentence that you do not need.

1 ___   2 ___   3 ___   4 ___

a You will be given training.
b The employer hasn't decided the pay yet.
c You can earn more than the advertised pay.
d This job is suitable for a young person.
e This job involves shift work.

4 **SPEAKING** Describe the jobs in the photos. Talk about: the name of the job, the activities, the hours, the pay, whether you'd like to do the jobs and why.

> I think the woman in photo 1 is a … .

> She's working in a …

> She probably earns …

> Her job looks challenging. …

Activities at work	
answer the ¹_____	deal with the ²_____
use a computer	work on your ³_____
do paperwork	work in a ⁴_____
do manual work	be in ⁵_____ of
serve ⁶_____	supervise people

Hours of work	
work ⁷_____	do ⁸_____ work
work nine-to-five	work a 35-⁹_____ week

Pay		
salary	well-¹⁰_____	badly-paid
¹¹_____ (money)	£6 an ¹²_____	

Describing work			
stressful	busy	fun	tedious
¹³_____	menial	easy	rewarding
skilled		¹⁴_____	

5 **SPEAKING** If you could choose any job in the world, what would it be? Why? Think about hours of work, pay, responsibilities, etc.

> I'd be a …

> I'd work with / in …

⟫⟫⟫ VOCABULARY BUILDER 3.1: PAGE 129 ⟪⟪⟪

⟫⟫⟫ VOCABULARY BUILDER 3.2: PAGE 129 ⟪⟪⟪

3B GRAMMAR Defining relative clauses

I can describe a person, thing or place using defining relative clauses.

1 Read the text. Who does Tommy Lynch work for?

THE BEST JOB IN THE WORLD?

This is Tommy Lynch, a man whose job is to test water-slides. It's a job which almost every young person would love. He travels to holiday resorts which have waterslides, has a go on them and reports back to the travel company where he works. There are a lot of people who would like Tommy's job, so his company can expect a lot of applications when he leaves!

2 Underline the words *who, whose, where* and *which* in the text in exercise 1. Then complete the rules in the *Learn this!* box.

> **LEARN THIS!**
>
> **Relative pronouns: *who, whose, where* and *which***
> 1 We use _____ for things and animals.
> 2 We use _____ for people.
> 3 We use _____ for places.
> 4 We use _____ to indicate possession.

3 Complete the text with *who, whose, where* and *which*.

A DREAM JOB

It's a job ¹_____ attracted over 34,000 applications from around the world. Everyone ²_____ applied had to send in a 60-second video ³_____ explained why they wanted the job and what skills they had to offer. And what was this amazing job? Caretaker of Hamilton Island, in the Great Barrier Reef. It's a place ⁴_____ it's sunny and warm all year round, and ⁵_____ probably has the most beautiful coral reefs in the world. The person ⁶_____ got the job had to explore the islands nearby, and report back to the world about their experiences. The sixteen people ⁷_____ videos most impressed the employers came to Australia for an interview. The lucky man ⁸_____ was finally chosen for the job was Ben Southall from the UK. Unfortunately for him the job was only for six months!

4 SPEAKING Work in pairs. Ask and answer these questions.
1 Which job would you like better, Tommy Lynch's or Ben Southall's? Give reasons.
2 Can you think of any other dream jobs?

5 Complete the defining relative clauses with *who, where, which* and *whose*. Then write the words they are defining.
1 clothing *which* nurses, police officers, soldiers, etc. wear: *uniform*
2 a person _____ job is to look after the passengers on a plane: _____
3 a place _____ a surgeon works: _____
4 a person _____ is in charge of a shop or an office: _____
5 the money _____ you receive for a job: _____
6 a person _____ place of work is a laboratory: _____
7 a place _____ workers answer phones and give out information: _____
8 a job _____ you do only for part of the time: _____

6 Read the *Look out!* box. In which sentences in exercise 5 could you use *that*?

_____

> **LOOK OUT!**
> We often use *that* instead of *which*. In informal English, we can also use *that* instead of *who*.

_____

7 Read the *Learn this!* box. Look at exercises 1 and 3. Where do we place the relative clauses in the sentences?

> **LEARN THIS!**
>
> **Defining relative clauses**
> A defining relative clause comes immediately after a noun and tells us which person, thing or place we are talking about. It can be in the middle or at the end of a sentence. We do not put a comma before the clause.
> *She's the nurse who looked after my mother.*
> *The farm where my cousin picks fruit is enormous.*

>>> GRAMMAR BUILDER 3.1: PAGE 112 <<<

8 SPEAKING Work in pairs. Take turns to define the words below, or choose other words relating to the world of work. Your partner has to guess what you are defining.

a building site   a civil servant   a computer   a customer
an electrician   a hotel   a nurse   manual work
part-time job   salary   shift work

It's a person who / whose …

It's a place where …

It's something which …

Education for life?

I can talk about education.

1 🎧 1.26 **Listen to five students talking about university. Match the speakers (1–5) with the sentences (a–f). There is one sentence that you do not need.**

a The speaker's degree was essential for their job.
b The speaker thinks people with degrees should be paid more.
c The speaker thinks university is a waste of time.
d The speaker thinks it's better to get a job first and go to university later.
e The speaker really enjoyed their university course.
f The speaker thinks you should choose your university course carefully.

UNIVERSITY IN THE UK: FACT FILE

- In the UK approximately 40% of school-leavers go
  ^{1}_____ to study at university, compared with 8% in ^{2}_____ early 1980s.
- 15% of all university students are ^{3}_____ outside the UK. The most popular subjects with foreign students are business studies and engineering.
- Most undergraduate courses take three years of full-time study ^{4}_____ complete.
- University education is subsidised ^{5}_____ the Government. British and EU students pay towards their tuition fees and have to pay their own living expenses. They can usually take out a Government loan for this, ^{6}_____ they pay back when they reach a certain level of income.
- Vocational courses are becoming more popular. 90% of people ^{7}_____ take degrees in the UK go on to get ^{8}_____ job or do further study.
- People with degrees are likely to earn ^{9}_____ average £100,000 more during their working lives than non-graduates.

2 🎧 1.26 **VOCABULARY** **Complete the speakers' opinions with the words below. Then listen again and check.**

course   degree   education   graduates   university

1 Working for yourself is the best education there is – much more useful than a _____ .
2 I think _____ get more interesting jobs.
3 A university _____ teaches you a lot about yourself.
4 It's really important to think how the particular _____ you plan to do is going to help you get a job.
5 You'll get more from _____ if you spend some time working first.

3 **SPEAKING** **Work in pairs. Do you agree or disagree with the opinions in exercise 2? Can you think of any other advantages and disadvantages of going to university? Use the phrases below to help you.**

<u>Expressing an opinion</u>
I (don't) agree that …   I think that …   To my mind, …
In my view, …   In my opinion …

<u>Agreeing and disagreeing</u>
Yes, I agree.   That's right.   I think so too.   I don't agree.
On the other hand …   That may be true, but …

> To my mind, university teaches you a lot about life, as well as about your subject, so it's important to go to university.

> Yes, but on the other hand, university costs a lot of money.

4 🎧 1.27 **Read the fact file and complete it with appropriate words. Then listen and check.**

5 **Answer the questions.**

1 How has the number of students entering university changed since the early 1980s?
2 What proportion of university students are from abroad?
3 What do students have to pay for at university?
4 Where can they get money for their fees and living costs?
5 According to the text, what advantage do graduates have over people who haven't been to university?

6 **SPEAKING** **Work in pairs. Discuss these questions. Give reasons for your answers.**

1 Do you intend to go to college or university? Why? / Why not?
2 If so, what do you plan to study and where do you plan to study?
3 Would you consider studying abroad? If yes, where would you go and why? If not, why not?

▶▶▶ **VOCABULARY BUILDER 3.3: PAGE 129** ◀◀◀

1 Read the text about Ted Ingram quickly. What is his job and why does he do it?

Ted Ingram, who is 91 years old this year, could enter the Guinness Book of Records as the world's oldest paperboy. He has delivered newspapers in the village of Winterborn Monckton, where he lives, since he was 23. Ted moved to the village in 1938 and got a job on a farm, where he drove a tractor. He started delivering papers in 1942 to earn a bit more money. The 91-year-old, whose wife died twelve years ago, loves his job as it allows him to meet the neighbours and have a chat. During his career, which has lasted nearly seven decades, Ted has delivered over half a million papers. 'I'm not a paperboy – I'm more like a paperman!' joked Ted, who has no plans to retire.

2 Read the text again, ignoring the relative clauses (the words in red). Does the text make sense without them?

3 Read the *Learn this!* box and choose the correct words to complete the rules. Use the relative clauses in red in exercise 1 to help you.

LEARN THIS!

Non-defining relative clauses
1 A non-defining relative clause comes immediately **before / after** a noun and gives us information about that noun.
2 It adds extra information to the sentence; the sentence **makes sense / does not make sense** without it.
My uncle lives in London. He's an accountant.
My uncle, who's an accountant, lives in London.
3 It **starts / ends** with a comma and **starts / ends** with a comma, or a full stop.

LOOK OUT!

In non-defining relative clauses, we use *who, which, where* and *whose*, but we do not use *that*.

4 Complete the text about Bill Hocking with the relative clauses (a–f).

a who worries about him every time he goes out to sea
b where he keeps his boat
c who is 81 years old this year
d which used to last up to 36 hours
e which he sells at the local market
f whose boat is called *Neptune's Pride*

Bill Hocking, [1]_____ , is Britain's oldest fisherman. Most mornings he gets up early and goes down to the harbour, [2]_____ . His fishing trips, [3]_____ , are now only a few hours long. Besides being very old for a fisherman, there are other things that are unusual about Bill. First of all, he can't swim. His wife, [4]_____ , says 'It's what he loves doing and I would never try to stop him.' Bill, [5]_____ , goes out in his boat in almost any weather to catch lobsters and crabs, [6]_____ . The other odd thing about Bill is that he doesn't eat fish. He says he prefers steak!

5 Combine the two sentences to make one complex sentence. Include the information in the second sentence as a non-defining relative clause, either at the end or in the middle of the new sentence.

1 My sister wants to be a vet. She loves animals.
   My sister, who loves animals, wants to be a vet.
2 My aunt earns a lot of money. She's a lawyer.
3 I'd like to go to Africa. I can work in a national park.
4 Her daughter works in a laboratory. She lives in France.
5 He loves his job. It involves dealing with the public.
6 Last summer I visited Thailand. My cousin lives there.
7 Matthew wants to be an interpreter. His mum is a translator.

>>> GRAMMAR BUILDER 3.2: PAGE 113 <<<

6 Work in pairs or small groups. Add non-defining relative clauses to this story to make it more interesting.

On 1st June, Dan Smith went for a job interview with a large company. The interviewer looked at his CV and asked some questions. Dan told her about his previous job. Dan received a letter and showed it to his wife. He got the job, but he wasn't happy with the salary.

On 1st June, which was his 95th birthday, Dan Smith ...

7 **SPEAKING** Read your story to the class. Which is the most interesting story?

READING Reversing roles

I can understand and react to a magazine article about gender and work.

1 Read the puzzle. What is the answer? Why do many people find it difficult to answer this puzzle?

> A man and his son are in a serious car accident. The man dies and the son is taken to hospital. When he gets there, the surgeon sees the boy and says: 'I can't operate on this boy. He's my son!'
>
> How can this be?

2 **VOCABULARY** Look at the photos. What jobs are the man and woman doing? Choose from the jobs below.

air-traffic controller   labourer   nursery schoolteacher
plumber   surgeon

3 🎧 1.28 Are the man and woman good at their jobs? Read the texts quickly and find out.

4 Are these sentences true or false? Correct the false sentences.

1 Jonathan was better than the other men who applied for the job.
2 Jonathan has lots of experience of looking after small children.
3 The percentage of male nursery schoolteachers is less than ten years ago.
4 People expect male nursery schoolteachers to behave like female nursery schoolteachers.
5 Jonathan's female friends admire him for his choice of career.
6 The number of women air-traffic controllers has risen over the past ten years.
7 Both Caroline and her dad are interested in planes.
8 Caroline wasn't surprised that the male air-traffic controllers viewed her with suspicion.
9 Quite a few of the women air-traffic controllers can't read a map.

5 Read the *Learn this!* box. Look at the words in red in the first paragraph of each text. Do they apply to (a) just men? (b) just women? (c) both men and women?

<table>
<tr><td>LEARN THIS!</td><td>

The suffix *-ess* indicates that the person doing a job is a woman:
actress   air hostess   manageress   waitress
However, it's now more usual to use the same term for both men and women:
actor   flight attendant   manager   waiter
The neutral words *assistant, worker, person* or *officer* are now often used instead of *-man* or *-woman*:
police officer   spokesperson
</td></tr>
</table>

6 Find six more neutral words in the texts.

▶▶▶ **VOCABULARY BUILDER 3.4: PAGE 130** ◀◀◀

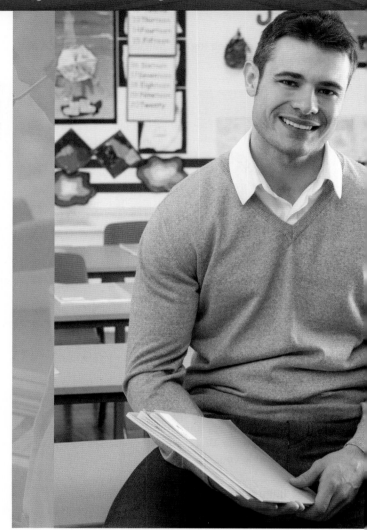

7 **VOCABULARY** Look at the list of jobs below. Decide which jobs involve:

a helping or looking after people.
b working with small children or babies.
c working with heavy machinery.
d getting dirty.

aircraft pilot   astronaut   beauty therapist   builder
coal miner   dental assistant   flight attendant   lorry driver
mechanic   nurse   secretary

8 **SPEAKING** Discuss these questions. Give reasons for your opinions.

1 Would you expect a man or woman to do the jobs in exercise 7?
2 Do you think men and women are better at different jobs, or equally good at all jobs?
3 Would you mind doing a job that is traditionally carried out by people of the opposite sex?
4 Would you like to do a job that involves a lot of travel or being away from home for long periods?

Woman's work?

ToddlerWorld Nursery was delighted to employ a trainee – twenty-two-year-old Jonathan Brown – as their first male nursery schoolteacher. He was also the only man who applied for the job, but, insists Margery Bowman, head teacher of ToddlerWorld, by far the best applicant. 'Both boys and girls will benefit from the experience of having a male role model in the nursery,' says mother of two, Margery.

Jonathan has always been interested in childcare. His own mother is a childminder and his father is a teacher. 'I've always helped Mum with looking after all the children,' he says. 'I'm used to changing nappies, feeding babies, reading stories and playing with Lego.'

But Jonathan is a rare male in a female world. Only 2% of nursery teachers are men and this hasn't changed for ten years. Roger Olsen of the National Nursery Trust said, 'Men are often viewed with anxiety and suspicion in a children's environment. Or they are expected to do things the way women would do them. But men bring different things into childcare and this has to be recognised.' Jonathan agrees. He is a qualified under-7s football coach, and plans to introduce football lessons to the nursery for boys and girls.

What do Jonathan's friends think of his choice of career? 'Actually, most of them are pretty cool about it now,' he says, 'though they do make jokes about nappies. And I've found that girls are actually quite impressed – so that's good!'

A man's world?

Ten years ago there were very few female air-traffic controllers. It was seen as a man's world. But now 25% of air-traffic controllers in the UK are women and the number is increasing.

Caroline Beck is one of them. She says, 'I've always been interested in planes because of my dad. He knew a lot about them. For a while we lived near Heathrow airport and we used to watch all the planes taking off and landing.' She was determined to be an air-traffic controller. 'The twelve months of training, the exams and the air-crash simulation exercises were tough,' says Caroline, 'but I was well-prepared for my career. What I wasn't prepared for was the reaction of some of the men, especially the older ones.' The new women controllers were viewed with suspicion and they had to work twice as hard to be accepted by their male colleagues. Nowadays things are better, but women are still in a minority. 'I'm the only woman in my team, but I get on well with my colleagues. There are still plenty of jokes about women – the men say that we can't read maps, which isn't true – but I generally don't mind. My job is highly responsible and stressful, but I know I'm good at it.'

1 🎧 1.29 Read the job adverts below. Then read and listen to the dialogue. Which job would suit Emily best?

> ▶ Confident, enthusiastic **assistant bartender** required for hotel on outskirts of town.
> Hours: 18.00–20.00 Monday to Friday.
> Experience not required. £7 an hour
>
> ▶ **Waiter / Waitress** needed for our new café. Hard-working and energetic, you will join our friendly, young team. Must enjoy dealing with customers. Shift work (lunch or dinner). £7.30 an hour plus tips

Manager	How did you find out about the job?
Emily	I saw it advertised on a recruitment agency website.
Manager	You've worked in catering before, haven't you?
Emily	Yes, I have. I used to help out at my uncle's restaurant.
Manager	What did you do there?
Emily	First of all just washing up in the kitchen. But then I took orders, and served food and drinks. Occasionally I answered the phone and took reservations.
Manager	Did you enjoy the work?
Emily	Yes, I did, though it was very tiring on busy nights.
Manager	And you worked there for about a year, didn't you?
Emily	Yes, about a year, part-time.
Manager	I see. And why do you think you're the right person for this job?
Emily	Because I'm hard-working and reliable, and I enjoy dealing with the public. I'm also good at working in a team.
Manager	Well, thanks for coming in, Emily. We'll be in touch before the end of the week.

2 Read the *Learn this!* box. Find two examples of question tags in the dialogue in exercise 1.

> **Question tags**
> **1** We use question tags when we want somebody to confirm what we are saying:
> *You worked in the kitchen, didn't you?*
> **2** We use auxiliary verbs (*do, have, would*, etc.) or the verb *be* in question tags:
> *You weren't serving customers, were you?*

🎧 1.30 **PRONUNCIATION** ⟫ GRAMMAR BUILDER 3.3: PAGE 114 ⟪

3 **VOCABULARY** Check the meaning of these words in a dictionary. Which qualities did Emily mention?

<u>Qualities needed for jobs</u> confident conscientious co-operative creative determined energetic enthusiastic fit flexible hard-working polite positive reliable self-motivated thoughtful trustworthy

4 **SPEAKING** Which qualities are (a) necessary (b) desirable for these jobs?

athlete banker chef farm worker fitness instructor police officer refuse collector research scientist sales representative

> To be an athlete, you need to be very / quite …

> It doesn't matter if you're not very …

5 🎧 1.31 Listen to the interview for a summer job. Which of the jobs in exercise 4 is it for?

6 🎧 1.31 Listen again. Number the questions in the order that you hear them. How many answers can you remember?

a What kinds of things did you do? ☐
b You're in good physical health, aren't you? ☐
c When can you start work? ☐
d You live locally, don't you? ☐
e Have you got any experience of this type of work? ☐
f Why do you want this job? ☐
g Why do you think you're the right person for this job? ☐

7 Work in pairs. Plan an interview for one of the jobs in exercise 4 following the guide below.

• where the applicant saw the job advertised
• the applicant's experience of similar jobs
• why the applicant wants the job
• when the applicant can start

8 **SPEAKING** Act out your dialogue to the class. The class votes on whether the applicant gets the job!

I can write a letter applying for a job.

1 Read the letter quickly. Answer the questions.

1 Why is Dan writing the letter?
2 Is the letter formal or informal?

The Manager
Manning's Electrical Store
Turnpike Lane
Bedford MK48 5FG

13 St Ann's Crescent
Bedford MK47 5RF

19 June 2012

Dear Sir or Madam

Post of part-time shop assistant

I am writing to apply for the post of part-time shop assistant which I saw advertised in the Luton Gazette.

Last summer, I worked for six weeks as an assistant in my local newsagent's. My responsibilities there included serving customers as well as shelf-filling and answering the phone.

I consider myself to be trustworthy, hard-working and enthusiastic. If necessary, I can supply references from the newsagent and also from a teacher at my school.

I would be grateful for the opportunity to visit your shop and discuss my application with you in person. I am available for interview any day after school or on Saturdays. If my application is successful, I will be available to start work on 22 July.

I am enclosing my CV.

I look forward to hearing from you soon.

Yours faithfully,

Dan Wilson

Dan P. Wilson

2 Look at the letter. Where can you see (a) the date? (b) the recipient's address? (c) the writer's address?

3 In which paragraph (1–4) does Dan mention:

1 references that he can send?
2 the job he's applying for?
3 when he can start work?
4 where he saw the job advert?
5 his personal qualities?
6 his experience of working in a shop?

4 Read the *Learn this!* box. How does Dan begin and end his letter? Why?

Forms of address in formal letters
If we don't know the recipient's name, we start with *Dear Sir or Madam*, and end with *Yours faithfully*.
If we do know the recipient's name, we start with *Dear Mr / Ms / Mrs* + surname, and end with *Yours sincerely*.

EXAM STRATEGY

Make sure you start and finish your letter in an appropriate way. Using some more formal expressions improves the style of your letter.

5 Read the exam strategy. Read Dan's letter again. Find more formal ways of saying the phrases in red below.

1 I am writing to ask you for the job of part-time shop assistant
2 The things I had to do there included serving customers and shelf-filling
3 I think that I am trustworthy, hard-working and enthusiastic
4 If I have to, I can give you references
5 I would really like to visit your shop
6 I can start work on 22 July
7 I'm sending my CV

6 Read the job advert. Think about what qualities and experience you might need for the job. Make notes.

❦ HOTEL RECEPTIONIST ❦
We need an experienced person to work at our hotel in Oxford from 15 July to 31 August.
Working hours are from 10 a.m. to 6 p.m.
Your duties will include:
• greeting guests • checking them in and out
• answering the phone and taking bookings

Please apply in writing to:
The Manager, **Queen Victoria Hotel**,
84–88 Beecham Rd, Oxford OX4 7UH

7 Write a formal letter of 120–150 words applying for the job in the advert. Follow the writing plan below.

• Mention the job you are applying for and where you saw the advert.
• Give details of previous work experience and responsibilities. Mention any relevant personal interests.
• Talk about why you are right for the job. List your personal qualities and offer to send a reference.
• Say when you are available for interview and when you could start work.

CHECK YOUR WORK

Have you:
☐ included the information in the task from exercise 7?
☐ used formal expressions?
☐ written no more than 150 words?

Reading

1 [**Get ready to READ**] Work in pairs. Imagine you could live in an unusual place or lead an unusual lifestyle. Where or what would it be? Discuss the ideas below and then try to think of other unusual places or ways to live.

1 on a ship sailing around the world with your family
2 with a small group of people on a small island
3 in a hut in the mountains alone
4 with a remote tribe away from civilisation

2 Do the exam task.

READING exam task

Read the text. Four sentences have been removed. Match each gap (1–4) with a sentence (A–E). There is one extra sentence that you do not need.

The way things were

When I think of my childhood, I think of water. I was born, and spent my early life, on a houseboat, along with my older sister and my parents. I remember the unsteady, but also comforting, feeling of being on the water. [**1**]
And I remember the rain – lots of it! When you're on a small boat, you feel and notice the weather more. I also remember going to the standpipe to fetch water. We regularly needed to fill up the water tanks on the boat, and that job belonged to me and my sister. We always had to be careful with how much water we used. [**2**]
We washed in a small tin bath, and washed our hair in the sink. We brushed our teeth with a mug of water. My mum washed all our clothes by hand and hung them out along the top of the boat in fine weather, but all over the inside of the boat on rainy days. A lingering memory of my childhood is the smell of damp clothes.

Our boat was fairly long, but extremely narrow. [**3**]
My parents' bedroom was at the far end of the boat, next to the little room where my sister and I had bunk beds. At the other end of the boat, there was a tiny bathroom, living space and kitchen area. When my sister and I wanted more space, we played beside the boat at the water's edge. We used to play outside in all weather.

Most of my early life we spent travelling along the canals of southern England. But when I was six, we came to stay in Oxford on a canal near the centre of the city, and my sister and I started formal education. [**4**] Until then we hadn't really realised that our way of life was unusual, but our new friends were fascinated by our home. As we were by theirs!

A	It was funny to be surrounded by water, but feel that we didn't have much of it.
B	It was strange at first to stay in the same place, but the pleasure of going to school helped a lot.
C	So there was a lot of hard work for my parents and my sister and me.
D	Our house was always rocking and moving slightly.
E	As a result, there wasn't much space, so we had to be very tidy.

Use of English

3 Do the exam task.

USE OF ENGLISH exam task

Complete the text with an appropriate word in each gap.

Early memories

My first memory is of my mother painting my cot. I remember the smell [1]_____ the paint. It probably wasn't very good [2]_____ me! I also remember falling [3]_____ of my pushchair and banging my head, although my mum says it was my brother [4]_____ did that. He's a year older [5]_____ me. Perhaps I saw him do it. I have a vague memory of my grandmother visiting us and giving me a bag of sweets, but she died when I was three, so I'm not sure [6]_____ this is a real memory or just based [7]_____ what my mum has told me about her. I remember my sister being born when I was four. My brother and I went to a neighbour's house while mum was [8]_____ hospital. I don't know why dad couldn't look [9]_____ us, but anyway, we were only there [10]_____ one night.

Speaking

4 Do the exam task.

SPEAKING exam task

Work in pairs. Imagine that you left school ten years ago and that you are now organising a reunion for members of your class. Agree on:

- where you should hold the reunion (restaurant? school hall? other venue?)
- what the reunion should involve (food and drink? entertainment? speeches?)
- how you will notify the former members of your class of your plans
- whether you should invite teachers too.

Listening

5 **Get ready to LISTEN**
Work in pairs. Describe the photo. Ask and answer the questions.

1 When did you last take an exam?
2 How did you feel? Why?
3 Do you find revising easy?

6 Use the words below to complete the expressions connected with exams.

do   get   hear from   mess up   revise   sit

1 _____ good marks
2 _____ for an exam
3 _____ a university
4 _____ an exam
5 _____ an exam
6 _____ well in an exam

7 🎧 1.32 Do the exam task.

LISTENING exam task

Listen to the conversation. Match each statement to the correct speaker, Angus or Dora. Tick the correct boxes.

Which speaker	A	D
1 has just sat a history exam?		
2 has just taken a difficult exam?		
3 isn't keen on chemistry?		
4 has a relative who found a biology exam difficult?		
5 has to get permission to visit another country?		
6 would like to go to America?		
7 hasn't had their place at university confirmed yet?		

Speaking

8 **Get ready to SPEAK** Work in pairs. Ask and answer the questions.

1 How often do you go to restaurants? What kind of restaurants?
2 How often do you go to museums or art galleries? What do you like / dislike about them?

9 Do the Speaking exam task.

SPEAKING exam task

Compare and contrast the two photos. Answer the questions.

1 What are main differences between the two places of work: a street café and a museum?
2 What could be good or bad about working in a street café or a museum?
3 What kind of personal qualities would you need to do each job well?
4 Which job would you enjoy more? Why?

THIS UNIT INCLUDES

Vocabulary ■ parts of the body ■ inside the body ■ nutrition ■ laws and rights ■ homonyms and homophones ■ symptoms
Grammar ■ past simple and present perfect contrast ■ present perfect continuous
Speaking ■ talking about diet and lifestyle ■ at the doctor's
Writing ■ an announcement

4A VOCABULARY AND LISTENING The human body

I can talk about parts of the body and injuries.

1 VOCABULARY Work in pairs. Match these parts of the body with the correct section of the photo (A–C).

<u>Parts of the body</u> ankle armpit calf chest chin eyebrow eyelash eyelid fingernail heel hip lip neck nostril palm scalp shin sole stomach thigh throat thumb toenail waist wrist

2 🎧 1.33 Listen and check your answers.

3 SPEAKING Work in pairs. Choose and describe a part of the body using one or more of the phrases below. Your partner guesses which part you are describing.

> It's part of your (face / leg / hand / etc.).

> It's at the front / back / end of your ...

> It's between your ... and your ...

4 SPEAKING Work in pairs. Complete the injuries (1–6) with the words below. Then ask and answer questions. If the answer is *yes*, ask a follow-up question using the past simple.

ankle eye leg lip ~~shin~~ shoulder

1 a bruised <u>shin</u>
2 a dislocated _____ / finger
3 a sprained _____ / wrist
4 a broken arm, _____ or finger
5 a black _____
6 a cut _____

> Have you ever had a bruised shin?

> Yes, I have.

> How did you get it?

> Somebody kicked me while I was playing football.

5 🎧 1.34 Listen to six dialogues. Complete each sentence with one of the words below and then choose the correct meaning for the idiom (a–c).

arm eyelid head hand leg neck

1 He was pulling your _____ .
   He was **a** angry with you. **b** joking. **c** embarrassed.
2 Did you give him a _____ ?
   Did you **a** help him? **b** lie to him? **c** make him happy?
3 You've twisted my _____ .
   You've **a** upset me. **b** told me everything.
   c persuaded me.
4 I'll stick my _____ out.
   I'll **a** take a risk. **b** think about it. **c** look.
5 She didn't bat an _____ .
   She wasn't **a** awake. **b** crying. **c** surprised.
6 You need to keep your _____ .
   You need to **a** be silent. **b** work hard. **c** stay calm.

6 Work in pairs. Write three short dialogues which include three of the idioms from exercise 5.

7 SPEAKING Act out your dialogues to the class. The class votes for the most entertaining dialogues.

>>> **VOCABULARY BUILDER 4.1: PAGE 130** <<<

1 **Look at the photo. Guess the answers to these questions. Then read the text and find the answers.**

1 What is the man doing?
2 Is it his job or just a hobby?
3 Which country is he in?

Inspired

Danny MacAskill grew up on a Scottish island, but has lived in Edinburgh, since 2006. Thanks to the Internet, he has become one of the most famous stunt riders in the world. Three years ago, he made a video called *Mountain Bike Trickster* and posted it on YouTube. Three million people watched it. His most recent video is called *Inspired Bicycles*. It has already had half a million views – and it hasn't been on YouTube for more than a few days! His videos are so successful that Danny has given up his regular job and become a professional mountain bike rider. Danny has always enjoyed doing stunts. Not surprisingly, he's had a lot of accidents. In fact, he can't ride at the moment because he's just broken his collarbone for the third time in the past six months!

2 **Look at the verb forms in red in the text. Which are present perfect and which are past simple? Read the *Learn this!* box and match the present perfect examples in the text with uses a–c.**

Present perfect and past simple
1 We use the **past simple** to talk about completed events in the past, often with words that refer to a specific time (*yesterday, two years ago*, etc.):
  I went to London last weekend.
2 We use the **present perfect**
  a to say how long a current situation has existed (often with *for* or *since*):
    I've worked here for a year. (and I still work here)
  b to talk about an experience at an unspecified time in the past:
    'Have you ever been to Paris?' 'No, I haven't.'
  c to talk about recent events that have a connection with the present. We sometimes use *already, just* or *yet*:
    'You look happy.' 'I've just got my exam result.'

▶▶▶ GRAMMAR BUILDER 4.1: PAGE 114 ◀◀◀

3 🎧 1.35 **Complete *Wave* magazine's interview with Adam Harvey, a 16-year-old kayak surfing champion. Use the past simple or present perfect. Then listen and check.**

Wave When ¹_____ you _____ (start) kayak surfing?
Adam Ten years ago. I ²_____ (go) kayaking a few times with my family. Later, my brother ³_____ (take) me to the beach and we went kayaking in the waves. I ⁴_____ (be) a fan since that day!
Wave Most people ⁵_____ (not hear) of kayak surfing. What is it?
Adam It's like surfing, but you're in a kayak, not on a board. The sport ⁶_____ (become) a lot more popular in the past few years.
Wave ⁷_____ you _____ (have) much success in the sport?
Adam Yes. I ⁸_____ (win) several medals so far including the junior world championship.
Wave When ⁹_____ you _____ (win) that?
Adam In 2009.

4 **Find these time expressions in the dialogue in exercise 3. Then add them to the chart below.**

in [2009]   in the past few years   later   since …   so far
[ten] years ago

past simple		present perfect
yesterday		yet
last week	this morning	already
a year ago	for a week	today
1_____		4_____
2_____		5_____
3_____		6_____

5 **SPEAKING Work in pairs. Ask and answer questions about what you have done in the past few months. Use the phrases below or your own ideas. Ask follow-up questions in the past simple.**

do any sport?   eat out?   go shopping?
play computer games?   read any good books?
see any good films?

> Have you been shopping in the past few months?

> Yes, I have.

> What did you buy?

> I bought a new MP3 player.

1 VOCABULARY Describe the food in the photo. What does each food contain a lot of?

calories carbohydrate fat fibre protein salt sugar vitamins

A healthy appetite?

In Britain, school children usually have lunch at school, and recently the Government has encouraged schools to offer healthier food.

At the start of the autumn term, John Lambert, the head teacher at Rawmarsh Comprehensive School in Yorkshire, introduced healthier school meals that he says help the children to concentrate better. He also reduced the lunch break from one hour to thirty minutes, and banned children from going out to local takeaways during the break.

But two mothers, Mrs Critchlow and Mrs Walker, believe that the new rules don't give pupils enough choice or enough time to enjoy their lunch. So two weeks ago, they started passing burgers, fish and chips and fizzy drinks over the school fence. Soon, they were delivering up to 60 food orders!

Mr Lambert has described the two mothers as unwise, and said they were undermining the school and their children's education. He claims there have been improvements in behaviour and learning in the afternoons since the new healthy eating regime was introduced.

After a meeting with Mr Lambert, the two mothers have agreed to stop their deliveries while they try to resolve the problem. Speaking before their meeting, Mrs Critchlow argued that the children have the right to choose their food. 'We are not against healthy eating – it's about the freedom of choice.'

2 🎧 1.36 Read and listen to the text and answer the questions.

1 When did the school introduce the new rules?
2 What has the school banned students from doing during lunch break?
3 Why are the two mothers unhappy about the new rules?
4 What did the mothers do after the new rules were introduced?
5 What are the benefits of the new regime, according to the head teacher?

3 SPEAKING Work in pairs.

1 Explain the disagreement between Mr Lambert and the two mothers in your own words.
2 Do you think schools should try to improve their students' diets, or should students be able to choose what they eat? Justify your answer.

4 🎧 1.37 Listen to five people in Britain talking about health issues. Which two speakers think that the Government should not tell us what to eat?

5 🎧 1.37 Complete each speaker's opinion (a–e) with the words below. Then listen again and match the speakers (1–5) with the opinions.

children diet Government issues treatment

a _____ and fitness are personal matters – the Government shouldn't pass laws about them.
b If people don't look after their health, the Government will have to raise taxes to pay for _____ .
c People have the right to eat unhealthy food, but not to give it to their _____ .
d The _____ would make a lot more things illegal, if they could.
e The Government has launched successful campaigns in the past to raise awareness of health _____ .

6 VOCABULARY Find and complete these collocations from exercise 5. Then write an example sentence for each collocation.

have ~~launch~~ make pass raise raise

1 _launch_ a campaign (to do something)
2 _____ a law
3 _____ awareness (of something)
4 _____ something illegal
5 _____ taxes
6 _____ the right (to do something)

The Government has launched a campaign to improve the diet of families.

▶▶▶ VOCABULARY BUILDER 4.2: PAGE 130 ◀◀◀

7 Work in pairs. Decide on three ways to make your diet and lifestyle healthier. Think about:

• foods you should cut down on or give up completely.
• foods you should have more of in your diet.
• ways of getting more exercise.

8 SPEAKING Tell the class your three ideas from exercise 7. The class votes for the best ideas.

> We think we should cut down on fried food and give up sugar in coffee.

> We also think ...

> And finally, we think ...

1 SPEAKING Read the text. What is the scientific study trying to find out? How would you summarise the results?

Brain workouts

Kevin Wilson is not usually a fan of computer games, but recently he has been playing one particular game a lot. In fact, he's been playing it every day for six weeks. It's a special kind of game which is designed to increase brainpower by giving the player mental exercises.
'I'm definitely improving,' he says. 'I've been getting much better scores recently.'
Wilson is one of 11,000 volunteers who have been taking part in a scientific study organised by a Cambridge scientist called Adrian Owen. Its purpose is to find out if brain-training really works. Half of the volunteers haven't been using the brain-training programs at all; they've been surfing the Internet instead.

Owen has conducted several studies of this kind, and they have all shown the same thing: brain-training has a small positive effect on mental abilities, but surfing the Internet is just as good!

2 Look at the verbs in red in the text. Complete the rule.

> We form the present perfect continuous with
> *have* / ¹_____ + ²_____ + the *-ing* form of the verb.

3 Read the *Learn this!* box. Complete the examples with the correct form of the present perfect continuous.

Present perfect continuous
We use the present perfect continuous to talk about:
1 an action that began in the past and is still in progress. We often use *for* or *since* to say how long it has been in progress.
We ¹_____ *(play) tennis for an hour.*
How long ²_____ *you* _____ *(wait)? Since midday.*
2 an action that has recently stopped and which explains the present situation.
I ³_____ *(carry) these heavy bags. That's why I'm tired.*

4 Complete the sentences with the present perfect continuous form of the verbs below.

drink eat play pull wear work

1 You _____ that computer game for hours. Haven't you finished yet?
2 I feel sick. I _____ chocolates all day!
3 I'm sure you'll pass your exams; you _____ all term.
4 Who _____ my orange juice? My glass is half empty!
5 Luke isn't Lady Gaga's cousin – he _____ your leg.
6 The weather's great. We _____ shorts every day.

>>> GRAMMAR BUILDER 4.2: PAGE 114 <<<

5 Read the *Learn this!* box. Find two examples in exercise 1 of the present perfect simple which describe actions that are finished and complete.

Present perfect simple or present perfect continuous?
We use the present perfect simple, not continuous:
1 if the action is finished and complete.
I've written a letter. I'm going to post it now.
2 if we want to say how often an action has happened.
She's broken her leg three times.
3 with state verbs (*like, love, know,* etc.).
I've known Joe for years. ✓
I've been knowing Joe for years. ✗

6 Complete the email with the present perfect simple or present perfect continuous form of the verbs in brackets.

✉ Inbox

Hi Tom! So, we're halfway through the summer holiday. ¹_____ you _____ (enjoy) it? Aunt Vera ²_____ (stay) with us. Dad and Aunt Vera ³_____ never _____ (like) each other. They ⁴_____ (not have) any big arguments yet, but that's probably because Dad ⁵_____ (spend) his evenings up in the attic! He says he ⁶_____ (work), but when I went up there, he was making a model aeroplane. He ⁷_____ (make) about ten of them – they're all on his desk.

>>> GRAMMAR BUILDER 4.3: PAGE 115 <<<

7 SPEAKING Work in pairs.
Student A: Make a comment from the list (1–5).
Student B: Give a reason, using the present perfect simple or continuous.
You look
1 ... confused.   3 ... pleased.   5 ... fed up.
2 ... tired.   4 ... guilty.

You look confused.   I've been trying to do my maths homework.

1 Look at the photos and the main title of the text. What do you think the people in each photo are doing? What connects the photos?

MIND OVER MATTER?

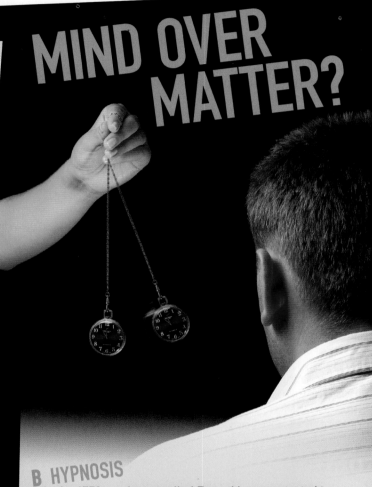

A FIREWALKING

Walking across burning coals or red-hot stones has a long tradition. 1 ☐ It became popular in Europe and the USA in the 1970s, and <u>many people went on training courses</u> to learn the skill. They believed that firewalking was good for their mind and body and might even give them mystical powers. Actually, the ability to walk over hot coals has more to do with physics than mind over matter. The heat doesn't pass quickly from the coals to the walkers' feet, particularly if they keep moving. If you do it properly, there is little risk of injury.

2 ☐ In 2002, 30 managers from the KFC fast food chain went on a team-building trip which included firewalking. <u>Twenty of them had to go to hospital</u> in order to get medical treatment for burnt soles. They used red hot wood instead of coal.

B HYPNOSIS

In the 1770s, a doctor called Franz Mesmer started to treat his patients in Paris with a strange new technique: he held their thumbs, pressed their stomachs, and then played music on an instrument made of glass. 3 ☐ Mesmer didn't know it, but he was using a form of hypnosis. These days, hypnosis still has medical uses, but most people are familiar with it because of stage hypnotists. <u>These performers ask for volunteers from the audience</u> so that they can hypnotise them. In this state, the volunteers do all kinds of strange and funny things: they eat onions as if they were apples, or they act like animals or giant babies. The hypnotist seems to have control over their minds. Although the main purpose is entertainment, some people find the idea of mind control worrying. The <u>British Government even passed a law in 1952</u> in order to protect the public from irresponsible hypnotists! 4 ☐ Most scientists believe stage hypnotism does not involve real mind control. The volunteers are extroverts who want to help the performer to put on a good show.

2 🎧 1.38 Read the text, ignoring the gaps. Match each section of the text (A–C) with two of the questions (1–6).

Which mind-over-matter activity:
1 is sometimes used by doctors?
2 caused an injury?
3 did ordinary people start practising?
4 was first studied in the 1800s?
5 often takes place on stage?
6 was an American performer suspicious of?

C TELEKINESIS

In the nineteenth century, scientists became interested in the possibility that some people had the power to move a physical object without touching it. They named this power telekinesis, and over the years several people have claimed to have it. In 1980, American James Hydrick became famous overnight after appearing on a TV show. Millions watched him as he made the pages of a book turn without touching them. 5 ☐ But James Randi, an American magician, was sceptical. He knows the different tricks people use when they pretend to have psychic powers. Randi appeared on a live TV show with Hydrick in order to test his claims. He put small pieces of polystyrene around a book and then challenged Hydrick to turn the pages using telekinesis, without moving the polystyrene. Hydrick couldn't do it. Later, Hydrick publicly admitted that he had never had special powers. So, how did the pages move? Simple: he blew them! But he had practised blowing hard without moving his lips or chest.

3 Match sentences a–f below with gaps 1–5 in the text. There is one extra sentence that you do not need.

a However, using the wrong materials can be a disaster.
b On the other hand, many people doubted that his powers could be genuine.
c It has been part of ceremonies in many different countries for at least 3,000 years.
d Most viewers were convinced that he had genuine psychic powers.
e Many of these patients showed dramatic improvements.
f In fact, this was probably unnecessary.

4 Find the five underlined phrases in the text and look at the words which follow them. Read and complete the *Learn this!* box.

> **Clauses expressing purpose**
> 1 We can use an infinitive to explain the purpose of an action.
>   *He went to the Alps to go skiing.*
> 2 We can also use these phrases:
>   ¹_____ _____ *to* + base form
>   ²_____ *that* + subject + verb (usually a modal verb, e.g. *could*)

5 Answer questions 1–5 about the underlined parts in the text. Use a different clause expressing purpose from that used in the text.

1 Why did people go on training courses? [Text A]
2 Why did the managers go to hospital? [Text A]
3 Why did the performers ask for volunteers? [Text B]
4 Why did the British Government pass a law in 1952? [Text B]
5 Why did Randi appear on a live TV show with Hydrick? [Text C]

6 **VOCABULARY** Read the *Look out!* box. Then look at the red words in the text and decide whether they are nouns or verbs.

LOOK OUT! Homonyms

Homonyms are words which have the same spelling, but are not the same word. Sometimes homonyms are different parts of speech. The meaning can be similar or completely different.
Let's talk. I had a talk with him. (similar meaning)
Meet me at the park. Park your car over there. (different meaning)

⟫⟫ **VOCABULARY BUILDER 4.3: PAGE 130** ⟪⟪

7 Do the experiment below in pairs. Then count the total number of correct answers in the class.

Student A: Choose one of the shapes below, but don't tell Student B. Stare at it and try to send your thoughts to Student B for thirty seconds.

Student B: After thirty seconds, look at the shapes. Guess which shape Student A chose.

8 **SPEAKING** Discuss the results of your experiment with the class.

- Did more than 25% of the class guess correctly? (25% is the result you might expect to get on average, just by chance.)
- Do you think the people who guessed correctly have a special ability?
- If your result was over 25%, can you suggest why?
- Do you believe that some people have psychic powers? Why? / Why not?

1 🎧 2.02 **Complete the dialogue with the doctor's questions (a–e). Then listen and check.**

a Are you allergic to penicillin?

b Have you had any other symptoms?

c Have you put any drops in it?

d Is it painful?

e When did it start?

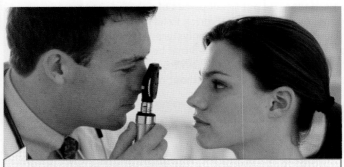

Doctor	Good morning. What can I do for you?
Patient	Well, I've got a problem with my eye.
Doctor	Oh, yes. I can see that. ¹_____
Patient	Three or four days ago.
Doctor	I see. ²_____
Patient	Yes, it's very sore. It hurts when I blink.
Doctor	Let me have a look at it. Yes … the eyelid is very swollen. ³_____
Patient	Yes. I got some eye drops from the chemist's, but they didn't do anything.
Doctor	I think you need antibiotics. You've got an eye infection. ⁴_____
Patient	No, I'm not. I've taken it before.
Doctor	OK. I'm going to prescribe some eye drops as well.
Patient	Good. Thank you.
Doctor	⁵_____
Patient	No, I haven't. I've been feeling fine.
Doctor	Good. Now, I think you should come back next week. I want to make sure it's getting better. And you must call immediately if it gets worse.

2 VOCABULARY **Complete the sentences with the words below. Underline the two symptoms that are in the dialogue in exercise 1.**

Symptoms blocked up dizzy itchy rash sore stiff
swollen temperature

1 If a part of your body is _____ , it has got bigger.

2 If you're _____ , you feel as if you might fall over.

3 If a part of your body is _____ , you can't move it easily.

4 If you've got a _____ , your body is hotter than usual.

5 If a part of your body is _____ , you want to scratch it.

6 If you've got a _____ nose, you can't breathe through it.

7 If you've got a _____ , an area of skin is red.

8 If part of your body is _____ , that part hurts.

⟫⟫⟫ VOCABULARY BUILDER 4.4: PAGE 131 ⟪⟪⟪

3 🎧 2.03 **Listen to four patients. Match the patients with the symptoms. Each person has got two different symptoms. Write patient 1, 2, 3 or 4.**

headache   ___ ___   feel sick   ___ ___
temperature ___ ___   upset stomach   ___ ___

> **LEARN THIS!**
>
> **Giving advice**
> We can use these expressions to give advice.
> *I (really) think you should … I don't think you should …*
> *If I were you, I would / wouldn't … Try (not) to …*
> *In your position, I would / wouldn't … You need to …*
> *It's (very) important (not) to … You must / mustn't …*
> *The best thing would be to … You (really) ought to …*
> *It would be a good idea (not) to …*

4 **Read the information in the *Learn this!* box above. Which of the expressions is used for giving very strong advice?**

5 🎧 2.04 PRONUNCIATION **Listen and repeat the phrases, copying the intonation.**

6 **Write the doctor's advice using suitable expressions from the *Learn this!* box. There may be more than one correct answer.**

1 <u>You need to</u> drink lots of water.

2 _____ worry about food until you're better.

3 _____ cycle home.

4 _____ be careful about head injuries.

5 _____ to cook meat properly.

6 _____ take extra care washing your hands.

7 _____ to stay at home for a few days.

8 _____ rest as much as possible.

7 **Work in pairs. Prepare a role-play between a patient and a doctor. Decide:**

• how long the patient has been feeling unwell.

• what the patient's symptoms are (see Vocabulary Builder 4.4: Page 131).

• what the doctor's advice is.

8 SPEAKING **Act out the following dialogue using your ideas from exercise 7. Use expressions from the *Learn this!* box for giving advice.**

Student A: You are staying in England on an exchange trip and you've started to feel unwell. You are now at the doctor's. Tell the doctor your symptoms and answer any other questions.

Student B: You are a doctor. An exchange student has come to see you, feeling unwell. Listen to the symptoms and ask relevant questions. Give advice.

1 Read the announcements. Which activity appeals to you most? Why?

DO YOU WANT TO EXPLORE THE COASTLINE?

Are you a strong swimmer and generally fit?
THEN COME AND TRY COASTEERING!

The North Devon Coasteering Society meet every weekend to explore the beautiful, rocky coastline from Lynton to Bideford. It's a great way to make friends too!

Time: 4.30 p.m. every Saturday
Venue: meet by Watermouth Castle
Cost: £15 per session
Come along for one session – and you'll be hooked!

Meditation

Meditation is not only relaxing and enjoyable, but it also boosts your natural immune system. Follow our ten-week course and learn a new skill which will have real benefits for your health.

Meditation is ideal for people who suffer from:
• frequent headaches • memory failures • anxiety • backache • loss of concentration

The new course starts on 10 May at 7.30 p.m. at Frume Village Hall and costs £45 for ten sessions.

Why don't you try it? It could change your life!

DO YOU WANT TO GET FIT?
Do you prefer dancing to working out?

Then our new STREET DANCE class could be perfect for you. You can learn new steps, meet new people, have fun, and get a new, fitter body. And of course, the soundtrack is COOL!

Time and place - 6.30 p.m. at Mango Dance Studio Cost - £5 per session. Don't delay. Book today!

2 Match the activities in exercise 1 with the sentences (1–6).
1 It includes music.
2 It is probably the quietest.
3 You do it outdoors.
4 It is the cheapest per session.
5 It claims to be good for both the mind and the body.
6 It is only for fit people.

WRITING STRATEGY
When we write an announcement, we often:
1 use capitals to emphasise key words or phrases.
2 present key information (the time, date, place, cost, etc.) in note form or
3 in a list with bullet points (•).
4 use rhetorical questions (questions that are asked to create an effect rather than to get an answer).
5 end with a strong and memorable final message.

3 Read the writing strategy. Then answer these questions.
1 Which announcements use capitals to emphasise key words? Underline the words.
2 Which announcement does not present key information in note form? Rewrite that part in note form.
3 Which announcement uses bullet points? Find a list in another announcement and rewrite it with bullet points.
4 How many rhetorical questions do the three announcements contain in total? Underline them.
5 Do all three announcements end with a final message? Which is the most memorable, in your opinion?

4 **SPEAKING** Work in pairs. Look at the photos. Discuss how the activities might benefit your mind and / or body.

I think walking would be good for your mind because it's relaxing.

5 Choose one of the activities from exercise 4 or your own idea. Imagine you are organising regular sessions. Decide on the details (price, venue, time, etc.).

6 Write an announcement to publicise your sessions.
• Inform people what the activity is and describe it briefly.
• Mention the benefits for mind and / or body.
• Inform people of the time, place and cost of sessions.
• End with a strong and memorable final message.

CHECK YOUR WORK
Have you:
☐ included the information in the task in exercise 6?
☐ ended with a strong final message?
☐ included ideas from the writing strategy?

Unit 3

1 Match words 1–5 with a–e to complete the verb phrases.

1 serve   a manual work
2 work   b people
3 do   c £5 an hour
4 supervise   d customers
5 earn   e nine-to-five

Mark: ____ /5

2 Complete the sentences with *who*, *whose*, *which* or *where* and the clauses below.

checks your eyesight   I applied for   sister was on TV
likes us to be on time   my mum works

1 That's the building _____ _____ .
2 My boss is someone _____ _____ .
3 That's the job _____ _____ .
4 Do you know the boy _____ _____ ?
5 An optician is someone _____ _____ .

Mark: ____ /5

3 Rewrite the sentences, including the information in brackets as a non-defining relative clause.

1 My uncle works for Fiat. (He's just got a new car.)
2 Sally's new job is stressful. (She started it last month.)
3 John can't draw at all. (His mum is an artist.)
4 My maths teacher is going to join a band. (She's a great singer.)
5 My interview went well. (It took two hours.)

Mark: ____ /5

4 Complete the sentences with the adjectives below.

conscientious   creative   flexible   polite
self-motivated

1 A _____ person has lots of new ideas.
2 A _____ person doesn't mind changing plans if necessary.
3 A _____ person works hard to make sure that every job is done properly.
4 A _____ person doesn't need anyone to tell them what to do.
5 A _____ person speaks to other people in a nice way.

Mark: ____ /5
Total: ____ /20

Unit 4

5 Match words 1–5 with the correct part of the body (a–e).

1 nostril   a hand
2 palm   b foot
3 waist   c leg
4 sole   d body
5 thigh   e nose

Mark: ____ /5

6 Complete the mini-dialogues with the correct form of the verbs in brackets. Use the past simple or present perfect.

1 A When _____ you _____ (buy) that jacket?
  B On Saturday. Do you like it?
2 A I _____ already _____ (do) my homework.
  B Good for you. I haven't!
3 A Sally _____ (go) on holiday yesterday.
  B Lucky her. Where to?
4 A I _____ (win) my swimming race last week!
  B Oh, congratulations!
5 A I _____ just _____ (finish) a great book.
  B Oh, really? Who wrote it?

Mark: ____ /5

7 Complete the dialogue with the correct form of the verbs in brackets. Use the present perfect simple or continuous.

Boy What [1]_____ you _____ (do) lately?
Girl I [2]_____ (read) detective stories! I [3]_____ (read) four this week! They're fantastic!
Boy I [4]_____ (play) computer games all week. I [5]_____ (not read) any books. Can I borrow one of yours?
Girl Of course.

Mark: ____ /5

8 Complete the doctor's questions with the words below.

allergic   dizzy   do   painful   symptoms

1 What can I _____ for you?
2 Have you had any other _____ ?
3 If I touch your stomach, is it _____ ?
4 Are you _____ to penicillin?
5 Do you feel sick or _____ ?

Mark: ____ /5
Total: ____ /20

Lead-in

1 Imagine you needed to work part-time to earn some extra money. What job would you like to do? Why?

Speaking

2 Describe the photo.
Then answer the questions.

1 How do you think the waiter in the photo is feeling?
2 What do you think young people can learn from doing part-time jobs?
3 Tell me about the last time you saw somebody who seemed unhappy at work.

Reading

3 Read the job adverts (A–E). Which job looks the most interesting, in your opinion? Why?

A

Are you hard-working and reliable?

If you are, then come and join the team at Left Field Bookshop and Café. We need people to work 9–5 Tuesday–Saturday in our busy sandwich bar and in the bookshop too: please state your preference when you apply. Send your CV and a covering letter to the shop manager. Pay: £8 an hour.

B

Part-time job at the Museum of Liverpool

We are looking for hard-working and enthusiastic people to work a two-hour shift (morning or afternoon) every day between Tuesday and Sunday. Applicants must be good at dealing with the public. Languages an advantage. Apply online or phone for an application form.
Pay: £10–£12 an hour depending on age and experience.

C

ALFREDO'S

Waiters required to work at our busy, city-centre restaurant, lunchtime or evening shifts (11–3 p.m. / 7–11 p.m.), Monday to Friday. £7 an hour. Successful applicants will be flexible, hard-working and polite. Please apply by sending a hand-written letter addressed to the restaurant manager, Ms Tara Cox.

4 Match each sentence to one or more of the job adverts (A–E).

1 The job involves working six days a week.
2 Applicants need to write a letter.
3 Successful applicants must be reliable.
4 Successful applicants must work in the evening.
5 Successful applicants will have a choice of hours.
6 The job pays £8 an hour or more.
7 Speaking another language will help.
8 There is an application form for this job.

Listening

5 🎧 2.05 Listen and answer the questions.

1 Which job from exercise 3 does Anna apply for and get?
2 Why doesn't she start work on the agreed day?

6 🎧 2.05 Listen again. Are these sentences true or false?

1 The interviewer hasn't seen Anna's application.
2 Anna tells the interviewer that the job matches her experience and personality.
3 Anna says she can speak English, Polish, German and a little Russian.
4 Anna doesn't remember correctly what the job advert said about working hours.
5 Anna prefers to work in the afternoon because she has classes in the morning.
6 Anna can't speak to Julian Lloyd because he isn't in the office.

Writing

7 Choose one of the other job adverts from exercise 3 and write an application letter. You do not need to include addresses. Remember to state:

• where you saw the advert (invent this).
• what your personal qualities are.
• what relevant experience you have (invent if necessary).
• what you are enclosing with the letter.

D

Wanted

Receptionist for busy sports and fitness club in Liverpool city centre. Must be polite, friendly and reliable. An interest in sport and / or keep-fit is essential and foreign languages would be an advantage.
Hours: 6–10 p.m., Monday to Saturday   Pay: £6 an hour
Apply by email to: manager@fitnessforall.com

E

EARN MONEY

Did you know you can earn £9 an hour delivering important letters and packages?
We need couriers to work seven evenings a week from 8 p.m.–10 p.m.

Applicants should be honest and enthusiastic. They must also have their own car and a full driving licence.
To apply, phone 07753 27166528.

THIS UNIT INCLUDES

Vocabulary ▪ computing ▪ noun prefixes ▪ verb and noun allocations ▪ making, accepting and declining suggestions
Grammar ▪ zero conditional ▪ speculating and predicting: *will, may, might,* etc. ▪ first conditional ▪ future perfect and future continuous ▪ *will, going to,* present continuous ▪ future time clauses
Speaking ▪ talking about the future ▪ making and agreeing plans
Writing ▪ an informal email

5A VOCABULARY AND LISTENING Computing

I can talk about computers and computing.

1 SPEAKING Work in pairs. Discuss this question.

How often do you use a computer and what different things do you use it for?

2 🎧 2.06 VOCABULARY Complete the questionnaire using the words below. Use a dictionary to help you if necessary. Then listen and check.

Computing app autocomplete blog browsers channel data desktop links network podcast social-networking USB username web page webcam Wi-Fi

ARE YOU A COMPUTER GEEK?

1 Have you ever …
 a downloaded and listened to a _____ ?
 b uploaded photos to a _____ site?
 c located a _____ hotspot?
 d installed an _____ on your phone?
 e joined a file-sharing _____ ?
 f published a _____ ?
 g subscribed to a YouTube _____ ?
 h used a _____ to video chat?
 i used _____ to fill in forms on web pages?

2 Explain these sentences in your own words.
 a Please contact the webmaster if any of the _____ on this page are broken.
 b Your _____ and password are case sensitive.
 c Click on the red button to bookmark this _____ .

3 Can you name three different …
 a companies that make _____ computers?
 b things you could connect to the _____ port of a computer?
 c means of _____ storage?
 d Internet _____ ?

3 SPEAKING Answer the questionnaire in exercise 2. Then compare answers with your partner. Who is more geeky?

4 🎧 2.07 Look at the description of a computer. Then listen to a customer in a shop and write the missing numbers.

> This laptop has a 1.66 Ghz processor and
> ¹_____ MB of RAM. It has a ²_____ GB
> hard drive and a ³_____ " LED display.
> It has a ⁴_____ x DVD writer and two
> built-in ⁵_____ W speakers.

5 🎧 2.07 PRONUNCIATION How do you pronounce the abbreviations in red in exercise 4? Say them aloud. Then listen again and check.

6 Match the first part of the sentences about smartphone apps (1–6) with the endings (a–f). Which app sounds most useful? Give reasons.

With this new phone app:
1 your phone tells you what song is playing
2 if you visit a tourist attraction,
3 you can make free calls
4 you can exchange information between two phones,
5 if you take the phone outside at night,
6 if you point the phone at something in a shop,

a your phone knows where you are and gives you interesting information about the place.
b it tells you where you can buy the same thing at a cheaper price.
c it tells you the names of the stars in the sky.
d if you bump the phones gently together.
e if you hold it in front of a speaker.
f if the person you are calling has the same app.

⟫⟫ GRAMMAR BUILDER 5.1: PAGE 115 ⟪⟪

7 SPEAKING Work in pairs. Invent a new app for a smartphone. Think about:
- the type of activity (games, work, music, photos, etc.).
- a name for your app and what it can do / how you can use it.

8 SPEAKING Describe your smartphone app to the class. The class votes for the best app.

⟫⟫ VOCABULARY BUILDER 5.1: PAGE 131 ⟪⟪

GRAMMAR **Speculating and predicting**

I can speculate about the future and make predictions.

1 SPEAKING Read the text. Do you think Ray Kurzweil's predictions will come true? Give reasons.

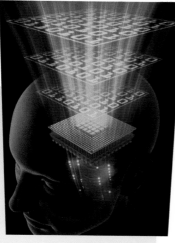

'**Man won't fly** for 50 years,' said Wilbur Wright in 1901. Two years later, he and his brother made the world's first successful flight. Predicting the future is difficult, but at the Singularity University in California, you can actually study futurology. The University's director is Ray Kurzweil, who predicts that huge increases in computer power will change the world dramatically. By 2045, we'll probably be only the second most intelligent creatures on Earth, after computers. These computers might think, communicate and act so quickly that ordinary humans won't be able to understand them. But of course, ordinary humans might not exist then – everybody may have computer chips inside their brains. Technology may also eradicate disease and increase life expectancy. If life expectancy increases faster than people age, nobody will die. This could cause other problems for the Earth!

2 Read the *Learn this!* box. Find examples of these structures in the text: *may, might, could, won't, might not, will* and *will probably*.

LEARN THIS!

Speculating and predicting

0%		100%

won't → probably won't → may / might / could → will probably → will

1 To talk about possibility in the future, we can use *may, might* or *could* followed by a base form:
She may / might / could leave school next year.

2 We use *may not* or *might not* for the negative – we do not use *could not.*

3 To make predictions, we can use *will.* When we are not certain, we use *I think* ... or *probably*:
I think it will rain later. / It will probably rain later.

3 How likely are these events to happen in the next five years? Write sentences using expressions from exercise 2.

there's an earthquake in Britain
there's a major flu epidemic
Brazil wins the football world cup
you fail an important exam
you move abroad
you learn to drive
you go to university
you get married

There probably won't be an earthquake in Britain.

4 Read the *Learn this!* box. Find an example of the first conditional in the text in exercise 1.

LEARN THIS!

Predicting: first conditional

1 We often make predictions with the first conditional. We use the present simple in the *if-* clause and *will* in the main clause:
If the hotel has Wi-Fi, I'll check my emails.

2 We can use *may, might* or *could* in the main clause if the prediction is only a possibility:
If you refresh the page, it might load.

5 Match the two halves of the predictions and write the verbs in brackets in the correct tenses (present simple and *will* or *may / might / could*).

1 If there _____ (be) a major flu epidemic,
2 Ordinary tourists _____ (go) into space
3 Governments _____ (ban) cars
4 If the Earth _____ (become) too crowded,
5 Everybody _____ (be) online 24 hours a day
6 If young people _____ (put) too much personal information on social-networking sites,

a humans _____ (live) on Mars.
b if tickets _____ (not be) too expensive.
c if the number of Wi-Fi hotspots _____ (increase).
d millions of people _____ (die).
e they _____ (regret) it when they're older.
f if global warming _____ (get) worse.

>>> GRAMMAR BUILDER 5.2: PAGE 115 <<<

SPEAKING STRATEGY

We can use these phrases to agree or disagree with other people's opinions:
I think that's true. / I don't think that's true.
I agree / don't agree with (you / him / that opinion).
I believe / don't believe that's right.
That seems / doesn't seem very likely.

6 SPEAKING Read the exam strategy. Say whether you agree or disagree with the predictions in exercise 5. Give reasons.

7 SPEAKING Work in pairs. Complete these predictions about the future with your own ideas. Then tell the class. Do they agree?

1 If everybody lives forever, ...
2 If computers become more intelligent than humans, ...
3 If the world becomes too crowded, ...
4 If humans have computer chips in their brains, ...
5 If we don't use less energy, ...

1 SPEAKING Look at the picture of the Westinghouse time capsule. Work in pairs and discuss these questions.

1 What is the point of a time capsule?
2 What kinds of items do you think would be interesting to people in the future? Give reasons.

2 VOCABULARY Complete the compound nouns using the words below. Check in a dictionary to see if they are written as one word or two.

alarm base can light lip news tape tooth

1 _____ clock
2 _____ opener
3 _____ measure
4 _____ brush
5 _____ stick
6 _____ ball
7 _____ switch
8 _____ reel

3 🎧 2.08 PRONUNCIATION Listen, repeat and check your answers. Which part of the compound nouns is stressed?

4 Work in pairs. Think about the items in exercise 2, which are all in the time capsule. Decide whether each item:

1 is in the picture in exercise 1.
2 would be interesting for people in the future. Why?

5 🎧 2.09 Listen to a radio programme. What has been buried in the park in New York?

6 🎧 2.09 Listen again. Choose the correct answers.

1 The interview is taking place in Flushing Meadows Park
   a because there is a World Fair taking place there.
   b because Professor Wolfson works at a university near the park.
   c because the time capsules are buried in the park.

2 Why are there two time capsules?
   a They made a copy of the first capsule.
   b They couldn't fit everything into one capsule.
   c Because there were two World Fairs.

3 How were the 35 items inside the first time capsule chosen?
   a They were all made of different materials.
   b They showed what everyday life was like in 1939.
   c They were all invented in the 20th century.

4 What is the connection between Albert Einstein and the time capsule?
   a He invented the material the capsule is made of.
   b There's a biography of Einstein in the capsule.
   c There's a message from him in the capsule.

5 What does the capsule contain to help people in the future understand the contents?
   a A complete guide to the English language.
   b A grammar book.
   c Translations of the contents into different languages.

6 What does the *Book of Record* contain?
   a A list of libraries and museums around the world.
   b Information about the time capsule.
   c Information about things in libraries and museums.

7 SPEAKING Work in groups or pairs. Imagine you are going to bury a time capsule with ten items inside. Choose two items for each category A–E below.

A Culture (music, literature, etc.)
B Technology
C Politics and world affairs
D Home life
E Language

Let's include a …

8 PROJECT Write a message to the people who will open your time capsule 1,000 years from now. Include this information:

• Who you are.
• When and why you are burying the time capsule.
• An explanation of your choice of items from exercise 7.
• One or two problems the world is facing today (e.g. climate change, war, poverty, etc.).
• When the time capsule should be opened.

Our names are … we live in …
The year is … and we're burying this capsule because …
We are including … because …
The world today faces the problem of …
The capsule should be opened in the year…

9 SPEAKING Present your project to the class. The class votes for the best choice of items and the best message.

1 **SPEAKING** Read the text. Which of the three jobs do you think would be the most interesting? Give reasons.

What new jobs will we be doing 20 years from now? Many of today's jobs will have disappeared, but what will replace them? Nobody knows for sure, but here are three ideas from employment experts.

Vertical farmer: Our cities will have become so over-populated that farmers will be growing crops in skyscrapers in order to feed everyone.

Weather police: Global water shortages will have become so serious that people will be stealing clouds from their neighbours.

Memory surgeon: Medical scientists will have learned how the human brain works. Doctors will be adding extra memory to people whose brains are full.

2 Read the *Learn this!* box. Underline all the examples of the future perfect and future continuous in the text in exercise 1. Then complete the rules.

> **Future perfect and future continuous**
> **1** We form the future perfect with:
> *will have* + past participle
> *By next Friday, we'll have finished school.*
> **2** We form the future continuous with:
> *will be* + *-ing* form
> *This time next week, I'll be revising.*
> **3** We use the future ¹_____ to talk about a completed action in the future.
> **4** We use the future ²_____ to talk about an action in progress in the future.

3 Complete the text. Use the future perfect or future continuous form of the verbs in brackets.

This is my final year at school. Six months from now, I
¹_____ (study) at university. It's a three-year course, so
four years from now, ²_____ (finish) it. I'd love a career
in fashion. Maybe, in five years' time, I ³_____ (work)
for a fashion designer. I ⁴_____ (live / probably) in a
big city: London, New York, Paris or Milan. That's where the
jobs are. Hopefully, by the time I'm 35, I ⁵_____ (learn)
enough about the fashion industry to start my own fashion
label. With luck, I ⁶_____ (run) my own successful
company by then and a few young fashion graduates
⁷_____ (work) for me!

≫≫ GRAMMAR BUILDER 5.3: PAGE 116 ≪≪

4 Look at the chart. Do you think these things will have happened, or will be happening, by the years suggested? Write *Y* (yes) or *N* (no) next to each prediction.

prediction	date	Y / N
1 doctors / find a cure for all major diseases	by 2025	
2 tourists / go on trips into space	by 2030	
3 scientists / invent zero-emissions cars	by 2035	
4 people / often live to the age of 200 or more	by 2040	
5 humans / make contact with aliens	by 2045	
6 a robot / become president of a country	by 2050	
7 Earth / completely run out of oil	by 2055	
8 teenagers / spend all day in a virtual world	by 2060	
9 humans / destroy the Earth	by 2065	

5 **SPEAKING** In pairs, ask and answer questions about the chart in exercise 4. Use the future perfect or future continuous.

> Will doctors have found a cure for all major diseases by 2025?

> Yes, I think so. / No, do I don't think so.

> Will tourists be going on trips …

6 Work in pairs. Choose a year between 2025 and 2065 and decide on:
- one current job that will have disappeared.
- one new job that people will be doing.
- one new gadget that people will be using.
- one new item of clothing that people will be wearing.
- one new place where people will be living.
- one major discovery that scientists will have made.

7 **SPEAKING** Present your ideas to the class. Do they agree or disagree? Which idea is the most interesting or unusual?

> We think that by 2040, the job of teacher will have disappeared because students will be learning at home using personal robots. One new job that people will be doing is …

1 SPEAKING Describe the pictures. They show visions of the future fifty years from now. Which one do you think is the most likely to come true? Give reasons.

2 🎧 2.10 Read the texts. In your opinion, whose prediction is:

1 the most optimistic?
2 the scariest?
3 the most likely to come true?

READING STRATEGY

When you're looking for specific information in a text, reading the first sentence of a paragraph often tells you what the whole paragraph is about.

3 Read the reading strategy. Then match paragraphs A–F with predictions 1–8. There are two extra predictions that you do not need.

1 We will be able to choose how long our own life is.
2 We will be communicating directly with search engines as if they were people.
3 We will use computers to help us talk to people who do not speak our language.
4 We will be able to get any new body parts we need.
5 We will develop a new technology that will make the human race extinct.
6 Some humans will have gone to live on another planet.
7 We will have made contact with life in other parts of the galaxy.
8 We won't be living in most of the areas we inhabit now.

4 VOCABULARY Match the verbs (1–7) and nouns (a–g) to make phrases from the text.

1 reduce   a a catastrophe
2 treat   b information
3 suffer   c damaged parts
4 start   d discoveries
5 replace   e carbon emissions
6 provide   f a colony
7 make   g illnesses

5 Complete the sentences with phrases from exercise 4.

1 When poorer countries _____ like a flood or an earthquake, it causes enormous destruction.
2 Is it possible to _____ without drugs?
3 Using public transport helps to _____.
4 Today, surgeons can _____ of your heart.
5 I asked the university to _____ about their degree courses.
6 It would be difficult to _____ on the moon because there's no water.
7 Every year, scientists _____ about our universe.

6 Work in pairs. Make three predictions about the world in fifty years' time. Use the ideas below to help you and some of the nouns and verbs from exercise 4.

buildings   climate   computers   education
entertainment   health   space   transport   work

7 SPEAKING Tell the class your predictions. Do they agree or disagree?

⋙ **VOCABULARY BUILDER 5.2: PAGE 131** ⋘

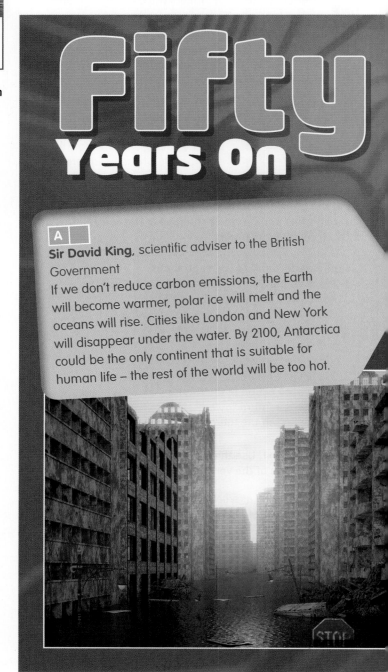

Fifty Years On

A

Sir David King, scientific adviser to the British Government

If we don't reduce carbon emissions, the Earth will become warmer, polar ice will melt and the oceans will rise. Cities like London and New York will disappear under the water. By 2100, Antarctica could be the only continent that is suitable for human life – the rest of the world will be too hot.

 B

Francis Collins, geneticist
Fifty years from now, millions of people will live past the age of 100 and remain healthy. This will happen because we'll be able to study each person's genetic code and find the best way to treat illnesses in that individual. In about fifty years' time, the most important question for our society might not be 'How long can humans live?', but 'How long do we want to live?'

C

J Richard Gott, physicist
During the next fifty years, our planet might suffer a catastrophe. Humans could disappear, just like the dinosaurs and hundreds of other species. The best way to make humans safe from extinction is to start a colony on Mars. This is not a prediction, but a hope. Will we be smart enough to do it?

D

Ellen Heber-Katz, biologist
I believe that soon we will be able to repair the human body in the same way that we can replace damaged parts of a car or a washing machine. Five years from now, we will be able to grow new fingers, and, a few years after that, new arms and legs. Within fifty years, replacing your whole body will be normal.

E

Peter Norvig, director of research at Google
Today, people all over the world have access to billions of pages of text on the Internet. At the moment, they use search engines to find information, but fifty years from now, people will simply discuss their needs with their computer, and the computer will make suggestions and provide usable information, not just a list of links.

F

Eric Horvitz, principal researcher at Microsoft Research
In fifty years' time, computers will be much more intelligent than today, and this will change people's lives. Computers will help people work, learn, plan and decide. They will help people from different countries to understand each other by automatically translating from one language to another. Intelligent computers will work as scientists, and will start to make important discoveries on their own.

1 🎧 2.11 **VOCABULARY** Read and listen to the dialogue. What are Blake and Lauren planning to do this weekend? Write *L* (Lauren) and *B* (Blake) next to the activities you hear.

Activities do some schoolwork ☐ go bowling ☐
go ice skating ☐ go for a pizza ☐ go for bike ride ☐
go skateboarding ☐ go to bed early ☐
have a barbecue ☐ have lunch / dinner with relatives ☐
have some friends round ☐
meet (somebody) for a coffee ☐

Lauren	What are you up to at the weekend?
Blake	I'm going skateboarding on Saturday morning.
Lauren	Have you got any plans for the afternoon?
Blake	Yes, I have. I'm going to finish my science project. But maybe we could meet up in the evening?
Lauren	I can't, I'm afraid. I'm having a barbecue.
Blake	That's a shame. Do you fancy doing something on Sunday?
Lauren	Sure! The afternoon is better for me. I might be going for a bike ride with my sister in the morning.
Blake	Actually, I'm going bowling with some friends on Sunday afternoon. But you're welcome to join us.
Lauren	Thanks. I'd love to. What time?
Blake	Four o'clock, And we'll be going for a pizza after.
Lauren	Great idea. Let's speak again on Sunday.
Blake	OK. I'll call you.

2 Read the *Learn this!* box and underline all the examples of the tenses in the dialogue.

> **LEARN THIS!**
>
> **will, going to, may / might, present continuous and future continuous**
> 1 We use *will* for things we decide to do as we are speaking (instant decisions, offers, promises).
> 2 We use *going to* or the future continuous for things we have already decided to do (intentions).
> 3 We often use *may* or *might* if we aren't sure.
> 4 We use the present continuous for things we have already agreed to do, usually with somebody else (arrangements).

3 **SPEAKING** Work in pairs. Practise reading the dialogue in exercise 1 replacing the words in blue with other activities from exercise 1 or your own ideas.

4 🎧 2.12 Listen to two dialogues. Why are the speakers calling each other? Who is more keen to meet up? Katie or Joe? Jack or Olivia? Explain your answer.

5 🎧 2.12 Listen again. What arrangement do they make?
1 Katie & Joe _____
2 Jack & Olivia _____

6 Match these phrases from the dialogues with the groups A–C in the *Learn this!* box. Then add one more phrase to each group from the dialogue in exercise 1.

I'm not up for it. ☐ I've already got plans. ☐ Let's ... ☐
I was wondering if you'd like to ... ☐ Next time maybe. ☐
OK. Why not? ☐ No, thanks. I'm not very keen on ... ☐

> **LEARN THIS!**
>
> **A Making suggestions**
> Shall we ... ?   Why don't we / you ... ?
> How about (+ -ing)?   Maybe we could ...
> What about (+ -ing)?
> **B Accepting suggestions**
> Great idea.   I'd love to.
> Yes, that sounds fun.   Yes, I'd be up for that.
>   That's a good idea.
> **C Declining suggestions**
> Sorry, I can't.   I don't really fancy (+ -ing).

7 **SPEAKING** Work in pairs. Practise making suggestions and reacting to them using phrases from the *Learn this!* box. Use activities from exercise 1 and your own ideas.

> Why don't we watch a DVD?

> Yes, I'd be up for that.

8 **SPEAKING** Work in pairs. Prepare a dialogue. Remember to use the correct verb forms from the *Learn this!* box and appropriate phrases from exercise 6.
- Ask about your partner's plans.
- Tell your partner about your own plans.
- Make suggestions for an activity you could do together.
- Accept or decline your partner's suggestions.
- Agree on one activity you can do together.

9 **SPEAKING** Act out your dialogue to the class.

⫸ **GRAMMAR BUILDER 5.4: PAGE 117** ⫷

An informal email

I can write an informal email about future plans and ambitions.

1 Read the email. Why is Archie writing to Carl?

2 Find four different activities that Archie is planning to do during the Easter holiday. What tenses does he use in his email?

✉ **Inbox**

Dear Carl,

Thanks for your email. It's great that you're planning to visit us next month.

As soon as term finishes, I'm going camping in the New Forest with my dad and my brother, Kieran. We're planning to be away for three or four days. I really want to go fishing a few times, and while we're there, I'm hoping to catch some fish to eat in the evenings. After we get back I'll be working in my uncle's café for a few days over Easter.

You could visit any time during the last week of the holiday. I'll be re-taking a couple of exams next term, so I need to do some revision before I go back to school. But I reckon I'll be able to work when you're here.

I'd be grateful if you could confirm the dates of your visit as soon as possible. I won't make any more plans until I hear from you!

All the best
  Archie

3 Find one sentence that is too formal. How could you rewrite it in a more informal style?

4 Read the *Learn this!* box. Underline examples of *want*, *hope*, *plan* and *reckon* in Archie's email.

1 We can use an infinitive after the verbs *want*, *hope* and *plan*.
  I'm hoping to visit some friends.

2 We use a clause after the verbs *think* and *reckon*. We cannot use an infinitive.
  I think I'll stay at home.
  I don't reckon I'll enjoy this film.

5 Complete the sentences using the verbs in brackets and a clause or an infinitive.

1 I'm not planning _____ (go) to university next year.
2 I don't reckon _____ (pass) all my exams.
3 We're hoping _____ (spend) a few days abroad.
4 I think _____ (look) for a job in a restaurant.
5 I don't think _____ (visit) any relatives this holiday.
6 We want _____ (stay) in a hotel by the sea.

6 Read the writing strategy. Find and underline an example of all six conjunctions in Archie's email.

WRITING STRATEGY

In sentences referring to the future, we use the present simple after: *when*, *as soon as*, *until*, *after*, *before* and *while*, but NOT will.

7 Choose the correct conjunction in these sentences.

1 We can't go to the beach **until** / **while** it stops raining.
2 I'm going to buy a car **after** / **as soon as** I can afford to.
3 I'll believe it **before** / **when** I see it.
4 You must visit the Eiffel Tower **until** / **while** you're in Paris.
5 I need to get to the bank **as soon as** / **before** it closes.
6 They won't let us into the cinema **after** / **while** the film starts.

>>> GRAMMAR BUILDER 5.5: PAGE 117 <<<

8 Read the exam task below. Which parts of Archie's email include the information required in the task?

A British friend wants to stay with you for a few days over the holiday. Write an email (120–150 words) to him / her.
- Say how you feel about his / her plans to visit and why.
- Give some information about what you will be doing in the holidays and when.
- Explain when the best time for his / her visit would be, and why.
- Ask when he / she plans to arrive and how long the visit will be.

9 Make notes for the exam task. Write down one or two ideas for each piece of information required in the task. Invent a name for the person you are writing to.

10 Write your email using your notes from exercise 9.

CHECK YOUR WORK

Have you:
☐ included the information in the task in exercise 8?
☐ written in an informal style?
☐ used future time clauses correctly?
☐ written the correct number of words (120–150)?

Reading

1 `Get ready to READ` **Work in pairs. Ask and answer the questions.**

1 Do you like cooking? Why? / Why not?
2 Who's the best cook in your family?

2 Match the cooking verbs (1–4) with the definitions (a–d).

1	steam	A	cook in liquid that is gently boiling
2	stir-fry	B	cook quickly in hot oil
3	poach	C	cook under or over very strong heat
4	grill	D	cook over boiling water

3 Do the Reading exam task.

READING exam task

Read the text and decide if the sentences are true or false. For each sentence, write the line number where you find evidence for your decision.

Healthy cooking with Jordi Francisco

Jordi Francisco, the world-famous prize-winning Spanish chef, has been cooking healthy food in his restaurant for over ten years. Here he takes us through some of his top tips for healthy eating.

5 'Healthy eating really starts with healthy cooking. It's not only about what you eat, but how you cook it. A burger can be incredibly unhealthy if it's made from low quality meat, deep-fried in cheap oil and served in processed white bread. However, if you make a burger from premium beef,
10 brush it with a small amount of good-quality oil, grill it and serve it with a generous portion of salad and wholemeal bread, you've transformed it into a nourishing and well-balanced meal.

Light steaming is perhaps one of the healthiest cooking
15 methods to use. I've always liked cooking vegetables this way, in a basket over simmering water, as all the flavours and nutrients are retained – all you have to do is add seasoning and you're done. Easy, quick, delicious and nutritious!

20 Another healthy cooking method I've used a lot is stir-frying. It's no coincidence that in Asian countries, where this is the most common form of cooking, there are very low rates of heart disease. You only need a splash of oil to stir-fry and you cook things for a very short time, so your
25 meat or vegetables retain their nutrients, as well as texture, flavour and colour.

Grilling can also be great for preparing low-fat meals. In my opinion, it adds a delicious smoky flavour to meat, fish or vegetables. The fat drips away from the food as it cooks.

30 Perhaps the most under-rated healthy cooking method is poaching: gently simmering food in water until it is cooked

through. Just thinking about a lightly poached egg on toast makes my mouth water! Fish works fantastically well
35 poached. You have to be careful with fish, as it's so easy to overcook it and make it go dry and flavourless. With poaching, however, you can cook it very gently and keep it moist and full of flavour.'

		T	F	Line no.
1	Burgers cooked with fat can never be healthy.			
2	Jordi recommends steaming vegetables because it keeps all the goodness in the food.			
3	People in Asia use stir-frying more than any other cooking method.			
4	Jordi suggests adding some fat to grilled vegetables.			
5	Jordi doesn't often poach fish as it is easy to overcook it.			

Use of English

4 Do the exam task.

USE OF ENGLISH exam task

A design student has created a 'walking chair' which he hopes will one day help [1]_____ (able) people to get around more [2]_____ (easy). Its 21-year-old [3]_____ (create), Martin Harris, said the machine operates like a conventional electric wheelchair, with one important [4]_____ (different). Instead of wheels, Harris' [5]_____ (invent) has got six metal legs on each side. This gives the user far greater [6]_____ (free) of movement. The chair can be [7]_____ (use) indoors while also having the [8]_____ (able) to cross soft surfaces such as sand or grass, which can prove difficult for wheelchairs. Harris came up with the idea after being [9]_____ (inspire) by the 'walking sculptures' of Dutch [10]_____ (art) and engineer Theo Jansen, whose giant skeletons can walk across beaches.

Speaking

5 **Get ready to SPEAK** Work in pairs. Read the task and think of three arguments in favour of the statement and three against. Then compare your ideas with the class.

SPEAKING exam task

Do you agree or disagree with this statement?
Give reasons.

Computers have made the world a better place.

6 Do the Speaking exam task.

Listening

7 **Get ready to LISTEN** Work in pairs. Make a list of the five most important inventions in recent times. Explain why you think they are important.

8 Match the words (1–6) with the definitions (a–f).

1 artificial
2 monitor
3 detector
4 concentrate
5 launch
6 highway

a main road
b not natural; made by people
c focus on something
d watch closely; observe
e machine used for finding or noticing something
f start; activate

9 🎧 2.13 Do the exam task.

LISTENING exam task

Listen to five speakers talk about various inventions. Match each invention 1–5 with a sentence A–F. There is one extra sentence that you do not need.

Speaker 1		Speaker 3		Speaker 5	
Speaker 2		Speaker 4			

A This invention will help people with communication difficulties.
B This invention is designed to make people's lives safer.
C This invention is used to create realistic images.
D This invention enables people to control their mental activity.
E This invention is only for people who live in big cities.
F This invention is a combination of two different vehicles.

Writing

10 **Get ready to WRITE** Work in pairs. Ask and answer these questions.

1 What special cultural traditions do you have in your country? Think about music, dances, clothing, etc.
2 What is one of the most important characteristics of the culture of your country? Write a slogan to advertise it.

11 Do the exam task.

WRITING exam task

You are staying in the UK, studying English at a language school in London. You want to organise a cultural evening to celebrate the traditional food, music, costumes, etc. from your own country. Write an announcement in which you:

- Inform the reader about the party you are planning
- Say when and where it is going to take place
- Give information about food and entertainment
- Encourage everybody to come.

6 Mystery

THIS UNIT INCLUDES
Vocabulary ■ compound nouns ■ easily confused words ■ inseparable phrasal verb
Grammar ■ reported speech (statements) ■ *say* and *tell* ■ reported speech (questions
■ *must have, might/could have, can't have* ■ indirect questions ■ verbs with two object
Speaking ■ deciding who committed a crime ■ speculating about an event
Writing ■ a formal letter

6A VOCABULARY AND LISTENING Crime at the manor

I can suggest solutions to a mystery.

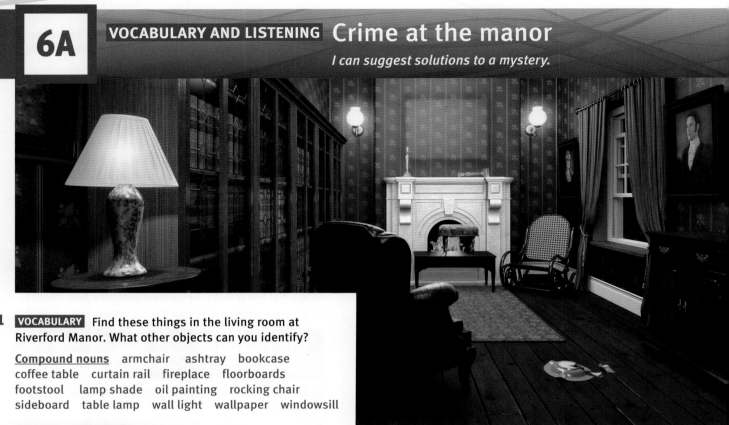

1 VOCABULARY Find these things in the living room at Riverford Manor. What other objects can you identify?

Compound nouns armchair ashtray bookcase
coffee table curtain rail fireplace floorboards
footstool lamp shade oil painting rocking chair
sideboard table lamp wall light wallpaper windowsill

2 🎧 2.14 VOCABULARY Match the objects in exercise 1 with the materials they are made from. (Some objects are made from more than one material.) Then listen and check.

Materials china fabric glass leather marble paper
wood

The armchair is made of wood and leather.

> **LEARN THIS!**
> A compound noun is formed from two words. Some compound nouns are written as two words, others as one word. They are always written as two words when the first word ends in *-ing*:
> *a living room*   *a bedroom*
> They can refer to a specific part of something:
> *a garden path*   *a door handle*
> Or they can specify the purpose of an object:
> *an ironing board*   *a carwash*

3 VOCABULARY Read the *Learn this!* box. Then complete the compound nouns using the words below. Check in a dictionary to see if they are written as one word or two.

book chair flower hair key light window writing

1 _____ hole   5 _____ bed
2 _____ ledge   6 _____ brush
3 _____ shelf   7 _____ paper
4 _____ shade   8 _____ leg

4 Look at your answers to exercise 3. Which nouns refer to a specific part of something and which specify its purpose?

»» VOCABULARY BUILDER 6.1: PAGE 132 «««

5 SPEAKING Work in pairs. Look at the picture of the living room at Riverford Manor. There has been a burglary last night. Decide what happened and tell the class your ideas.

> A thief climbed in through the window. He put the footstool on top of the ...

6 🎧 2.15 Listen to Inspector Dalton talking to his assistant. Who does he think took the painting? Are his ideas similar to your ideas in exercise 5?

7 🎧 2.15 Listen again. What three clues help the Inspector reach his conclusion? Talk about:

1 the flower bed   2 the windowsill   3 the coffee table

8 SPEAKING Work in pairs. Decide what happens next in the story. Then tell the class.

»» VOCABULARY BUILDER 6.2: PAGE 132 «««

1 Read the text. What did André Poisson get for his money?

  a Secret documents.   **b** The Eiffel Tower.   **c** Nothing.

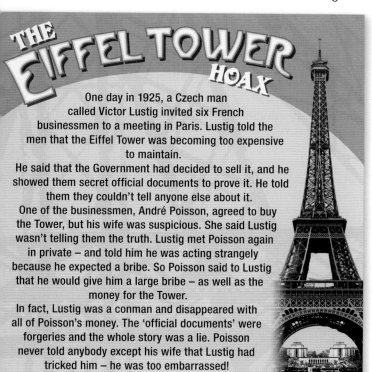

THE EIFFEL TOWER HOAX

One day in 1925, a Czech man called Victor Lustig invited six French businessmen to a meeting in Paris. Lustig told the men that the Eiffel Tower was becoming too expensive to maintain.
He said that the Government had decided to sell it, and he showed them secret official documents to prove it. He told them they couldn't tell anyone else about it.
One of the businessmen, André Poisson, agreed to buy the Tower, but his wife was suspicious. She said Lustig wasn't telling them the truth. Lustig met Poisson again in private – and told him he was acting strangely because he expected a bribe. So Poisson said to Lustig that he would give him a large bribe – as well as the money for the Tower.
In fact, Lustig was a conman and disappeared with all of Poisson's money. The 'official documents' were forgeries and the whole story was a lie. Poisson never told anybody except his wife that Lustig had tricked him – he was too embarrassed!

2 Read the quotations below. Underline the parts of the text in exercise 1 that match them.

  1 'The Eiffel Tower is becoming too expensive to maintain.'
  2 'The Government has decided to sell it.'
  3 'You can't tell anyone else about it.'
  4 'Lustig isn't telling us the truth.'
  5 'I'm acting strangely because I expect a bribe.'
  6 'I'll give you a bribe.'
  7 'Lustig tricked me.'

3 Compare the quotations in exercise 2 with the parts of the text that you underlined. Then complete the table.

	Direct speech	Reported speech
1	present simple	past simple
2	present continuous	
3	past simple	
4	present perfect	
5	*can / can't*	
6	*will / won't*	

4 Read point 1 in the *Learn this!* box. Find examples of pronouns that are different in direct speech and reported speech in exercise 2.

5 Read point 2 in the *Learn this!* box. Match time expressions 1–6 with their equivalents in reported speech a–f.

1	today	a	the next week
2	tonight	b	the month before
3	next week	c	that day
4	yesterday	d	that night
5	this year	e	the day before
6	last month	f	that year

6 Read the direct speech and complete the reported speech with the correct tenses, pronouns and time expressions.

  1 'I'm doing my homework today,' he said.
    He said _____ homework _____ .
  2 'I don't understand your question,' she said to me.
    She said _____ question.
  3 'We sold our car last month,' he said.
    He said _____ car _____ .
  4 'I'll give you your book back tomorrow,' he said to her.
    He said _____ book back _____ .

⟫⟫ **GRAMMAR BUILDER 6.1: PAGE 117** ⟪⟪

7 Read the *Look out!* box. Underline all the examples of *say* and *tell* in the text in exercise 1.

8 Complete the sentences with *said* or *told*. Then rewrite the direct speech as reported speech.

  1 'I'm not feeling well,' my sister <u>told</u> me.
    My sister told me she wasn't feeling well.
  2 'You've done really well,' my dad _____ me.
  3 'It will be great show,' the singer _____ .
  4 'I can't find my purse,' she _____ to her boyfriend.
  5 'I'm going on holiday next week,' my aunt _____ me.
  6 'You don't need your books today,' our teacher _____ us.

9 **SPEAKING** Think of something that somebody told you which you didn't believe. Why didn't you believe it? Tell the class.

> My mum once told me that she'd met Johnny Depp, but I didn't believe her. It was probably a dream!

Crime writers

I can talk about mystery stories.

1 SPEAKING **What is a crime novel? What characters and events would you expect to see in a crime novel?**

2 Read the first paragraph of a story by the crime writer Edmund Crispin. Then work in pairs and decide what '*the job*' is.

Max Linster went through the small side gate and saw the large house in front of him. Not far away, a church clock told him that it was ten o'clock. He had half an hour to do the job. At midnight, a private plane would take off for Europe from a lonely field in Norfolk, and Linster planned to be on it even if his last job in England was not successful.

3 🎧 2.16 **Listen to the next part of the story and check your ideas for exercise 2.**

4 🎧 2.16 **Listen again. Choose the correct word in these sentences.**

1 Linster **climbs** / **looks** into the servants' room.
2 Mr Elliston has only got one arm – his **left** / **right** arm.
3 Linster will get the money when Elliston's **brother** / **wife** is dead.
4 Linster agrees to use two **guns** / **hands** for the murder.
5 Linster agrees to **hide** / **steal** a jewellery box so the murder looks like a burglary.
6 **Elliston** / **Linster** goes into another bedroom to hide.

5 Read the final part of the story. Does Linster follow Elliston's instructions?

6 VOCABULARY **Complete these expressions from the text with the correct preposition.**

1 to move _____ of a cupboard
2 to go _____ behind somebody
3 to watch somebody _____ a mirror
4 to pull something from _____ a blanket
5 to jump _____ (when you get a shock)
6 to put something _____ somebody's hands
7 to look _____ a window
8 to climb _____ of a window

7 SPEAKING **Work in pairs. Work out the answers to these questions. Then compare your ideas with the class.**

1 Does Linster kill the servant by mistake? How do you know?
2 Why does Linster only use one hand to kill her?
3 Why does Linster hide the jewellery box under the bed?
4 Why does Linster say 'You will' at the end?

Linster hides in a cupboard. But instead of Mrs Elliston, the next person to enter the room is Josephine, a servant, who tries on Mrs Elliston's coat and some of her jewellery.

It was then that Linster moved out of the clothes cupboard. He went silently up behind her. He watched her face in the mirror and was still a metre or two away when she saw him and turned around. But his left hand was large and fast. It closed around her narrow throat. She made no sound as she died …

Linster gently put her body on the bed, then covered her with a blanket. It took only a few minutes to open the cupboards and make them look untidy. He looked at the little jewellery box, then threw it under the bed.

When Elliston entered the room again, he looked at the shape under the blanket. He said, 'It – it's done?'

'Yes,' said Linster. 'It's done.'

'You're sure she's …?'

'Yes, Mr Elliston, she's dead.' Linster pulled a white hand from under the blanket. 'If you don't believe me, feel this.'

But Elliston jumped back, shaking. 'That ring,' he said slowly. 'It's one she almost never –'

Linster dropped the hand. 'The money, Mr Elliston. Five thousand.'

The money was put silently into his hands.

'I'm going now, Mr Elliston,' said Linster. And then, with a smile, he said, 'Sorry I can't stay and talk to that pretty little servant that your wife has.'

Elliston looked surprised. 'The – the girl?'

'The girl,' said Linster. 'I looked through the window of your servants' room before I climbed up here, and there she was. A pretty girl. I'd recognise her again, anywhere. But I had this job to do. And you don't get paid until you've done the job, do you? It's cash on delivery. And a man must live.'

'I don't understand what you're talking about,' said Elliston.

But Linster was already climbing out of the window. 'You will Mr Elliston,' he said. 'You will.'

1 SPEAKING Describe the picture. Do you think encounters between humans and aliens really happen? Give reasons for your opinion.

2 🎧 2.17 Listen to the press conference with Vernon, a man who claims to have encountered an alien. Complete the reported questions with the words below.

aliens contact encounter night police spacecraft

1 They asked him if he could remember the previous _____ clearly.
2 They asked him where he'd seen the _____.
3 They asked him how many _____ there had been.
4 They asked him if he felt different after his _____.
5 They asked him if the aliens would try to make _____ again.
6 They asked him if the _____ were investigating his story.

3 🎧 2.17 Work in pairs. Listen again.
Student A: Write the exact words spoken in questions 1, 3, and 5 in exercise 2.
Student B: Write the exact words spoken in questions 2, 4 and 6 in exercise 2.

4 In pairs, compare your answers to exercise 3 with the reported questions in exercise 2. Then choose the correct words in the *Learn this!* box to complete the rules.

LEARN THIS!

Reported questions
1 The reporting verb is *ask* / *say* / *tell*.
2 The tense changes **are** / **aren't** the same as for reported statements. (See Lesson 6B, page 55).
3 Pronouns and time expressions **change** / **don't change** in the same way as for reported statements.
4 The subject comes **before** / **after** the verb.
5 We **use** / **don't use** *do* or *did*.
6 We use *if* / *that* when we report *yes* / *no* questions.

5 Read some other questions that reporters asked Vernon. Rewrite them as reported questions.

1 'Did you take any photos?'
   They asked him if he'd taken any photos.
2 'Were you scared?'
3 'Do you drink every night?'
4 'Will you give more interviews tomorrow?'
5 'Can you describe the spacecraft?'
6 'Are you telling the truth?'

⟫⟫⟫ GRAMMAR BUILDER 6.2: PAGE 118 ⟪⟪⟪

6 Read the dialogue between Vernon and his wife. Then complete the text with reported speech (questions and statements).

Marie	Are you going to tell me the truth, Vernon?
Vernon	What do you mean?
Marie	You didn't really meet any aliens last night.
Vernon	How do you know?
Marie	I can tell when you're lying. We've been married for ten years! Why did you invent the story?
Vernon	I can make money from it!
Marie	It's wrong to lie.
Vernon	Do you want to be rich?

Marie asked Vernon if he was going to tell her the truth .
Vernon asked her ¹_____ . Marie said that Vernon ²_____ the previous night. When Vernon asked her ³_____ , Marie replied that she ⁴_____ because they ⁵_____ for ten years. She asked him ⁶_____ the story. Vernon replied that he ⁷_____ from it. When Marie told him ⁸_____ to lie, Vernon asked her ⁹_____ rich.

7 Write down six questions on any topic to ask your partner. Use a different tense or verb below in each question.

can past simple present continuous present perfect present simple will

What kind of films do you like?

8 SPEAKING Play a class game in two teams. One pair from team 1 asks and answers a question from exercise 7.

What kind of films do you like?

I like horror films.

One person from team 2 has to remember and report the question and answer.

Catherine asked Mark what kind of films he liked. Mark said that he liked horror films.

1 You are going to read about a famous German mystery story. What other famous mystery stories do you know?

2 🎧 2.18 Read the text quickly. Match the paragraphs (A–E) with the headings (1–6). There is one extra heading that you do not need.

1 His fame spreads
2 Were his stories true?
3 Reunited with his real parents
4 Alone in a strange city
5 A mysterious murder?
6 A strange childhood

KASPAR HAUSER

A ☐

ON 26TH MAY 1828, THE PEOPLE OF NUREMBERG IN GERMANY FOUND A TEENAGE BOY WHO WAS WANDERING ALONE THROUGH THE STREETS. When they came across him, he had no possessions except for two old letters. Because of his behaviour and appearance, they took him to the police station. Kaspar spent the next two months in prison, where he hardly spoke and refused all food except for bread and water. Some people assumed that Kaspar had grown up alone in the forest, like a wild animal. But gradually, a different picture emerged.

B ☐

Kaspar said he had spent his whole childhood in a small dark cell. He had never seen the world outside or left his cell. He had never met or spoken to another human being. The cell was empty apart from a small bed and one toy – a wooden horse. He claimed that he had found bread and water in his cell every morning. According to Kaspar's account, a mysterious man had begun to call on him shortly before his release. The man never showed his face.

C ☐

Kaspar became well-known throughout Germany and in other countries too, and people found his story fascinating. Some suggested that Kaspar was the son of a rich and powerful man – a prince perhaps – who wanted to keep his identity secret. A schoolteacher called Friedrich Daumer met Kaspar and agreed to look after him. Daumer taught him various subjects and encouraged Kaspar's talent for drawing.

D ☐

One day in 1829, Kaspar was found with a knife wound to his head. He claimed that a man with a hood over his face had attacked him – the same man who had brought him to Nuremberg. It wasn't a serious injury, and Kaspar got over it. But in 1833, Hauser came home with a deep knife wound in his chest, saying someone had attacked him in a garden. Three days later, Kaspar died from the wound. Just before he died, Kaspar told the police that his attacker had given him a bag, so the police went to the garden and looked for it. They found it, with a note inside. The note was in mirror writing and said in German: 'I want to tell you about myself. I come from the Bavarian border, on the river.'

E ☐

Over the years, books have been written about Kaspar's stories and various historians have looked into them. Most have concluded that the stories were untrue and that Kaspar Hauser was a liar who killed himself (possibly by mistake). But for some people, Kaspar Hauser's life and death remain one of the most mysterious stories in history.

EXAM STRATEGY

The order of the questions usually follows the content of the text. Read the questions first, then the text and if you are not sure of the answer, eliminate the options which are definitely incorrect first. This should help you to narrow down your answers and focus your reading.

3 Read the exam strategy and choose the correct answers.

1 People in Nuremberg took Kaspar Hauser to the police station because
  a he was carrying two letters.
  b he said he wanted to be a soldier.
  c he was acting strangely.
  d he had no possessions.

2 Before Kaspar told his story, some people believed that he had grown up
  a in prison.
  b with his father, in a forest.
  c without any people around him.
  d in a normal home.

3 According to his story, Kaspar spent the first years of his life
  a in a dark cell with a mysterious man.
  b in a dark cell with absolutely nothing in it.
  c in the garden of a mysterious stranger.
  d alone and always indoors.

4 Some people suggested that Kaspar Hauser was
  a from another country.
  b really an artist.
  c the son of a schoolteacher.
  d from a wealthy family.

5 Between 1829 and 1833, Kaspar Hauser suffered
  a two knife wounds, but they weren't serious.
  b two knife wounds, one small and one fatal.
  c two very serious knife wounds.
  d two knife wounds on the same occasion.

6 Police found a mysterious letter inside a bag
  a in Kaspar Hauser's room, after his death.
  b in the place where Kaspar Hauser died.
  c near a river in Bavaria.
  d in the place where Kaspar Hauser was attacked.

7 Most historians today believe that Kaspar Hauser
  a was the son of a Bavarian prince.
  b was one of the most mysterious people in history.
  c invented the story of his life.
  d did not really die from the knife wound.

4 **VOCABULARY** Match the highlighted phrasal verbs in the text with the definitions below.

1 to study or investigate something
2 to visit somebody
3 to recover from something
4 to try to find something
5 to take care of somebody or something
6 to find somebody or something by chance

▶▶▶ VOCABULARY BUILDER 6.3: PAGE 132 ◀◀◀

5 **SPEAKING** Which of these events from Kaspar Hauser's life do you find strangest? If his story wasn't true, how would you explain them?

1 He was found wandering the streets alone.
2 He could only say a few words when they found him.
3 He was found with a knife wound.
4 He was attacked in a garden and died three days later.
5 A note containing a mysterious message was found after his death.

6 **SPEAKING** Work in pairs. Discuss whether you think Kaspar Hauser's story is true. Then have a class vote.

7 **SPEAKING** Work in pairs. Look at the film posters. Do you know any of these films in which the main character's true identity is kept secret? Discuss (a) Why you think the character's identity needs to be a secret, and (b) other possible reasons for hiding your true identity.

1 **SPEAKING** Read the news report. Work in pairs and decide what happened to the people on board the boat. Tell the class.

We think they probably … | Perhaps they … | Maybe …

YACHT FOUND DESERTED

A large, luxury yacht has been found deserted off the coast of Monaco. There were no signs of an accident or a fight. According to records, the yacht left port with twelve people on board: the owners – a Russian billionaire and his wife – and ten crew members. The personal possessions of the twelve missing people were still on the yacht.

2 🎧 2.19 Read and listen to two teenagers discussing the news report. Do they mention any of your ideas from exercise 1? Which explanation do they agree is most likely?

Tyler	Have you seen this story about a deserted boat?
Kayla	Yes. It's weird. What do you think happened?
Tyler	They could have been attacked by pirates, I guess.
Kayla	I doubt it. There aren't any pirates in the Mediterranean.
Tyler	Hmm. Or they might have gone swimming and been killed by sharks.
Kayla	That isn't very likely. They can't have all gone swimming at the same time.
Tyler	I see what you mean. That would be crazy!
Kayla	The crew could have killed the owners, stolen their money and then escaped.
Tyler	Yes, that's quite likely. But where are the bodies?
Kayla	They must have thrown the bodies into the sea.
Tyler	Hmm. Yes, I think you're right.

3 Read the Learn this! box. Underline the examples of *could have*, *might have*, *must have* and *can't have* in the dialogue in exercise 2. Match them to the opinions of the speakers a–c.

a It's impossible – it didn't happen.
b It's possible – maybe it happened.
c It's definite – it happened.

LEARN THIS!

Speculating about the past
We can use these phrases – *could / might have*, *must have, can't have* – to speculate about the past. They are all followed by a past participle.
*Where's my phone? I **must have** left it somewhere.*
*I **can't have** left it at school – I didn't take it there.*
*My sister **might have** picked it up.*

>>> GRAMMAR BUILDER 6.3: PAGE 119 <<<

4 Work in pairs. Read the newspaper headlines and think about what might have happened. Make notes.

1 $3,000 Ferrari destroyed by fire in car park
2 Footballer found unconscious in hotel room
3 Missing cat returns home after ten years

5 🎧 2.20 Listen to teenagers talking about the headlines in exercise 4. Do they mention any of your ideas?

6 🎧 2.20 Listen again. Which explanation (a, b or c) do they agree is most likely in each case?

1 a It was an accident.
  b Somebody was jealous of the car's owner.
  c The owner had argued with somebody.
2 a The footballer took drugs.
  b He hit his head during a match.
  c He was attacked by a robber.
3 a The cat found its old house by accident.
  b The cat's new owner died.
  c The cat's new owner moved away.

7 🎧 2.21 **PRONUNCIATION** Read the speaking strategy. Then listen and repeat the phrases, copying the intonation.

SPEAKING STRATEGY

We can use these phrases to react to another person's speculation.
No way!   No, that's not possible.   I don't think so.
I doubt it.   That's unlikely.   That's not very likely.
Maybe.   Perhaps.   Yes, that's possible.
Yes, that's quite likely.   I suppose so.
Yes, you're probably right.   Definitely!

8 **SPEAKING** Work in pairs. Read the headline below and think about possible explanations. Use the words below to help you or your own ideas.

drug-dealers   in hiding   kidnapped   murdered
on the run   robbers   stolen

25-YEAR-OLD BUSINESSMAN DISAPPEARS FROM HOTEL IN MEXICO, LEAVING $100,000 IN CASH IN SUITCASE

9 In pairs, write a dialogue like the one in exercise 2. Use your ideas from exercise 8. Include three possible explanations and agree on the most likely. Include phrases from the speaking strategy.

10 **SPEAKING** Act out your dialogue to the class. How many of your classmates agree with your conclusion?

I can write a letter asking for information.

1 Read the advert. Would you enjoy this holiday? Why? / Why not?

Murder Mystery Tour!

Combine a trip to London with the chance to take part in a special weekend event: a ~~murder mystery party~~.

Involves acting?

Your holiday begins with two days of sightseeing in the UK's historic capital. On Thursday and Friday, you visit all the major landmarks, and spend a whole afternoon at the Sherlock Holmes Museum in Baker Street. On Friday evening, you see Agatha Christie's *The Mousetrap* at the theatre. On Saturday and Sunday, the excitement really begins. Someone at your hotel is found dead, and it's your job to be a detective: question witnesses, collect clues and try to solve the mystery.
For more details, contact Bob Clarke at MM Tours.

free time
included?

dates? fully booked?   *which hotel?*

2 Read the notes that Oscar added to the advertisement. Then read his letter. What information does he forget to ask for?

Dear Mr Clarke,
Having read your advertisement in *News Weekly*, I am very interested in attending one of your Murder Mystery Tours, but would be grateful if you could give me some more information about some of the arrangements.
Could you tell me if there is any free time on Thursday or Friday, and also if the cost of the theatre ticket is included in the price of the holiday?
I'd also like to know which hotel in London we will be staying at, so I can look at its website. Ideally, I would like to book the holiday before the end of the year. Would you mind sending me a complete list of dates for September and October? Please let me know which of the tours are already fully booked.
I look forward to hearing from you in due course.
Yours sincerely,
Oscar Deer
Mr O Deer

WRITING STRATEGY

Direct questions often sound too familiar for a formal letter. It is more polite to use indirect questions beginning with these phrases:
Could you tell me …?   Could you please let me know …?
I'd be interested in knowing …   Please let me know …
I'd appreciate it if you could tell me …   I'd like to know …
I'd be grateful if you could tell me …

3 Read the writing strategy. Find questions in Oscar's letter which are formal equivalents of:

1 Is there any free time on Thursday or Friday?
2 Which hotel will we be staying at?
3 Which of the tours are already fully booked?

>>> GRAMMAR BUILDER 6.4: PAGE 119 <<<

4 Work in pairs. Write three direct questions that you could ask about a restaurant. Then swap questions and rewrite your partner's questions as indirect questions.

What time does the restaurant close?
I'd like to know what time the restaurant closes.

5 Read the *Learn this!* box. Find two verbs with two objects in the letter.

Verbs with two objects
Some verbs can be followed by both an indirect and a direct object. The indirect object comes first and is usually a person.
Sam bought his mum some flowers.
My friend sent me an email.

>>> GRAMMAR BUILDER 6.5: PAGE 119 <<<

6 Imagine you are interested in booking the Murder Mystery Tour. Plan a formal letter to Mr Clarke. Ask for information about these aspects of the holiday:

• meeting time and meeting place in London.
• costumes for the weekend event and acting involved.
• cost of meals and availability of vegetarian meals.
• reduced prices for students and for sharing rooms.

7 Write a formal letter asking for information. Write 120–150 words using your notes from exercise 6.

CHECK YOUR WORK

Have you:
☐ included the information in the task in exercise 6?
☐ followed the formal letter writing style?
☐ used the phrases in the writing strategy?

Unit 5

1 Choose the correct word and complete the sentences.

1 Plug the printer into the _____ port.
   a blog   b desktop   c USB
2 Email me from the airport. There's a _____ hotspot there.
   a Wi-Fi   b links   c channel
3 I downloaded an _____ that helps me with my English.
   a username   b app   c autocomplete
4 This hard disk can store a huge amount of _____ .
   a social networking   b data   c Wi-Fi
5 Go to the home page and click on the _____ to the booking form.
   a browsers   b podcast   c link

Mark: _____ /5

2 Choose the correct word.

1 If we're lucky, it **could** / **might** not rain for the picnic tomorrow.
2 She probably **won't** / **may not** come to the party tomorrow.
3 I'll buy you a present if I **will have** / **have** enough money.
4 They **may** / **will** have Wi-Fi in the hotel, but we're not sure.
5 You could win the race next Saturday if you **will run** / **run** as fast as that.

Mark: _____ /5

3 Correct the sentences.

1 By the end of term, we have done all our exams.
2 This time next week, they will be lie on the beach.
3 A year from now, I will have learn to drive.
4 At 10 p.m., I'll still have doing my homework.
5 I'll be leave for the airport at 7 a.m. tomorrow.

Mark: _____ /5

4 Complete the dialogue with the phrases below.

Do you fancy   I'd be up for   Maybe we could
Sorry, I can't.   Yes, that sounds

Boy Hi, Bella! ¹_____ going to the cinema on Saturday evening?
Girl ²_____ I'm going out with friends. But what film is it?
Boy It's *I Am Number Four*, that science fiction film.
Girl Oh, I want to see that film! ³_____ go on Sunday afternoon?
Boy ⁴_____ that. I'll find out what time it's on.
Girl Great. And how about a pizza before?
Boy ⁵_____ fun. I'll call you later.

Mark: _____ /5

Total: _____ /20

Unit 6

5 Complete the compound nouns using the words below.

flower   hole   lamp   ledge   shelf

1 Could you get me the dictionary from the book _____ ?
2 There are some wonderful plants in that _____ bed.
3 Can you see inside if you look through the key _____ ?
4 Shall I switch the table _____ on so you can read?
5 The cat's sitting on the window _____ again!

Mark: _____ /5

6 Report the direct speech with *said* or *told*.

1 'I didn't finish my project yesterday,' said John.
2 'We're having our lesson outside,' our teacher told us.
3 She said, 'I can't do it on my own.'
4 'I'll do it for you tomorrow,' Mum said to us.
5 'Our plane leaves tonight,' they told me.

Mark: _____ /5

7 Rewrite the questions as reported speech.

1 'Did you have a nice time yesterday?' I asked her.
2 'When are you going home?' he asked me.
3 'Will you give me a call?' she asked him.
4 'Where were you last night?' I asked him.
5 'Are you working this evening?' he asked her.

Mark: _____ /5

8 Imagine you want information about a business meeting. Rewrite these questions formally as indirect questions. Start each question in a different way.

1 What time does the meeting start?
2 What time will it finish?
3 Will there be a break for lunch?
4 Do we have to bring food?
5 How many people will be there?

Mark: _____ /5

Total: _____ /20

Lead-in

1 Work in pairs. Discuss these questions. Then compare your ideas with the class.

Why are museums important? What can you learn from them?

Reading

2 Look quickly at the text. What kind of text is it? Choose a, b, c or d.

a A review of a new exhibition.
b A formal letter from a museum.
c A publicity leaflet about an exhibition.
d An article about a new museum.

3 Match the headings (1–7) with paragraphs A–E in the text. There are two extra headings that you do not need.

1 Artificial intelligence
2 The future of entertainment
3 Shopping in the 25th century
4 A multimedia experience
5 Half human, half machine
6 Homes of the future
7 Science fiction films of the future

Writing

4 Imagine you are Anna. Your boss Julian Lloyd has asked you to write an announcement for a local newspaper to advertise the new exhibition. Include this information:

- where the exhibition is and when it opens
- what the exhibition is about and what you can see there (choose information from the text)
- how much the tickets are and who can get a reduction (invent this information)
- what the opening times are and how people can get more information (invent this information).

Speaking

5 Read the text message from Anna to her friend Libby. What might have happened? Discuss your ideas using *could / might have*, *can't have* and *must have*.

> WENT TO OPENING PARTY FOR EXHIBITION AND INVITED MIKE. WHAT A DISASTER! SO ANGRY WITH HIM. NEXT TIME, I'LL GO ON MY OWN! :-(

Listening

6 🎧 2.22 Listen to what happened at the exhibition. Were any of your ideas from exercise 5 correct?

7 🎧 2.22 Listen again. Complete each sentence with between one and three words.

1 Anna tells Mike that she _____ in class.
2 She invites Mike to the party on _____ afternoon.
3 They arrange to meet _____ the museum.
4 While Anna is talking to Julian, Mike goes to the _____ .
5 Daisy guesses Anna is not British because of her _____ .
6 Anna tells Mike that she felt _____ when he disappeared.

Into the Future

A

A new exhibition at the Museum of Liverpool opens on 1 July. It looks at current trends in four different areas and asks where they are heading. It includes videos, interactive displays and virtual reality exhibits.

B

[C]omputers are [b]ecoming more and more [p]owerful each year. Will they [s]oon be more intelligent than people? If the [an]swer is yes, then how will that change [ou]r relationship with computers? Might [th]ere be dangers for the human race? This [p]art of the exhibition explores this question [an]d other related issues.

C

What will the kitchen of the future look like? Will domestic robots finally become a reality? In this part of the exhibition you can find out what day-to-day life may be like fifty years from now. From a fridge that does your shopping online, to a wardrobe that tells you what to wear, it seems certain that everything around us will soon be 'smart', not just our phones!

D

At the moment, 3D TV and films are a new and exciting development. But what will the next development be? Will TV become genuinely interactive? Or perhaps nobody will watch TV or films at all. Instead, they will put on a headset and find themselves a new world of virtual reality. These technologies already exist; come and try them, and get a taste of the future. The fun has only just started …

E

We all know about superheroes from comic books and science fiction films. As science advances, will some of their 'superpowers' be found in ordinary humans? Perhaps – if we are prepared to let technology and our bodies mix. In this part of the exhibition, you can try out a bionic hand and let a mind-reading computer explore your thoughts. You'll be amazed!

THIS UNIT INCLUDES

Vocabulary ■ dating and relationships ■ time expressions ■ phrasal verbs ■ idioms with *heart* and *head* ■ noun + preposition ■ expressing contrast
Grammar ■ comparative and superlative forms ■ second conditional ■ *I wish, If only, I'd rather*
Speaking ■ telling the story of a relationship ■ stimulus description
Writing ■ a for and against essay

7A VOCABULARY AND LISTENING Relationships

I can talk about dating and relationships.

1 VOCABULARY Work in pairs. Put the phrases below into the order that they might happen in a relationship. There is more than one correct answer.

<u>Dating and relationships</u>
ask somebody out ☐ chat somebody up ☐
fancy somebody ☐ fall in love (with somebody) ☐
fall out (with somebody) ☐
get back together (with somebody) ☐
get divorced ☐ get engaged (to somebody) ☐
get married (to somebody) ☐ get on well (with somebody) ☐
go out (with somebody) ☐ make up (with somebody) ☐
split up (with somebody) ☐

2 Complete the sentences with *back, in, on, out, up, with* or – (nothing).

1 He fell _____ love _____ her the moment he saw her, and asked her _____ .
2 Jake and Sue split _____ last month, but got _____ together a few days later.
3 Tom and Ann didn't use to get _____ well, but now they're going _____ .
4 If you fancy _____ her, why don't you chat her _____ ?
5 Jo and Kevin had a big row and fell _____ , but they made _____ a few days later.
6 Did they get engaged _____ before they got married _____ ?

3 Rewrite the sentences using phrases from exercise 1.

1 Phil and Tanya had a big argument.
   Phil and Tanya fell out.
2 Dave is attracted to Helen.
3 Harry and Diana have ended their relationship.
4 Kate and Ian's marriage has ended.
5 Pete and Sarah have a good relationship.
6 Linda and Rob have started going out again.
7 Tina and Bruce have become friends again after their argument.

4 🎧 2.23 Listen to people talking about couples. Match the conversations (1–5) with the sentences (a–g). There are two sentences that you do not need.

a They're divorced.
b They're married.
c They're going out.
d They're engaged.
e They've split up.
f They're just good friends.
g They've got back together.

5 Look at the photostory of Ryan and Hannah's relationship. Make notes about what happened in each picture. Use phrases from exercise 1 to help you.

1 They met at a party. Ryan fancied ...

6 SPEAKING Tell the story of Ryan and Hannah's relationship. Use the pictures, your notes from exercise 5 and the time expressions below to help you.

<u>Time expressions</u> after a (few days) after that before finally first for (two months) in the end (two years) later the moment ... the same day

▶▶▶ VOCABULARY BUILDER 7.1: PAGE 133 ◀◀◀

STAYING IN TOUCH

Modern life is getting busier and busier. And the busier it gets, the more isolated people can feel. These days, people have fewer opportunities to meet friends, because they work harder, and have less time to socialise. Some say that social-networking sites allow them to stay in touch with friends more easily. Sue Weeks decided to test this theory. She stayed in for a week and only contacted her friends via Facebook, one of the most popular social-networking sites. Her view? 'It was great for staying in touch with friends I don't see very often or who live far away, but it wasn't the most exciting week I've ever had.' The least appealing aspect for Sue was not seeing the people she gets on with best. Her final verdict: 'It was more fun than I expected, but it's less satisfying than meeting people face to face.'

1 Read the text. Do you use social-networking sites to contact friends? Why? / Why not? Do you agree with Sue's opinions?

LEARN THIS!

Comparative and superlative adverbs
We usually form comparative and superlative adverbs with *more* and *most*. However, we add *-er* and *-est* to some adverbs:
Please speak more slowly. Tom works harder than Sam.
less and least
less is the opposite of *more*, *least* is the opposite of *most*. We can use them with adjectives, adverbs and uncountable nouns:
My dad bought the least expensive TV in the shop.
Who earns less money, teachers or nurses?

2 Read the *Learn this!* box. Then match the words in red in the text with the descriptions (1–7).
1 A comparative form of an adjective with *less*.
2 A superlative form of an adjective with *least*.
3 A comparative form of an adverb with *more*.
4 A comparative form of an adverb with *-er*.
5 An irregular superlative form of an adverb.
6 An uncountable noun with *less*.
7 A superlative form of an adjective with *most*.

>>> GRAMMAR BUILDER 7.1: PAGE 120 <<<

3 Read the *Learn this!* box. Then match the words in blue in the text with points 1–4.

LEARN THIS!

Comparison
1 We often use a superlative with the present perfect and *ever*:
That's the least funny film I've ever seen.
2 We can make comparisons with simple nouns:
She's more confident than her brother.
and also with clauses:
She's less talkative than she used to be.
3 We use double comparatives to say that something is changing:
You're getting taller and taller!
4 We use *the ... the* and comparatives to say that one thing changes with another:
The more I eat, the fatter I get.

4 **SPEAKING** Work in pairs. Ask and answer questions using a superlative form and the present perfect with *ever*. Use the prompts below and your own ideas.
1 interesting book / read
2 good friend / have
3 boring film / see
4 attractive person / meet
5 long phone call / make
6 good party / go to

> What's the most / least interesting book you've ever read?

>>> GRAMMAR BUILDER 7.2: PAGE 121 <<<

5 Complete sentence B so that it means the same as sentence A. Use the words in brackets.
1 A I didn't expect speed dating to be so easy. (than)
  B Speed dating was _____ .
2 A Mum is a faster driver than Dad. (slowly)
  B Dad _____ Mum.
3 A My partner's got more money than me. (less)
  B I _____ my partner.
4 A This is the cheapest TV in the shop. (expensive)
  B This is _____ TV in the shop.
5 A No team scored fewer goals than Plymouth. (fewest)
  B Plymouth scored _____ .
6 A It's getting increasingly difficult to meet people. (and)
  B It's getting _____ to meet people.

6 **SPEAKING** Complete the sentences using structures from the *Learn this!* boxes. Then read them to your partner and compare your answers.
1 The older you get ...
2 Britain is much ...
3 I'm getting more and more ...
4 The harder I work ...
5 I'm ... than I was ...

I can understand a poem.

1 How many poets can you name:
  1 from your country?
  2 from other countries?

2 Try to complete the poems with the verbs below. Remember that poems often rhyme.

came by   chose   depart   get   knew   met   ~~move~~   said
suppose   told   took

Love's Secret
Never seek to tell thy love,
Love that never told can be;
For the gentle wind does ¹move
Silently, invisibly.

I ² _____ my love, I told my love,
I told her all my heart;
Trembling, cold, in ghastly fears,
Ah! She did ³ _____ !

Soon as she was gone from me,
A traveller ⁴ _____ ,
Silently, invisibly
He ⁵ _____ her with a sigh.

William Blake

One Perfect Rose
A single flow'r he sent me, since we ⁶ _____ .
All tenderly his messenger he ⁷ _____ ;
Deep-hearted, pure, with scented dew still wet --
One perfect rose.

I ⁸ _____ the language of the floweret;
'My fragile leaves,' it ⁹ _____ , 'his heart enclose.'
Love long has taken for his amulet
One perfect rose.

Why is it no one ever sent me yet
One perfect limousine, do you ¹⁰ _____ ?
Ah no, it's always just my luck to ¹¹ _____
One perfect rose.

Dorothy Parker

3 🎧 2.24 Listen and check your answers.

4 SPEAKING Answer these questions about each poem. Give reasons for your opinions. Is the poem:
  1 funny or serious?
  2 old or modern?
  3 pessimistic or optimistic?
  4 likely to be written by a woman or by a man?
  5 about lost love or about the poet's present partner?

5 VOCABULARY Check the meaning of these words in a dictionary. Then use them to complete the sentences.

mystical   patriotic   professional   religious   renowned   romantic

  1 Christianity and Islam are _____ beliefs.
  2 Watching the sunrise was an almost _____ experience.
  3 _____ people love their country.
  4 Joe is very _____ . He's always buying flowers for his girlfriend.
  5 Everyone has heard of Shakespeare. He's England's most _____ playwright.
  6 My mum's a _____ musician. She plays in a big orchestra in London.

6 🎧 2.25 Listen to a radio documentary about the life of William Blake, a famous poet. Which of these things does the speaker talk about?

growing up   relationships   school   travel   writing

7 🎧 2.25 Listen again and choose the correct answers.
  1 Blake was
    a a poet.   c a poet and a musician.
    b an artist and a poet.
  2 Blake was
    a uneducated.   c educated at school.
    b taught at home.
  3 When Blake was 21, he
    a got a job as an engraver. c made his first engraving.
    b started to write poems.
  4 His wife Catherine
    a never learned to read or write.
    b was taught to read and write by her husband.
    c taught herself to read and write.
  5 Blake lived in London
    a for most of his life.   c for all of his life.
    b during his marriage.
  6 The majority of his poems are
    a romantic love poems.
    b mystical and religious poems.
    c poems about dead people.

8 SPEAKING Work in pairs. Ask and answer these questions. Give reasons.
  1 Did you like writing poems when you were younger?
  2 Do you ever write poems now?
  3 Do you like reading poetry?
  4 Do you agree that the lyrics of rappers like Jay-Z or Kanye West can be described as poetry?

>>> VOCABULARY BUILDER 7.2: PAGE 133 <<<

1 🎧 2.26 Read and listen to the conversation. Are there ever arguments about clothes in your family?

Mum	I wish you'd throw those old jeans out. They're so scruffy.
Sam	I like them. If I had more money, I'd buy some new ones. But I don't.
Mum	If you didn't buy so many computer games, you would have more money.
Sam	If only I could leave school and get a job.
Mum	Don't be silly. Anyway, I'd rather you didn't wear those jeans this evening. We're going to a very nice restaurant.
Sam	I'd rather stay in and watch TV.
Mum	No. It's your dad's birthday. We're all going out together.

2 Read and complete the *Learn this!* box. How many examples of the second conditional are in the dialogue?

> **LEARN THIS!**
> **Second conditional**
> We use the second conditional to talk about an imaginary situation or event and its result.
> We use the ¹_____ simple for the situation or event and ²_____ + base form for the result.

3 Complete the sentences with your own ideas.
1 If I didn't have to go to school, …
2 I'd leave home if …
3 If I could live anywhere in the world, …
4 If I could drive, …
5 If I had €3,000 for a holiday, …
6 If I found €100 in the street …
7 I'd never tell anyone if …
8 If I fell out with my best friend, …

>>> GRAMMAR BUILDER 7.3: PAGE 121 <<<

4 Read the *Learn this!* box. Underline an example of each expression in the dialogue in exercise 1.

> **LEARN THIS!**
> **I wish, If only, I'd rather**
> 1 We use *I wish …* or *If only …* with the past simple to say that we really want a situation to be different:
> *I wish it was Saturday. If only I had more money.*
> 2 We use *I wish …* or *If only …* with *would* + base form to say that we really want somebody's (or something's) behaviour to be different:
> *I wish he wouldn't speak so loudly. I wish it would snow.*
> 3 We use *I'd rather* with a base form to express a preference:
> *'Do you want a cup of tea?' 'I'd rather have a coffee.'*
> 4 We use *I'd rather* with the past simple to say that we really want somebody's (or something's) behaviour to be different:
> *I'd rather you didn't phone me after 10 p.m.*

5 Complete the sentences with *I wish* (or *If only*) and *I'd rather*.
1 I don't like living in the city. _____ live in the country.
2 I hate wet weather. _____ it would stop raining.
3 I'll give you a lift to town if you want, but _____ you took the bus.
4 I hate camping. _____ stay in a hotel than in a tent.
5 _____ my sister wouldn't keep following me around.
6 I can't afford those trainers. _____ they were less expensive!

6 How many sentences can you make using this chart?

	I had a better job.
I wish	she didn't have to work.
If only	get up later.
I'd rather	we took more holidays.
If she worked harder,	she'd do better in her exams.
She'd be less tired if	our teachers wouldn't give us so much homework.

7 **SPEAKING** Work in pairs.
Student A: Make comments using *I wish …* and the ideas below or your own ideas.
Student B: Ask why.
Student A: Say how life would be different.
Swap roles halfway through the exercise.

1 I / live / in the mountains
2 I / have / eight brothers and sisters
3 I / have / a new smartphone
4 it / be / my birthday
5 I / can / draw really well
6 I / own / a private jet
7 I / not have to / go to school on Friday

> I wish I lived in the mountains.

> Really? Why?

> If I lived in the mountains, I could go skiing every day in the winter.

>>> GRAMMAR BUILDER 7.4: PAGE 121 <<<

1 **SPEAKING** Discuss these questions with the class.

1 Can you fall in love with somebody without meeting them face to face?
2 In what ways can online relationships be dangerous?
3 Do you know anybody who has used an online dating agency or started a relationship online?

READING STRATEGY

Be aware of what type of text you are reading and what kind of information you expect to find in it. This will make it easier to understand the text.

2 Read the reading strategy. Then look quickly through the text and decide what type of text it is. Choose a, b, c or d.

a a blog
b an email
c an online article
d a Wikipedia entry

3 🎧 2.27 Read the text. Which sentence best summarises the writer's opinion?

1 Science can definitely help you to find a partner.
2 Science definitely can't help because it doesn't take account of personal attraction.
3 Science may help some people, but not all.

4 Are the sentences true or false? Correct the false sentences.

1 Over 50% of adults who aren't in a relationship think that Internet dating sites are a good way of meeting a life partner.
2 A psychometric test consists of a personality profile, and a hobbies and interests questionnaire.
3 Psychometric tests were first used about 100 years ago.
4 Cathy liked David the moment she saw him.
5 Simon had a lot in common with the women he met through online dating.
6 Dr Kenton thinks that psychometric testing will help you find someone with the opposite personality to you.

5 **VOCABULARY** Find and complete the noun + preposition combinations. Look in the text between lines 20 and 45.

1 a chance _____
2 an attitude _____
3 a date _____
4 an interest _____
5 take account _____
6 an attraction _____

6 **SPEAKING** Read the comments about online dating. Work in pairs. Discuss which are advantages and which are disadvantages of online dating.

1 It's impossible to know if you are really attracted to the person until you actually meet them.
2 You can find out a lot about a person before you meet.
3 You can meet lots of potential partners without leaving your home.
4 You have to fill in a long psychological questionnaire.
5 You can meet people from other countries.
6 You can't be sure if the other person is telling the truth about their sex, age or appearance.

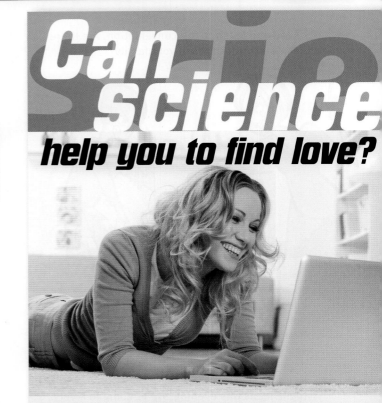

Can science help you to find love?

In our busy, stress-filled modern times, how do people meet their life partner? In Britain, over 50% of single adults think that online dating provides the answer. Internet dating sites have become the most popular way to meet people.

5 But is the Internet the ideal way to find true love? The dating agencies think so. They are using science in an attempt to match people more closely with suitable partners. In the past, dating agencies just used a simple personality profile, and a hobbies and interests questionnaire to put people together.

10 Now, however, more and more of them are using psychometric tests. These detailed psychological questionnaires were developed by scientists at the beginning of the twentieth century to recruit good spies for the First World War. Later they were used in business to find the right people for the right

15 jobs. And now online dating agencies are using the same techniques. If you logged on to a dating agency today, you might have to answer over 200 questions about yourself and the kind of person you would like to meet. It would take a very long time!

20 But does it work? 'Yes,' says Dr Jan Fellowes, a senior research scientist at one of the most popular agencies. 'It allows us to match people far more closely with compatible partners, so that there is a greater chance of success.'

7 🎧 2.28 **Listen and complete the song with the words below.**

cruel   cried   lost   man   mess   remember   scared   tired

8 🎧 2.28 **Listen again and choose the best summary of the song.**

1 You were very unfair to me and you left me. I hope I never see you again.
2 You left me and now I feel terrible. But I'll soon be strong again.
3 You left me and now I feel terrible. If you don't come back to me, I'll never be strong again.

So how does this work in real life? Here are two people's
25 stories.
Cathy is an attractive fitness instructor. 'I was working long hours and wasn't meeting men that I was interested in, so I joined a dating agency,' says Cathy. 'I was matched with several men and one of them was David. When I first met him I wasn't impressed. But as we
30 started talking, I discovered that we had a huge amount in common. I liked his attitude to life and the way he talked, and I realised that I really liked him. So, as a fitness instructor, I told him he had to get in shape!' Seven months later, Cathy and David got married. 'And now I think he is the most gorgeous man in the world!' she says.
35 Simon's experience was different. 'I wanted a serious relationship and a friend suggested online dating. I had some very pleasant dates with some very nice women and had a good time. All of them shared my interest in films and travel, so we were compatible, but there just wasn't that spark of attraction. It was strange.'
40 Dr Sarah Kenton agrees. She is the author of *How to meet your Soulmate*. She says, 'Psychometric testing is useful, but can't take account of attraction. And sometimes you can feel attraction for someone because they have something you haven't got. As the old saying goes, "Opposites attract".'
45 So, perhaps science can help you find your perfect partner, but sometimes it's just down to chemistry.

This ain't a love song

Every night I [1]_____ that evening,
The way you looked when you said you were leaving,
The way you [2]_____ as you turned to walk away,
The [3]_____ words and the false accusations,
The mean looks and the same old frustrations.
I never thought that we'd throw it all away,
But we threw it all away.

Chorus
   And I'm a little bit [4]_____ without you,
   And I'm a great big [5]_____ inside.
   And I'm a little bit lost without you.
   This ain't a love song. This is goodbye. (ooh)
   This ain't a love song. This is goodbye. (ooh)

I've been lost, I've been out, I've been losing.
I've been [6]_____, I'm all hurt and confusion.
I've been mad, I'm the kind of [7]_____ that I'm not.
I'm going down, I'll be coming back fighting.
I may be [8]_____ and a little bit frightened,
But I'll be back, I'll be coming back to life,
I'll be coming back to life.

Chorus

And you could try, (you could try)
And you can try, but you'll never keep me down.
And you could try, (you could try)
And you can try, but you'll never keep me down.

La la la la la la la la

Chorus

It's alright (It's alright)
'Cause you can try, but you'll never keep me down.
It's alright (It's alright)
I may be lost, but you'll never keep me down.
You could try, (you could try)
You can try, but you'll never keep me down.
You could try, (you could try)
I know I'm lost, but I'm waiting to be found.
You'll never keep me down.

1 SPEAKING Look at the photos. Compare the restaurants. Use the adjectives below.

<u>Adjectives to describe venues</u> boring bright cheap crowded dark expensive formal friendly informal lively noisy quiet romantic traditional trendy

> The restaurant in photo 1 looks livelier than the one in photo 2.

2 🎧 2.29 Look again at the photos and read the exam task below. Listen to a student answering the questions. Which restaurant did she choose and why?

You need to talk about a problem with a good friend who is visiting from the UK. Which of these places would you choose to meet in and why? Why wouldn't you choose the other places?

3 🎧 2.29 Complete the sentences with the words below. Then listen again and check.

best certainly choose looks might opt overall problem too

1 I'm going to _____ the restaurant in photo 1.
2 The _____ with the restaurant in photo 3 is that it's _____ crowded.
3 I wouldn't _____ for the restaurant in photo 2 because it _____ too formal.
4 It _____ be quieter than the other restaurants, but it _____ wouldn't be cheap.
5 So, _____ the restaurant in photo 1 would be _____ .

4 Do you agree with her choice? Why?

5 Read the *Learn this!* box. Check the meanings of the words in red. Use a dictionary to help you, if necessary.

> **Expressing contrast**
> We can use expressions like *however*, *in contrast*, *nevertheless*, and *on the other hand* at the start of a sentence to make a contrast with a point in the sentence before.
> *The café in photo 1 looks quite cheap. In contrast, photo 3 looks really posh.*
> We can use expressions like *whereas*, *but* and *although* to make a contrast between two points in the same sentence.
> *The restaurant in photo 1 is informal, whereas the one in photo 2 is formal.*

6 🎧 2.30 PRONUNCIATION Listen and repeat the phrases from the *Learn this*! box, copying the intonation.

EXAM STRATEGY

> Make sure you mention things that you can see in the photos when you compare and contrast them, and justify your choice.

7 SPEAKING Read the exam strategy. Then look at the photos and do the exam task. Use the adjectives in exercise 1 and the phrases in exercise 3 and the *Learn this!* box to help you.

You are planning a surprise birthday party for a friend who is coming from the USA. Which of these restaurants would you choose and why? Why wouldn't you choose the other places?

I can present arguments for and against an issue.

1 **SPEAKING** Work in pairs. Ask and answer this question.

If you could have fewer or more brothers and sisters, how many would you have? Why?

2 Read the exam strategy and the introduction to the essay. Which two of the techniques (a–c) does the writer use?

EXAM STRATEGY

In the introduction to the essay, you should show that you understand the title of the essay, and what the essay needs to cover. You can do one or more of these things:

a make one or two general statements which relate to the topic and / or give some background information.

b rephrase the statement to show that you understand the main issue.

c give a brief introduction to both sides of the argument.

3 Read the essay. Which paragraph puts forward arguments (a) for the statement in the title? (b) against the statement?

It's better to be an only child than to come from a large family. Discuss.

In the past it was common for married couples to have a lot of children. Nowadays, couples are increasingly choosing not to have children at all, or to have just one child. The question we need to answer is: is life better for children who grow up without brothers and sisters?

It is hard to deny that children with no brothers or sisters get more attention from their parents than children in large families. This can make them feel more confident and secure. It is also true that brothers and sisters in large families often argue a lot. They have to share possessions and living space, a bedroom for example, and this can lead to conflict. An only child does not face this problem.

On the other hand, children with no brothers or sisters may sometimes feel lonely, as they have no one at home to play with. They have to find friends to play with in their free time, and this may be difficult if they do not live in a large community. It can also be argued that they are often 'spoilt'. Their parents give them whatever they want, and so they don't learn to share or to co-operate with other people.

To sum up, there are clearly some advantages to being an only child, but also some disadvantages. It depends on personal experience and individual circumstances. In my view, it's better to have brothers and sisters, but I'm from a large family!

4 Read the *Learn this!* box. Find four of the phrases in paragraphs 2 and 3 of the essay.

Presenting an argument
It is true / clear that …   *It is hard to deny that …*
It can be argued that …   *Some people argue that …*
Presenting an opposing argument
On the other hand, …
However, some people argue that …
Other people take the opposite view and claim that …

5 Read the exam strategy. Identify an example or a supporting statement for each argument in the essay.

EXAM STRATEGY

Follow each argument in your essay with an example or a supporting statement.

1 Argument followed by example:
Only children get more privacy. For example, they don't have to share a bedroom.

2 Argument followed by supporting statement:
Children from large families are rarely lonely. There's always someone to talk to.

6 Read the *Learn this!* box and the conclusion of the essay. What is the writer's opinion? Do you agree with him / her? Why? / Why not?

For and against essay conclusion
1 You can begin the conclusion with:
To sum up / In summary, I would say that …
2 You should give your opinion. This could be a balanced view, or you may agree with the statement in the title, or you may disagree with it.

7 You are going to write an essay entitled *Friends have more influence than family on teenagers*.

1 Plan the second and third paragraphs. Think of two arguments for the statement and two against.

2 Think of an example or a supporting statement for each of the arguments.

3 Read the exam strategy in exercise 2 and plan the introduction.

4 Read the second *Learn this!* box again. Decide what *your* opinion is and plan the conclusion.

8 Write the essay (200–250 words).

CHECK YOUR WORK

Have you:
- [ ] followed all the instructions in exercise 7?
- [ ] checked your spelling and grammar?

Reading

1 [Get ready to READ] Work in pairs. Make a list of the advantages and disadvantages of living in the city and living in the country. Then compare your answers with your partner.

2 Do the exam task.

READING exam task

Read the text and choose the correct answers: A, B, C or D.

A few years ago I moved with my family from the city to the country, and we now live in an old farmhouse on the edge of a village. The house itself was built in the 1800s and looks like something out of a novel. It's an old stone house with very thick walls. These walls make the house slow to heat up in the winter, so we always have a fire in the living room fireplace in the winter months. And it is always cool inside in the summer – too cool, actually, as the English summers never get that warm!

For an old house, the ceilings are quite high, but they are also very thin. They are just the wooden floors of the upstairs rooms. When the lights are on in the kitchen, they shine through the floorboards into the bedroom above! And when you walk around upstairs, you can hear every step downstairs. Downstairs, the floors are made of black stone and are old and uneven. In fact, the whole house isn't straight. If you put a ball in the middle of the dining room, it rolls immediately into the far right-hand corner.

The best thing about the house is the living room. It is a lovely, light room and I can spend hours looking out of the window. The view is made even more interesting because the window has the original glass in it, and each small pane of glass is different and alters the view outside. From the sofa you can look straight out into the garden, and to the fields beyond. The scene is always changing and there is always something to see, including lots of different wildlife.

It has taken me a while to appreciate this view, though. For a long time I missed the noise and the bustle of city life. I preferred to see people, shops and buses on my way to school, not fields and trees. And it took me a long while to be able to sleep well at night – it was too quiet! Now I've got used to country life. I cycle everywhere and I like the space and freedom. But I never wait too long before going back and visiting my old friends in the city!

1 The old farmhouse
- **A** was built by the narrator's family.
- **B** was described in a book a long time ago.
- **C** takes a very long time to get warm.
- **D** is better for the summer than for the winter.

2 Inside the farmhouse
- **A** there's enough room to play ball games.
- **B** the stairs make a lot of noise.
- **C** there are very interesting lights.
- **D** the floors upstairs aren't very thick.

3 Which is true about the living room?
- **A** It's a bit dark as the windows are very small.
- **B** Each window looks out onto different scenery.
- **C** The window had to be changed recently.
- **D** The window is good for observing animals.

4 The narrator
- **A** can't wait to move back to the city.
- **B** used to like the city sights and sounds.
- **C** sleeps only a few hours a day.
- **D** wanted to move here for the views.

5 According to the text, the narrator
- **A** still prefers the city.
- **B** has got used to living in the country but doesn't feel happy.
- **C** is happy living in the farmhouse in the country.
- **D** is planning to move back to the city.

Speaking

3 Do the exam task.

SPEAKING exam task

Compare and contrast the two photos. Answer the questions.

1 What are the main differences between the two places to live: a flat in the city and a house in the country?

2 What could be good or bad about living in the city or the countryside?

3 Is it better to rent a place or save up and buy your own?

4 Which place would you prefer to live in? Why?

Use of English

4   Do the exam task.

USE OF ENGLISH exam task

Complete the text with an appropriate word in each gap.

Birth order theory

In 1908, Alfred Adler, a contemporary ¹_____ Freud and Jung, first put forward the idea that a child's personality is deeply affected by *when* it is born in relation to its siblings. He suggested that eldest children are socially dominant, highly intellectual, and extremely conscientious. Unfortunately, they're also less open ²_____ new ideas, and prone to perfectionism and people-pleasing – the result ³_____ losing both parents' undivided attention ⁴_____ an early age, and working throughout their lives ⁵_____ get it back.

Middle children, sandwiched ⁶_____ older and younger siblings, often develop a competitive nature – making them natural entrepreneurs later in life. They tend to be the ⁷_____ diplomatic and flexible members of the family and, eager for parental praise, often develop musical or academic skills.

Youngest children, according ⁸_____ Adler's theory, tend to be dependent and selfish – as they're used to others providing for them. ⁹_____ , despite the negatives, they're also quite often fun, confident, and good ¹⁰_____ entertaining others.

Listening

5   **Get ready to LISTEN**   Work in pairs. Ask and answer the questions.

1   Are your parents very strict?
2   Should parents give their children everything they want? Why / Why not?
3   How can parents help their children to be successful?

6   Complete the phrases (1–6) using the prepositions below.

about   for   for   in   of   on

1   to live in the USA _____ some of the time
2   to know something _____ advance
3   to have a huge influence _____ someone
4   to be obsessive _____ something
5   to win an Oscar _____ a screenplay
6   to be proud _____ your children

7   🎧 2.31   Do the exam task.

LISTENING exam task

Listen and decide if the sentences are true or false.

		T	F
1	When his father left, Matt lived with five other members of his family.		
2	Matt's mother encouraged her sons to be creative.		
3	As a child, Matt loved to pretend he was someone else.		
4	His first success came when he met Ben Affleck.		
5	*Good Will Hunting* was successful thanks to Matt's fame.		
6	Matt doesn't devote all his time and energy to acting.		

Speaking

8   **Get ready to SPEAK**   Work in pairs. Read the situations (1–4) and discuss what you think might have just happened.

1   Children are laughing.
2   A businessman is running and looking at his watch.
3   A girl is holding her head.
4   A man is standing next to a car in the middle of the road.

9   Do the exam task.

SPEAKING exam task

Describe the picture. Then answer the questions.

1   What do you think has happened to the child?
2   Would you like to look after very young children? Why? / Why not?
3   Describe a situation when you comforted someone who was really sad.

THIS UNIT INCLUDES
Vocabulary ▪ travel-related compound nouns ▪ travel and transport adjectives
▪ phrasal verbs ▪ acronyms ▪ accommodation problems ▪ tourist attractions
Grammar ▪ the passive ▪ indefinite pronouns: *some-*, *any-*, *no-* ▪ introductory *it*
Speaking ▪ discussing different modes of travel ▪ planning an ideal holiday
▪ complaining and dealing with complaints
Writing ▪ a description of a place

8A   VOCABULARY AND LISTENING   Getting from A to B
I can talk about travel.

1 SPEAKING Work in pairs. What are some of the advantages
and disadvantages of travelling by bike, car, train, bus,
plane and ship? Use the adjectives below to help you.

<u>Useful adjectives</u>   cheap / expensive
comfortable / uncomfortable   fast / slow
dangerous / safe   reliable / unreliable
relaxing / stressful   convenient / inconvenient

> Travelling by bus is slower
> than travelling by train.

> That's true, but travelling
> by bus is cheaper.

> When you travel by train, you
> can see more on the journey.

2 VOCABULARY Make compound nouns by matching words in
column 1 with words in column 2.

arrivals hall

1		2	
~~arrivals~~	baggage	reclaim	desk
buffet	check-in	~~hall~~	car
departure	duty-free	control	shoulder
hard	passport	gate	shop
petrol	taxi	office	station
ticket	waiting	room	rank

3 🎧 3.02 PRONUNCIATION Listen and check your answers to
exercise 2, then repeat. Underline the word that is stressed
in each compound noun. Is it usually the first or the second
word?

4 Put the compound nouns from exercise 2 into the correct
group (A, B or C).

A air travel	B road travel	C rail travel
arrivals hall		

5 Work in pairs. How many other words (nouns or verbs) can
you add to each group from exercise 4?

A a plane, to fly, …

6 🎧 3.03 Listen to eight dialogues and match them to eight
of the locations from exercise 2.

1 a waiting room

7 🎧 3.03 Listen again. Complete these sentences with the
words below. Which sentences include compound nouns?
What are they?

belt   boarding   carriage   economy   flight   luggage
platform   unleaded

1 It left from the other _____ .
2 I'll have to go back to my _____ .
3 Did you have a good _____ ?
4 Can I see your _____ pass?
5 Don't forget your seat _____ .
6 Can I take it as hand _____ ?
7 You're in _____ class.
8 How much is the _____ ?

8 Work in pairs. Choose one of the twelve locations from
exercise 2. Write a short dialogue for that location.
You could be:

• meeting somebody
• buying something (tickets, food, gifts, petrol, etc)
• waiting to travel
• dealing with a problem or delay
• talking to an official
• talking to another traveller.

9 SPEAKING Act out your dialogue to the class. Can they
identify the location?

⟫⟫⟫ **VOCABULARY BUILDER 8.1: PAGE 134** ⟪⟪⟪

GRAMMAR The passive

I can identify and use different forms of the passive.

1 Read the text. Are these sentences true or false?

1 The Velocipede was the first bicycle ever built.
2 Bicycles with backrests are slower, but more comfortable.
3 China manufactures about 80 million bicycles a year.

In the 1860s, a two-wheeled bicycle with pedals was built by a Frenchman called Ernest Michaux. Other kinds of bicycle had been invented earlier in the century, but Ernest Michaux's invention, the Velocipede, was easier to ride and thousands were sold throughout Europe from 1869. Over the next few decades, several improvements were made: tyres were fitted to the wheels and later, a chain was added to the pedals.

More recently, bicycles have been invented with pedals at the front and a seat with a backrest. They're comfortable to ride, and they're fast too.

Bicycles are more popular today than ever before. About 80 million new bicycles are manufactured every year in China alone! In cities around the world, cycle lanes are being built and cycling is being encouraged by governments. It's possible that in ten or twenty years' time, cars will be banned from city centres and only cyclists and pedestrians will be allowed.

2 Complete the table with the examples of the passive in red in the text.

The passive	
present simple	
present continuous	
past simple	
present perfect	
past perfect	
future with *will*	

3 Read the *Learn this!* box. Match the examples of the passive in exercise 1 with a and b below.

We use the passive when:
a we don't know who or what performed the action.
b we want to focus mainly on the action itself.
We may know who performed it, in which case we can add *by …* to say who or what the agent is.

4 Make these sentences passive. If appropriate, write who or what performed the action.

1 Kirkpatrick MacMillan built the first bicycle in 1839.
  The first bicycle was built by Kirkpatrick MacMillan in 1839.
2 People ride bicycles all the time in Oxford.
3 Do they hold the Tour de France every year?
4 They've banned cars from the centre of Rome.
5 Sam Wittingham set the world record for the fastest speed on a bicycle.
6 People are designing faster bikes all the time.
7 They won't allow electric bikes to compete in races.

>>> GRAMMAR BUILDER 8.1: PAGE 122 <<<

5 Complete the text using the active or passive form of the verbs in brackets.

The Tour de France [1]_____ (hold) almost every year in France since 1903. About twenty teams of cyclists [2]_____ (take part) with nine riders in each team. The race lasts for 21 days and in that time, about 3,200 kilometres [3]_____ (cover). A few changes [4]_____ (make) to the route every year, but the race always [5]_____ (end) on the Champs-Élysées in Paris. The first Tour de France [6]_____ (win) by Maurice Garin. The following year, Garin [7]_____ (disqualify) because he [8]_____ (travel) part of the distance by train. In fact, in the early days, competitors often [9]_____ (cheat) and some competitors [10]_____ (attack) by fans of their rivals! Advertising [11]_____ (allow) since 1930, when organisers [12]_____ (agree) to allow lorries to follow the cyclists for the first time. Today, about 11 million free items [13]_____ (give) to spectators each year during the race.

6 **SPEAKING** In pairs, complete the sentences with a passive form of the verb in brackets. Then choose the correct information.

1 The world's first plane _____ (fly) by the Wright brothers in **1803 / 1903 / 1953**.
2 In 2000, the Channel Tunnel _____ (open) between England and **France / Ireland / Wales**.
3 Tickets for spaceflights _____ (sell) today by Virgin Galactic for **$2,000 / $20,000 / $200,000** each.
4 The construction of *Sagrada Familia* in **Barcelona / Paris / Milan** _____ (not finish) until 2026.
5 Skoda cars _____ (manufacture) in **Hungary / the Czech Republic / Romania**.
6 According to US plans, a manned spacecraft _____ (send) to **Saturn / Mars / Jupiter** in around 2030.

I can talk about explorers.

1 SPEAKING Describe the photo. Where do you think this man is? Why is he there?

A BRITISH TRADITION

The British tradition of explorers dates back centuries, when intrepid men set off across the ocean to discover new lands. The public have always looked up to these explorers as heroes, even if they were unsuccessful. These days, most
5 places in the world have already been discovered, but there are still plenty of remote regions where it's challenging – and at times dangerous – to get about. Ed Stafford, a former British Army captain, has continued the British tradition of exploration. In 2010, he completed a record-breaking journey
10 when he became the first person to trek the entire length of the Amazon River. He started at the source of the river, which is in the mountains of Peru, and finished 859 days and about 7,000 km later on the Atlantic coast of Brazil.

One of the biggest challenges was dealing with wildlife.
15 Stafford and his partner came across electric eels, lethal vipers and giant anacondas. As if that wasn't enough, Stafford suffered an estimated 50,000 mosquito bites and a tropical fly laid its eggs in the skin of Stafford's head. Three months into their gruelling journey, Stafford's partner gave up
20 and went home.

But some of the humans he encountered were even more threatening than the wildlife. Stafford had been warned to stay away from certain notorious villages, but on one occasion he was chased by five or six boats full of angry
25 locals. They were armed with guns and bows and arrows. Stafford thought they were going to kill him. But, in fact, the village chief accompanied Stafford for 47 days of the walk and they ended up becoming good friends.

2 🎧 3.04 Read the text and find the answers to the questions in exercise 1.

3 Are these sentences true or false?

1 British explorers only become national heroes if they are very successful.
2 Ed Stafford's expedition lasted more than two years.
3 His route crossed international borders.
4 Stafford walked on his own for part of the journey.
5 The biggest danger he faced was the wildlife.
6 Stafford was injured by some of the locals.

4 VOCABULARY Match the adjectives in red in the text with the definitions (1–8).

1 not having success
2 causing death
3 brave
4 well-known, for bad reasons
5 appearing dangerous
6 difficult
7 very tiring
8 a long way from other places

5 🎧 3.05 Listen to the account of Captain Scott's last expedition. Did Scott die on the way to the South Pole, at the South Pole or on the way back?

6 🎧 3.05 Listen again. Choose the correct answers.

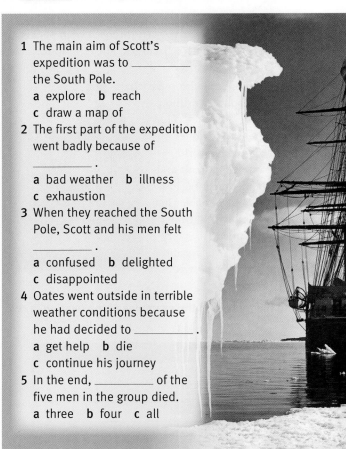

1 The main aim of Scott's expedition was to _____ the South Pole.
  a explore   b reach
  c draw a map of
2 The first part of the expedition went badly because of
  _____ .
  a bad weather   b illness
  c exhaustion
3 When they reached the South Pole, Scott and his men felt
  _____ .
  a confused   b delighted
  c disappointed
4 Oates went outside in terrible weather conditions because he had decided to _____ .
  a get help   b die
  c continue his journey
5 In the end, _____ of the five men in the group died.
  a three   b four   c all

7 SPEAKING Work in pairs. Discuss these questions.

1 What personal qualities are important for an explorer? Do you have those qualities?
2 Do you know any other famous explorers? What places did they explore and / or discover?
3 If you had to go on an expedition to explore a remote part of the world, where would you go? Do you think you would enjoy it or hate it? Give reasons.

⏵⏵⏵ **VOCABULARY BUILDER 8.2: PAGE 134** ⏴⏴⏴

8D GRAMMAR Indefinite pronouns: *some-, any-, no-, every-*

I can use indefinite pronouns.

1 Read the text. What is strange about the photo on Sarah's camera? Who might have taken it?

It was October, and three friends were on a walking holiday in the Lake District. It was seven o'clock in the evening and starting to get dark. They needed somewhere to spend the night. Jim looked at the map. 'There's nowhere within two hours' walk of here,' he said.
'Let's camp in this field then,' suggested Sarah.
'Good idea,' agreed Chris, sitting down on the grass. 'I'm exhausted. Can I have something to eat?'
'What do you want?' Sarah asked.
'I don't mind. Anything!' replied Chris. 'I've had nothing since breakfast.' Then he turned round. 'That's strange. I thought I heard somebody.'
'No, there's no one around here,' said Sarah. 'Just us. Maybe you heard a rabbit.' An hour later, everybody was fast asleep inside the tent.
The next morning, as Chris was making tea, Sarah came out of the tent looking confused. 'Did anyone touch my camera last night?' she asked.
Jim and Chris shook their heads. 'Is anything wrong?' asked Jim.
Sarah didn't say anything – she just held out the camera so everyone could see the picture. It showed all three friends fast asleep in their sleeping bags.
Nobody said anything for a few moments. Then Sarah started packing her bag. 'It's time to go,' she said.
'Where?' asked Jim.
'Anywhere,' replied Sarah. 'Let's just grab everything and go!'

2 Look at the examples of indefinite pronouns in red in the text. Complete the table.

Indefinite pronouns			
no one	1_____	2_____	everyone
3_____	anybody	somebody	everybody
nowhere	anywhere	4_____	5_____
6_____	7_____	something	everything

3 Study the examples of indefinite pronouns in red in the text. Then complete the rules with *affirmative*, *negative* and *interrogative* in the *Learn this!* box.

1 We use pronouns with *some-* in _____ sentences and in offers and requests.
2 We use pronouns with *any-* in _____ and _____ sentences.
3 We can also use pronouns with *any-* in affirmative sentences when we mean it doesn't matter *who / what / where*.
4 When we use pronouns with *no-*, we use _____ verbs, as the meaning is already negative.
5 When we use pronouns with *every-*, we use a singular verb, even when the meaning is plural.

>>> **GRAMMAR BUILDER 8.2: PAGE 122** <<<

4 Complete the dialogue with indefinite pronouns.

Sarah Look, 1_____ must have taken that photo. I mean, 2_____ has a logical explanation.
Chris Perhaps 3_____ went wrong with the camera.
Sarah It was in my bag when we went to bed!
Jim Maybe 4_____ came into the tent during the night and took the photo.
Chris Was 5_____ missing from your bag? Money?
Sarah No, 6_____ . 7_____ is still here.
Chris I knew 8_____ strange was going on. I'm sure I heard 9_____ walking around. Don't you remember, Sarah?
Sarah Yes, I do remember. But I couldn't see 10_____ in the field.
Chris But even if 11_____ was in the field, that doesn't really explain anything. How did they open the tent without waking us up?
Jim And how did they find the camera? Perhaps they were looking for 12_____ to steal.
Sarah But they didn't take 13_____ – and there was plenty of money in the bag. It's very odd! Are you sure it isn't one of your jokes, Chris? 14_____ knows you love tricking people.

5 Complete the questions with indefinite pronouns.
1 If you could visit _____ in the world, where would you go?
2 Do you think the world would be better or worse if _____ ever travelled by plane?
3 Would you prefer to live _____ very hot or very cold?
4 Do you think _____ will ever travel backwards in time?

6 SPEAKING In pairs, ask and answer the questions in exercise 5. Give reasons for your answers.

I can understand an article about gap years.

Travelling with friends

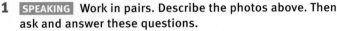

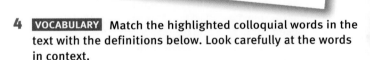

1 SPEAKING Work in pairs. Describe the photos above. Then ask and answer these questions.

1 What kind of holiday do you think these young people are having?
2 Do you prefer going away with friends or with your family? Give reasons.
3 Describe a holiday, trip or visit you went on recently (with or without your family).

> **READING STRATEGY**
>
> When you are reading a text and you need to establish the author's intention, it is a good idea to read the first and the last lines carefully. The author's intention is often described there.

2 Read quickly through the article. What is the author's main intention? Choose a, b or c.

a To narrate an experience of a trip abroad with friends.
b To give young people advice about travelling without their parents.
c To warn teenagers about the dangers of travelling alone.

3 🎧 3.06 Read the article again. Match the summary sentences (1–7) with paragraphs A–E. There are two extra sentences that you do not need.

1 You should think about your health.
2 You should contact home if you feel worried.
3 You should learn some useful phrases.
4 You should all agree on the type of holiday you want.
5 You should take care of each other while you're away.
6 You should be careful with your money.
7 You should take basic medical supplies with you.

4 VOCABULARY Match the highlighted colloquial words in the text with the definitions below. Look carefully at the words in context.

1 relaxing
2 friend
3 keep somebody safe, take care of somebody
4 parents
5 not sure, worried
6 cause problems or worries
7 aware of, thinking about

5 VOCABULARY Find these acronyms in the text. Do you know what they stand for? Try to fill in the missing words.

DIY: Do it _____
BBC: _____ Broadcasting Corporation
ASAP: As soon as _____
SMS: Short _____ service

🎧 3.07 **PRONUNCIATION** ≫ VOCABULARY BUILDER 8.3: PAGE 134 ≪

6 Work in pairs. Plan your ideal holiday with friends. Make notes about:

• the people you want to travel with
• the places you want to visit and why
• your accommodation and methods of transport
• the activities you plan to do.

7 SPEAKING Present your ideas to the class.

Going on holiday without your folks for the first time can be a great experience. Just be aware that they won't be at your side if it all goes wrong. A first-time holiday can be an experience you'll remember for life. So make sure you think ahead, and it won't be one you remember for all the wrong reasons. Here's a DIY guide to planning a holiday with friends!

A

So, you're going away with friends, with nobody around to give you grief? That might be how it seems in theory. In reality, disagreements can often happen. Before you even leave home, be honest with each other about what you want from this holiday. Don't wait until you arrive to discover you're the only person who wants to spend lots of chilled nights in watching BBC World. Be honest about what you want before you leave and discuss any problems ASAP.

B

This might be the first time you've had lots of money to spend on yourself. But don't forget that this money is supposed to last your whole holiday. Spending it all before you get as far as the airport departure gate isn't a good idea. Be sensible: work out how much you're going to spend each day and stick to it.

C

It's worth staying switched on about your diet. You can certainly have a break from your everyday dishes, but just remember that your body needs vitamins and minerals, not just chips and burgers! It's natural to want to relax on holiday, especially when you're parent-free, but that doesn't mean you should live like a pig. Personal hygiene still matters – and if it doesn't matter to you, it will to your friends!

D

You're on holiday from the stresses of the everyday world, but you're also away from your home and family. So try to look out for each other. And don't be selfish. A mate who won't make the effort should be left at home. Don't be the one who lets everyone down. Respect people's space and their needs, likes and dislikes. If you're staying in a self-catering apartment, make sure you all take turns to do the cooking and washing-up. With a little care and attention, you'll all get along just fine.

E

Right now, you might not think you'll miss home. But you may feel differently when you're hundreds of miles away, so be sure to keep in touch by phone, SMS or email. If possible, arrange for your family to call or text you at an agreed time, to keep your costs down. But don't be afraid to pick up the phone or send a message home at any time if you're feeling wobbly.

1 SPEAKING Work in pairs. Look at the titles of some hotel reviews on a travel website. How serious are the complaints, in your opinion? Put them in order from 1 (most serious) to 6 (least serious).

The rudest staff ever! ⊙○○○	Disco kept me awake all night ⊙⊙○○
Freezing cold swimming pool ⊙⊙○○	Tiny bathroom, no shower ⊙○○○
5-star hotel? No way! Only 3-star ⊙○○○	Warning: hidden extras add 50% to bill! ⊙○○○

2 In pairs, think of three more possible problems with hotels. Write titles following the style in exercise 1.

3 🎧 3.08 Listen to five dialogues. Match the problems (a–g) with the dialogues (1–5). There are two problems that you do not need.

a Some of the facilities they were expecting are not there.
b The passenger is going to have problems completing his journey.
c They have to pay extra for some of the facilities.
d The view is disappointing.
e The passenger is physically uncomfortable.
f The accommodation gets very cold when the weather is bad.
g Some of the facilities are very dirty.

SPEAKING STRATEGY

When we make a complaint, we often speak more slowly and emphatically than usual in order to make our point more strongly.

4 🎧 3.09 PRONUNCIATION Read the speaking strategy. Then listen and repeat these phrases from the dialogues, copying the intonation. Tick the ones which are slow and emphatic.

1 I'd like to make a complaint. ☐
2 That's just not acceptable. ☐
3 There's really nothing I can do about it. ☐
4 I'm very sorry to hear that. ☐
5 It's a disgrace. ☐
6 I'm running out of patience. ☐
7 I'm sorry to hear there's a problem. ☐
8 I'm really not happy about this. ☐
9 I'll sort it out immediately. ☐
10 I must apologise. ☐

5 Read the phrases in exercise 4 again. Who said them, the person making the complaint or the person dealing with it?

6 Add the phrases from exercise 4 to the chart below.

A Starting a complaint
I want to complain about …
1 _____

B Sympathising with a complaint
I do understand why you're unhappy about this.
2 _____ 3 _____ 4 _____

C Emphasising your discontent
Something needs to be done about this.
I'm sorry, it's just not good enough.
5 _____ 6 _____ 7 _____ 8 _____

D Agreeing to act
I'll see what I can do.
I'll do everything I can to sort this out.
9 _____

E Declining to act
That's really beyond our control, I'm afraid.
10 _____

7 SPEAKING In pairs, practise making and dealing with complaints. Use phrases from exercise 6. Choose a problem and prepare a dialogue following the guide below. Then swap roles.

<u>Accommodation problems</u> dirty room mosquitoes no clean towels no hot water noise room too hot / cold room too small TV / telephone / Wi-Fi not working uncomfortable bed unhelpful staff

Student A: Start a complaint. Say what it is.
Student B: Sympathise with the complaint.
Student A: Emphasise your discontent.
Student B: Agree or decline to act.

8 SPEAKING Do the speaking task below in pairs, taking turns to be A and B. Use phrases from exercise 6 and your own ideas.

Student A: You are a tourist. While staying at a hotel, you have to complain about the accommodation. Include these issues:
• There are too many noisy children.
• The restaurant closes early and the entertainment is terrible.
• Explain how the problems are affecting your stay.

Student B: You are the hotel receptionist.
It is very late at night. Deal with the tourist's complaints politely. Apologise and / or suggest solutions.

Description of a place

I can write a description of a place.

1 Look at the photo and read the description. What kind of text is it? Choose a, b, c or d.

a a newspaper report
b part of a geography textbook
c part of a tourism leaflet
d part of a biography

1 North Devon is the perfect setting for a holiday in the UK. It is situated in the south-west of England, and it takes only three hours to get there from London by train or car. But it is hard to imagine a bigger contrast – or a better place to escape from the stresses of urban life.

2 The North Devon Coast is an Area of Outstanding Natural Beauty, and for many visitors, it is the wide variety of breathtaking scenery which makes the region so attractive. There are tall cliffs and rocky headlands. There are wide, sandy bays and small, quiet coves. There are smooth, gentle sand dunes and steep, wooded hills. Or go inland and you can enjoy the wide open spaces of the moors, with their wild scenery and isolated villages.

3 North Devon is famous for its beaches, but there are plenty of other attractions for holidaymakers. A great place for families to visit is Watermouth Castle. It's a theme park as well as a historic building.

4 This region offers day trips to suit every taste, but for nature-lovers, a visit to Lundy Island is a must. Although it's less than five kilometres long and one kilometre wide, the island is home to a wide range of fascinating wildlife. It's a short boat trip from the coast or, if you are feeling adventurous, a thrilling helicopter ride! The place is a must-see for visitors.

EXAM STRATEGY

When writing a description, organise your ideas into paragraphs with separate topics: geographical location, physical description and scenery, activities and attractions, etc.

2 Read the exam strategy. Then match paragraphs 1–4 of the description with four of the topics below.

excursions   getting about   landscape   location
things to see and do   where to stay

3 **VOCABULARY** Find these adjectives in the text. Match them to the definitions below.

breathtaking   fascinating   historic   isolated   wild
wooded

1 _____ : amazing; extremely beautiful
2 _____ : covered with trees
3 _____ : not neat or tidy
4 _____ : important and from the past
5 _____ : very interesting
6 _____ : not close together

4 Use the adjectives in exercise 3 to describe places in your own country or region.

There are lots of historic buildings in the centre of Poznan.

5 Read the *Learn this!* box. Then look at the words in red in the description of North Devon and say which three are examples of introductory *it*.

Introductory *it*
1 We often use *it* as the subject in sentences referring to time, weather, temperature and distance.
It's midnight. It's Sunday. It took ages to do this exercise. It's raining. It's 20 °C. It's 10 km to the nearest town.
2 We can use *it* when we want to avoid starting a sentence with an infinitive, *-ing* form or clause, which often sounds unnatural or very formal.
It was nice to meet you. (= Meeting you was nice.)
It's hard to explain. (= To explain is hard.)
It doesn't matter what you say. (= What you say doesn't matter.)

>>> GRAMMAR BUILDER 8.3: PAGE 123 <<<

6 Read the exam task. Make notes for each point in the task.

A travel magazine has asked you to write a description of a region of your own country. Write a description designed to attract tourists and include information about:
• what part of the country you are describing
• the landscape and scenery
• places to see and visit
• an interesting trip or excursion.

7 Do the exam task in exercise 6. Write 200–250 words.

CHECK YOUR WORK

Have you:
☐ organised your ideas into separate paragraphs?
☐ used adjectives to make the text more interesting?
☐ checked your spelling and grammar?

Unit 7

1 Complete the text with the words below.

asked   engaged   fell   made   split

Guess what happened at Simon's party! Sally really liked Luke's brother, so she [1]_____ him out and he said yes! Jill and Mike had a huge row, and then they [2]_____ up and Jill went home. Stella and Fred also [3]_____ out with each other, but I think they've [4]_____ up now. And what about Kirsty and Mark? They've got [5]_____ ! How romantic!

Mark: _____ /5

2 Match the sentence halves and write the comparative or superlative form of the adjectives in brackets.

1 That's the _____ (good) pizza   ____
2 The _____ (early) we arrive,   ____
3 This exercise is much _____ (difficult) ____
4 This school is getting _____ (big)   ____
5 This is the _____ (far)   ____

a than I expected.
b we've ever cycled.
c I've ever tasted.
d and _____ (big).
e the _____ (good).

Mark: _____ /5

3 Complete the sentences with the phrases below.

I'd buy it for you   If I could sing   If only you
I wish I   I'd rather

1 _____ , I'd join a band!
2 _____ would stop annoying me!
3 _____ had a million pounds!
4 _____ go to the beach than the café.
5 _____ if I had the money.

Mark: _____ /5

4 Choose the correct adjectives.

1 It's a very **lively / quiet** café. They have music and dancing every evening.
2 This disco is too **bright / dark**. You can't see the person you're talking to!
3 It's a very **traditional / trendy** shop. Everything they sell is the latest fashion.
4 It's a **crowded / romantic** restaurant with candles on the tables and soft music.
5 It's quite a **friendly / formal** restaurant. The waiters all wear suits and call you 'sir' or 'madam'.

Mark: _____ /5

Total: _____ /20

Unit 8

5 Match words 1–5 with a–e to make compound nouns.

1 passport   a rank
2 hard   b gate
3 taxi   c control
4 departure   d shoulder
5 petrol   e station

Mark: _____ /5

6 Rewrite the sentences in the passive.

1 People are buying more electric cars now.
_____
2 They built a bridge over the river last year.
_____
3 The police have caught the criminals.
_____
4 The teachers had already written the new exams.
_____
5 They will award prizes later.
_____

Mark: _____ /5

7 Complete the sentences with some-, any-, every- or no-.

1 Have you seen my bag? I can't find it _____ where.
2 Shall I buy him _____ thing for his birthday?
3 'Who's at the door?' '_____ one. You're imagining things.'
4 Keep looking for Sara. Has _____ one seen her?
5 Where have you been? I've looked _____ where!

Mark: _____ /5

8 Complete the dialogue with the phrases below.

But that just isn't good enough
I'd like to make a complaint   I'll see what I can do
I'm running out of patience   I'm sorry to hear

Employee Can I help you?
Guest   Yes. [1]_____ .
Employee Oh. What's the problem?
Guest   The shower still doesn't work in my room. That's three days now. [2]_____ !
Employee [3]_____ that. I'll send someone to look at it immediately.
Guest   [4]_____ . I'd like to be moved to another room.
Employee Certainly, sir. [5]_____ .

Mark: _____ /5

Total: _____ /20

Lead-in

1 Work in pairs. What do you know about the history of your town? Did it use to be
- **a** bigger or smaller? **b** more or less important?

Listening

2 🎧 3.10 Listen to five short scenes. Are any of the characters in all five scenes? If yes, who?

3 🎧 3.10 Read the summary sentences a–g. Then listen again and match one sentence with each scene. There are two extra sentences that you do not need.
- **a** Anna and her friend make preparations for the evening.
- **b** Zara speculates about other people's feelings.
- **c** Libby tells Anna to make an arrangement with Mike.
- **d** Anna invites her flatmate to join them for dinner.
- **e** Mike tells Libby about his argument with Anna.
- **f** Mike recommends places to visit in Liverpool.
- **g** Libby and Mike make an arrangement to see each other.

Speaking

4 Imagine you and a friend want to go for a coffee and a chat. Look at the photos of two possible venues. Which place would you choose and why?

Writing

5 Imagine you are Libby. Write a postcard from Liverpool to a friend back home. Include this information:
- why you are there and where you are staying
- your first impressions of the city
- what you've done and what you're planning to do
- when you're coming home.

Reading

6 Read the text below, ignoring the missing sentences. Choose the best title: a, b or c. Explain your answer.
- **a** Famous Liverpudlians past and present.
- **b** A turning point in the history of Liverpool.
- **c** Liverpool through the centuries.

Liverpool attracts many thousands of tourists every year, and the city certainly has a lot to offer. It's a great place for culture-lovers. 1☐ And of course, football has always played an important part in the life of the city: Wayne Rooney and Steven Gerard are both famous Liverpudlians. Visit the old port where these days you can enjoy the modern, fashionable shops and restaurants. But if you stop to look at the old buildings, you may realise that this part of the city has a rich and interesting history.

During the 18th century, Liverpool's port was part of an important trade route. 2☐ This trade made the city rich and successful – but there is a dark side to its success. The same ships also took slaves from Africa to the West Indies, where they worked on the sugar plantations. About 10 million slaves were taken from their homes, until the slave trade became illegal in 1809.

The end of the slave trade did not mean the end of Liverpool's importance as a port. At that time, Britain had colonies all over the world. 3☐ The population of Liverpool grew; by 1880, it had reached 600,000. 4☐ But in fact, they found an overcrowded city with thousands of homeless children on the streets and frequent outbreaks of disease.

By the 20th century, Liverpool's port was becoming less important. 5☐ But the city now had a life of its own and soon became famous for other things, especially football, fashion and music. The most famous pop group ever, The Beatles, were from Liverpool. And now, at the start of the 21st century, the city still takes pride in all of its achievements, making Liverpool one of the most exciting places to visit in the UK.

7 Match the gaps (1–5) with the sentences (A–G). There are two sentences you do not need.
- **A** When ships brought sugar to England from the West Indies, they arrived at Liverpool.
- **B** Britain had lost most of its colonies and trade was declining.
- **C** And there's a second team in the football Premier League: Everton.
- **D** However, more and more people fought to put a stop to the slave trade.
- **E** Ships from Liverpool took steel, coal and other goods to these colonies.
- **F** There are more art galleries and museums in Liverpool than in any other UK city except London.
- **G** Some of these were immigrants from Ireland who came in search of a better life.

Money, money, money!

THIS UNIT INCLUDES

Vocabulary ▪ money and payment ▪ banking ▪ advertising ▪ prepositions and noun phrases ▪ linking words
Grammar ▪ *have something done* ▪ reflexive pronouns ▪ third conditional
Speaking ▪ advertising on TV ▪ photo description
Writing ▪ an opinion essay

9A VOCABULARY AND LISTENING Money and payment

I can talk about money and payment.

1 Look at the photo. What is happening? Have you ever bought anything in a sale?

2 🎧 3.11 **VOCABULARY** Listen and complete the signs with the nouns below.

Money and payment bargains cash change cheques credit cards offer price receipt reductions refunds sale stock till

1 Summer ¹_____ !
   50% off everything.
   ² _____ galore!

2 We accept all major ³ _____ .

3 Huge stock clearance!
   Massive ⁴ _____ !

4 *Please check your*
   ⁵ _____ .
   Mistakes cannot
   be rectified later.

5 This item is currently out of ⁶ _____ .

6 ⁷ _____ only at this ⁸ _____ .
   No ⁹ _____ or credit cards.

7 Special ¹⁰ _____ !
   Three for the ¹¹ _____ of two!

8 *Please retain your ¹² _____*
   as proof of purchase.

9 No ¹³ _____ or exchanges.

3 What is the purpose of the signs? Identify (a) three that are advertising things, (b) two that are requests to customers, and (c) four that are giving general information.

4 🎧 3.12 Listen to the conversation. Are the sentences true or false?

1 Bella's mum doesn't think that Bella spends her money wisely.
2 Alice thinks it's a good time to go shopping because there are lots of reductions.
3 Bella doesn't think the blue dress is a bargain.
4 Bella's aunt sent her a cheque for her birthday.
5 Bella pays in cash.
6 The assistant says Bella can return the dress if she keeps the receipt.

5 🎧 3.12 **VOCABULARY** Complete the sentences with the correct prepositions. Then listen again and check.

around   back   back   by   for   in   in   on   on   out   up

1 I've spent too much money _____ music and clothes lately.
2 She thinks I waste my pocket money _____ things I don't really need.
3 We can shop _____ for fantastic bargains.
4 I've been saving _____ for some boots.
5 I don't like being _____ debt.
6 I don't know when I can pay you _____ , though.
7 She could pay _____ the dress.
8 I can always take it _____ and get a refund.
9 Are you paying _____ cash or _____ credit card?
10 We've nearly sold _____ of that dress.

6 **SPEAKING** Work in pairs. Ask and answer these questions.

1 Have you ever bought something that was a waste of money? What?
2 Have you ever asked for a refund or an exchange? Why? What happened?
3 Do you always pay for things in cash? Why? / Why not?
4 Is there something that you'd like to buy, but can't afford? What?
5 Have you ever saved up to buy something? What?
6 Have you ever lent somebody some money? How much?
7 Have you ever borrowed some money from somebody? How much? What for?

⟫⟫ **VOCABULARY BUILDER 9.1: PAGE 135** ⟪⟪

1 Compare the two photos of Heidi Montag below. What has changed about her appearance?

2 Read the text. Why do you think Heidi Montag changed her appearance?

Botox Beauty

Heidi Montag is probably more famous for the plastic surgery that she has had carried out than for her TV career. Before she was 21, she had her nose altered, her lips made fatter and her breasts enlarged. And now the 23-year-old star of *The Hills* has admitted to having ten plastic surgery procedures in one day! She had work done on almost every part of her body. Heidi says she feels better and more confident. But many people think it is sad that she wanted to change her appearance at all.

3 Read the *Learn this!* box. Underline examples of the structure *have something done* in the text.

> **LEARN THIS!**
>
> **have something done**
> 1 You can use the structure *have* + object + past participle to say that you arranged for somebody to do something for you. (You didn't do it yourself.)
> He **had** his hair **cut.**
> He **had** his new car **delivered** to his house.
> 2 You can also use the structure for unpleasant things that have happened to you.
> I **had** my bag **stolen** yesterday.

4 Where do you have these things done? Write sentences with the present simple form of *have* and the words below.

dentist's ~~garage~~ hairdresser's jeweller's opticians tailor's

1 your car / service
2 your hair / cut
3 your teeth / whiten
4 your eyes / test
5 a suit / make
6 your watch / repair

1 You have your car serviced at a garage.

>>> **GRAMMAR BUILDER 9.1: PAGE 123** <<<

5 🎧 3.13 Complete the dialogue using the correct form of *have something done* and the words in brackets. Then listen and check.

Jim	Hey, Mark. Nice car! Was it expensive?
Mark	No. But I had to ¹_____ (a lot of work / do) on it. I ²_____ (new wheels / fit). And I ³_____ (it / repaint). It used to be blue.
Jim	Nice sound system. ⁴_____ (you that / fit) too?
Mark	No, I did that myself.
Jim	Can we go for a drive?
Mark	Er, no. It's broken down at the moment. I've got to ⁵_____ (it / repair). But I can't afford to!

6 Read the *Learn this!* box. Find an example of a reflexive pronoun in exercise 5. Is it use 1 or use 2? What are the reflexive pronouns for *she*, *you*, *we* and *they*?

> **LEARN THIS!**
>
> **Reflexive pronouns**
> 1 We use a reflexive pronoun when the object of a verb is the same as the subject.
> *He burnt himself on the hot cooker.*
> 2 We can use a reflexive pronoun to add emphasis.
> *He did his homework himself, without any help.*

>>> **GRAMMAR BUILDER 9.2: PAGE 124** <<<

7 Rewrite the sentences using *have something done*. Write a negative sentence using a reflexive pronoun.

1 Somebody took her photograph.
She had her photograph taken. She didn't do it herself.
2 Somebody has dyed my hair.
3 Somebody is repairing his bicycle.
4 Somebody washed our windows.
5 Somebody is going to paint her nails.
6 Somebody cleans their house every Friday.

8 SPEAKING Work in pairs. Find out if these things have ever happened to your partner. Use *Have you ever had your …?*

1 eyes / test
2 hair / dye
3 luggage / search
4 photograph / take
5 passport / steal
6 palm / read

1 SPEAKING **Describe the photo. Do you think that adverts change (a) the behaviour of people in general? (b) your own behaviour? Why do you think this?**

2 **Can you think of any famous advertising slogans? What do they advertise?**

3 **Complete each gap in the text with an appropriate word.**

4 🎧 3.14 **Read the text and answer the questions.**
1 Why do people nowadays pay less attention to adverts?
2 How are American companies trying to deal with this problem?
3 What kind of products were advertised in *Lara Croft: Tomb Raider* and *I, Robot*?
4 How do some people avoid watching the adverts on TV?
5 Which product is advertised in *American Idol*?
6 How are advertisers now targeting children?

5 🎧 3.15 **Listen to three people talking about advertising. Match two of the opinions (a–g) with each speaker (1–3). There is one opinion that you do not need.**
a Adverts aimed at children should be banned.
b Companies don't tell the whole truth in their adverts.
c Adverts don't influence most people to spend money.
d Many adverts are clever and entertaining.
e Adverts encourage people to buy things that they don't need.
f All TV advertising should be banned.
g People can switch off the TV if they don't want to watch the adverts.

6 SPEAKING **Say whether you agree or disagree with the opinions in exercise 5. Give reasons.**

I agree / don't agree that … because …

It's fair / It isn't fair to say that … because …

I think / I don't think it's true to say that … because …

>>> **VOCABULARY BUILDER 9.2: PAGE 135** <<<

PRODUCT PLACEMENT

People are getting tired ¹_____ advertisements. There are adverts everywhere – from the magazine in your hand to buses in the street. We see ads all day, every day. So people stop paying attention.

Therefore, in the USA the latest approach ²_____ to make advertising less obvious. Companies try to place their products within a film. This started ³_____ the 1980s, but now it happens ⁴_____ the time. There are even agencies to help companies do this. The next time you watch a Hollywood film, look ⁵_____ products or brands that you recognise. Pay attention ⁶_____ drinks, as it is likely you'll see one of the major companies represented. Is it Coke or Pepsi, ⁷_____ example? Then see how many times that product appears.

Car manufacturers are going further with product placement. The Hollywood action film *Lara Croft: Tomb Raider* became an advert ⁸_____ the new Jeep Wrangler Rubicon. And in *I, Robot*, Audi designed a futuristic car especially for the film. It looked amazing, but it was definitely still an Audi.

Product placement is also starting to happen more ⁹_____ American television. With hard disk recorders, people can now fast forward through the advertising breaks. So companies are paying to have their products placed in the programmes. If you watch *American Idol*, you will see ¹⁰_____ judges sitting behind huge red Coca-Cola glasses.

You can now find product placement in books, music videos, computer games and ¹¹_____ the Internet. ¹²_____ fact, children's learning books are one of ¹³_____ biggest new areas. Read these titles: *The Hershey's Kisses Addition Book, The Cheerios Christmas Play Book, The Oreo Cookie Counting Book.* The last book has children counting those little chocolate biscuits ¹⁴_____ every page.

Product placement is the future of advertising. There's no escape.

I can talk about an imaginary event in the past and its consequences.

1 🎧 3.16 Listen and complete the dialogue.

Mum Where have you been, Joe? Do you know what time it is? It's 1.30 in the morning!

Joe Sorry, mum! If I'd known the time, I ¹_____ have come home earlier.

Mum Oh, yes? So, what's your excuse then?

Joe I had to walk home. I was at Dave's house and I missed the last bus. If I ²_____ missed it, I wouldn't have had to walk.

Mum Oh, really? Well, you could have phoned me. I was worried sick!

Joe Sorry, mum. I ³_____ have phoned you if I'd had my mobile with me. But I think I left it at Dave's.

2 Answer the questions about Joe.

1 Did Joe know what time it was?
2 Did Joe miss the last bus?
3 Did Joe have his mobile with him?

3 Study the *Learn this!* box and complete the rule with *past participle* and *past perfect*.

> **Third conditional**
> 1 We form the third conditional with *if* + ¹_____ , *would have* + ²_____ .
> 2 We use the third conditional to talk about the imaginary result of things that did not happen.
> *If I'd known you were coming, I'd have cooked some more food.*
> 3 We often use it to express criticism or regret.
> *I'm sorry. If you hadn't lied to me, I wouldn't have got angry!*
> 4 We can also put the *if* clause in the second part of the sentence.
> *Argentina would have won the match if Messi hadn't been sent off.*
> 5 We often use short forms in third conditional sentences. The short form of both *had* and *would* is *'d*.
> *If I'd had more time, I'd have done my homework.*

4 Complete the sentences with the third conditional form of the verbs in brackets.

1 If you _____ (set) the alarm clock, you _____ (not be) late for school!
2 If I _____ (know) it was her birthday today, I _____ (send) her a card.
3 If I _____ (hear) the phone ring, I _____ (answer) it.
4 If you _____ (not waste) all your pocket money, you _____ (not have to) borrow money from me!
5 This coat _____ (be) cheaper if I _____ (buy) it in the sale.
6 Sally _____ (not fail) her exams if she _____ (revise) properly for them.
7 We _____ (play) tennis if the grass _____ (not be) wet.
8 He _____ (not crash) his car if he _____ (not drive) so fast.

5 Which sentences in exercise 4 express regret? Which express criticism?

6 🎧 3.17 PRONUNCIATION Listen and repeat the first three sentences in exercise 4. How is the word *have* pronounced?

7 Rewrite the sentences as third conditional sentences.

1 I didn't pay by credit card because I forgot my wallet.
   I'd have paid by credit card if I hadn't forgotten my wallet.
2 They didn't give you a refund because you didn't keep your receipt.
3 I didn't lend you any money because I was broke.
4 I didn't notice the mistake because I didn't check my change.
5 I didn't buy the dress because it wasn't in the sale.
6 I got into debt because I lost my job.

>>> GRAMMAR BUILDER 9.3: PAGE 124 <<<

8 SPEAKING Work in pairs. Ask questions and find out what your partner would have done if:

1 he / she had found a wallet on the way to school this morning.
2 he / she had forgotten to do his / her homework.
3 he / she had overslept.
4 he / she had lost his / her mobile on the way to school.
5 he / she had felt ill this morning.
6 it had been Saturday yesterday.

> What would you have done if you'd found a wallet on the way to school this morning?

> I'd have taken it to the police station.

1 SPEAKING **Can you think of anyone who is really lucky? In what way are they lucky?**

2 🎧 3.18 **Read the text, ignoring the gaps. Why does Frano Selak think that he is the world's luckiest man? Choose the correct answer.**

a Because he is now very rich, having narrowly escaped death on a number of occasions.

b Because he has survived seven serious accidents and then won the lottery.

c Because he has finally found happiness with his fifth wife.

EXAM STRATEGY

When completing a gapped text, look for words in the missing sentences that link with words that come before and after each gap (e.g. nouns, verb tenses, pronouns, time expressions, etc.).

3 **Read the exam strategy. Then do the tasks below.**

1 Look at the sentence before gap 2 in the text. Then read sentences a–h below and find two sentences that have words which link with 'freezing river'. Underline the key words in each sentence.

2 Only one of the sentences fits the gap. Which one? How do you know?

a Four people drowned, but – again – Selak swam to safety.

b Nineteen people were killed, but Selak fell clear of the crash and landed in a haystack.

c He turned sharply to avoid a collision, and went straight off the road.

d He never travelled by public transport again.

e He celebrated by buying his very first lottery ticket – and he won the jackpot!

f He had his hip replaced in hospital.

g Seventeen people drowned in the icy waters, but Selak survived.

h He managed to escape from it just before it exploded.

4 **Match the sentences (a–h) in exercise 3 with the gaps (1–7) in the text. There is one sentence that you do not need.**

5 **Are the sentences true or false? Correct the false ones.**

1 Selak got married after winning the lottery.

2 The third accident happened when Selak was travelling by bus.

3 Two of the accidents happened in the 1960s.

4 Selak was badly injured in the bus accident.

5 At the time of all seven accidents, Selak was travelling in a vehicle.

6 On three occasions Selak escaped from a burning car.

7 Selak feels that before he met his wife he had more bad luck than good luck.

8 Selak believes that money doesn't make him happier.

The World's Luckiest Man

Eighty-one-year-old Frano Selak is **known as the world's luckiest man.** Throughout his long life, he has survived seven disasters, all of which could have killed him. Then, at the age of 76, he got married for the fifth time. 1☐

Selak was born in a small town in Croatia. He was involved in his first accident in 1962. He was travelling by train from Sarajevo to Dubrovnik, when the train jumped from the rails and fell into a freezing river. 2☐ He managed to get to the riverbank with a broken arm, suffering from hypothermia. The following year Selak took a flight for the first – and last – time. The door opened and the passengers were thrown out of the plane. 3☐ If that haystack hadn't been in the field, he would have died.

A few years later, he was travelling by bus this time, when – again – it fell into a river. 4☐ This time he only had cuts and bruises. He was getting used to it. His next accident happened in 1970, but with a different method of transport. He was driving along the motorway, when suddenly his car caught fire. 5☐ Three years later, his next car caught fire at a garage. The fire swept through the car. Again, he escaped from the vehicle, but he lost most of his hair.

6 VOCABULARY **Complete the preposition + noun phrases. They are all in the text.**

1 _____ the (first) time

2 travel _____ train

3 be _____ foot

4 _____ the first place

5 _____ the end

6 _____ fact

▶▶▶ **VOCABULARY BUILDER 9.3: PAGE 135** ◀◀◀

Accident number six was caused by transport again, but this time Selak was on foot. He was walking in Zagreb, when a bus hit him. Amazingly, he wasn't too badly hurt. Was there no safe way for him to travel? His seventh accident happened the following year. He was driving in the mountains. He came round a bend and saw a huge lorry coming towards him. 6☐ Miraculously, he managed to jump out of the car. He watched as car number three rolled down the mountain and exploded.

Selak said, 'I never thought I was lucky to survive all my disasters. I thought I was unlucky to be in them in the first place.' In the end, however, Selak did feel lucky – not when he won the lottery, but when he met his fifth wife, Katerina. In fact, he has sold his luxury home and given away most of his lottery money. He said, 'All I need at my age is my Katerina. Money wouldn't change anything.'

But there was one thing that he did spend some of his money on. 7☐ Now, even if he never travels by car, bus or plane again, he can still keep walking!

Doesn't mean anything

Used to dream of being a millionaire,
Without a care,
But if I'm seeing my dreams,
And you aren't there 'cause it's over,
That just won't be fair.
Darling, rather be a poor woman
Living on the street, no food to eat,
'Cause I don't want nobody if I have to cry.
'Cause it's over when you said goodbye.

Chorus
All at once, I had it all,
But it doesn't mean anything, now that you're gone.
From above, seems I had it all,
But it doesn't mean anything since you're gone.

Now I see myself through different eyes,
It's no surprise.
Being alone will make you realise
When it's over that all in love is fair.
I shoulda been there, I shoulda been there,
I shoulda, shoulda.

Chorus

I know I pushed you away.
What can I do that would save our love?
Take these material things –
They don't mean nothing.
It's you that I want.

Chorus

7 SPEAKING Imagine that you had €1 million and wanted to give it away. Who would you give it to and why?

8 🎧 3.19 Listen to the song and choose the best summary (1–4).

1 I used to have lots of money. I lost it all, but it doesn't matter, because I've got you.
2 I'd love to be rich, but it doesn't matter if I never am because I've got you.
3 I'm very rich, but money means nothing to me now because I've lost you.
4 Let's throw away all our money and possessions and just be together.

9 Find colloquial equivalents in the song for the following:

1 I used to
2 I'd rather
3 I don't want anybody
4 should have
5 they don't mean anything

1 SPEAKING Work in pairs. Describe the photo.

2 Work in pairs. Read the first question and brainstorm ideas. Make notes.

1 What do you think the phone conversation is about? Why?
2 Do you and your friends buy a lot of things online? Why? / Why not?
3 Tell me about the last time you used a computer.

3 🎧 3.20 Listen to a student answering the first question. Compare your ideas with hers.

4 🎧 3.20 VOCABULARY Complete the student's sentences with the words below. Then listen again and check.

could   difficult   guess   looks   possibility   pretty
something   sure

1 I can't be _____, but I _____ the girl is buying something.
2 It certainly _____ like a credit card.
3 I'm _____ certain that she's giving her credit card details to the sales assistant.
4 Another _____ is that she's phoning her bank.
5 It _____ be that she's phoning the bank to set up a direct debit or _____ like that.
6 It's _____ to say.

5 🎧 3.21 Read and translate the phrases in the *Learn this!* box. Then listen to the student answering the second question. Which of the phrases does she use?

> **LEARN THIS!**
>
> **Giving an opinion (1)**
> *I'd say that …   I wouldn't say that …   I doubt that …*
> **Emphasising a point or giving extra details**
> *In fact, …   Actually, …   I also think that …*
> *My friend Sam often buys DVDs online. In fact, he bought one last week.*
> **Giving examples**
> *For example, …   For instance, …   For one thing, …*
> *… say, …*

6 🎧 3.22 Tick the tenses that the candidate is likely to use when answering the third question. Then listen and check your ideas. Which tense did the candidate use most frequently?

1 present simple ☐   5 past continuous ☐
2 present continuous ☐   6 past perfect ☐
3 present perfect ☐   7 *used to* ☐
4 past simple ☐   8 future perfect ☐

7 SPEAKING Work in pairs. Take turns to answer questions 2 and 3 in exercise 2.

8 SPEAKING Work in pairs. Describe the photo.

> **EXAM STRATEGY**
>
> When answering the examiner's questions, you should not limit yourself to succinct, single-sentence answers. Make sure you give reasons and arguments for your responses, and think about using a variety of tenses.

9 SPEAKING Work in pairs. Read the exam strategy. Then ask and answer these questions. Try to use the phrases in exercises 4 and 5, and a variety of narrative tenses.

1 Do you think the people are enjoying themselves? Why? / Why not?
2 Do you and your friends spend a lot of money on clothes? Why? / Why not?
3 Tell me about the last time you went shopping.

WRITING Opinion essay

I can write an opinion essay.

1 **SPEAKING** Work in pairs. Say whether you agree or disagree with each of these statements. Give reasons.

1 Worries about money are a cause of unhappiness.
2 Rich people are not always happy.
3 Love and friendship bring more happiness than money.

2 Read the opinion essay. What is the writer's opinion on the topic?

Do you agree that money can buy happiness?

In most parts of the developed world, people are richer today than they were fifty years ago. But has money made them happier? This is the question we need to answer.

I firmly believe that money is not the most important thing in most people's lives. They regard friends and family as more important. For example, if you are feeling miserable about a friendship that has ended, money cannot help you.

What is more, it seems to me that rich people are often the unhappiest. If money really could buy happiness, the rich would be the happiest people in the world. Judging by the stories about them in magazines and on TV, they clearly are not.

On the other hand, money is obviously necessary in today's world. It is very difficult to be happy if you do not have enough money for things like holidays. However, to my mind it is still possible to be happy and relatively poor, as long as you have enough to buy food and clothing.

In summary, I would say that money can improve the lives of people who do not have enough to live comfortably. However, money alone is not enough to bring happiness; love and friendship are far more important.

3 Read the exam strategy. In which paragraph is the opposing view and the counter-argument?

EXAM STRATEGY

In an essay which requires you to present your opinion, first write what your opinion is and then justify it. Then present the opposing view and explain why you disagree.

4 Add the highlighted expressions in the essay to the *Learn this!* box.

LEARN THIS!

Giving an opinion (2)
In my opinion, … 1_____
I think that … 2_____
As I see it, …
Introducing an additional point
Furthermore, … Moreover, …
Not only that, but … 3_____

5 Read the conclusion of the essay. What does the writer do?

1 Rephrases the question in the title, and restates his / her own opinion.
2 Summarises all of his / her opinions.
3 Mentions the opposing view, and restates his / her own opinion.

6 You are going to write an essay answering this question: *Do you agree that the best things in life are free?* Decide if you agree or disagree, then think of two or three arguments in support of your opinions, and one argument against. Think of supporting statements and / or examples for each.

7 Write the essay (200–250 words) following this plan. Use the phrases in exercise 4 and in exercise 4 on page 71 to help you.

- **Introduction** Introduce the topic. Show that you understand the title of the essay, and what the essay needs to cover.
- **Middle paragraphs** Give your own opinions, with supporting statements and / or examples.
- **Penultimate paragraph** Give an opposing view, with a supporting statement and / or example, followed by a counter-argument.
- **Final paragraph** Conclusion. Mention the opposing view, and restate your own opinion.

CHECK YOUR WORK

Have you:

☐ given your opinions, with supporting statements or examples?
☐ included an opposing view with a counter-argument?
☐ followed the advice for writing a conclusion?

Listening

1 Get ready to LISTEN Look at the picture. Where do you think these two men are going and why?

2 🎧 3.23 Do the exam task.

LISTENING exam task

Listen and write short answers to these questions.

1 How did Jason travel across the Atlantic Ocean?
  In a _____ .
2 How long was the race?
  It was _____ miles.
3 After finding a boat, what did Jason and Phil do first?
  They _____ .
4 How much food did they take?
  Enough to last _____ .
5 What happened on the third day?
  There was a _____ .
6 What could the shark have done if it had wanted to?
  It could have _____ .
7 Why did Jason have to go into the water?
  To _____ .
8 How many days did it take to travel across the ocean?
  It took _____ days.

Use of English

3 Do the exam task.

USE OF ENGLISH exam task

Choose the best word(s) (A–C) to complete each gap.

A 72-year-old man has [1]_____ a world record for the over-70 age group in the British 24-hour Cycle Championships. Arthur Puckrin [2]_____ a distance of 565 kilometres around the course at Chester in the north-west of England. The event started at 1 p.m. in the afternoon and finished at the same time [3]_____ day. 'I managed [4]_____ any punctures', said Arthur, 'though I had spare wheels with me just [5]_____ case. The only problem I had came at around 1 a.m. when I was feeling sleepy and thought I might fall [6]_____ the bike. I sorted that out with a coffee which kept me [7]_____ .'
[8]_____ his success in the race, it was a mere training run for Arthur, who has a much bigger target on the horizon. He [9]_____ a place in a triathlon in Mexico. It's a 38 km swim, a 1,800 km bike ride and a 422 km run over ten days. 'I'm looking forward [10]_____ it already!' says Arthur.

1 **A** put	**B** set	**C** done
2 **A** cycled	**B** had cycled	**C** was cycled
3 **A** next	**B** following	**C** the following
4 **A** avoiding	**B** avoid	**C** to avoid
5 **A** on	**B** in	**C** of
6 **A** over	**B** off	**C** down
7 **A** going	**B** go	**C** to go
8 **A** Although	**B** Despite	**C** However
9 **A** is offered	**B** offered	**C** has been offered
10 **A** over	**B** at	**C** to

Speaking

4 Get ready to SPEAK Work in pairs. Make a list of problems that can occur when you stay in a hotel, and possible ways to avoid them or solve them.

5 Do the exam task.

SPEAKING exam task

You are in a hotel where there are things you do not like. Complain to the manager about:

- The quality of the food in the hotel restaurant
- Noise from the bar at night
- Taps in the bath that do not work very well
- The possibility of swapping the room.

Reading

6 Get ready to READ Work in pairs. Ask and answer the questions.

1 Do you like watching reality TV shows and talent shows? Why? / Why not?
2 Would you like to take part in one? Why? / Why not?

7 Do the exam task.

READING exam task

Read the texts. Match the texts (A–E) to the statements (1–6). There is one statement that you do not need.

A

IS YOUR HOUSE UNTIDY?
HAVE YOU GOT ROOMS FULL OF JUNK?
ARE YOU BAD AT THROWING THINGS AWAY?

Then apply to appear on **Tidy Rooms**, the new reality TV show! We will tidy your house and sell your unwanted possessions on eBay. See how much profit you can make! Single people or married couples with no pets only. Sorry, no apartments.

B

We are looking for men and women of all ages who have extraordinary collections. It could be stamps, Star Wars models, shoes – it doesn't matter, as long you've got a lot of them! We'll film you telling us about your collection. We also need to speak to your spouse or partner about how your hobby affects your life together.

C

Can you sing? Have you dreamed of performing live on TV in front of millions of people?
Would you like to win a $1 million recording contract?

We are looking for just six talented but undiscovered singers. Auditions will be held in London from 21–24 July. The lucky six will appear on the live shows in the autumn.

D

ARE YOU SCARED OF GHOSTS?
Would you like to spend a week in a haunted house?

We are looking for volunteers to live alone for a week in a haunted house, and film their experiences. We will provide you with a camcorder. The only rule is: you aren't allowed to run away! Applicants must be fit, healthy and over 18.

E

The producers of '**HERE, BOY!**', a new talent show, are looking for audience members. The show is about trying to find Britain's most talented dog. Come and watch! The show will be filmed at Hazelwood studios in London. All applicants must be over 16 years of age. You will be required for approximately three hours. Tickets will be awarded on a first-come-first-served basis.

	Text
1 You can't apply if you have medical problems.	
2 You will make some money on the show.	
3 You have to bring your pet with you.	
4 The applicants have to compete to appear on the show.	
5 Only couples should apply.	
6 You won't star in the TV show.	

Writing

8 Get ready to WRITE Work in pairs. Think about the places you have stayed when you have gone on holiday. Have you ever been disappointed with your accommodation? What was wrong? Write a sentence explaining each complaint.

9 Do the exam task.

WRITING exam task

You have been on holiday to Los Angeles and during your stay you were very unhappy with your accommodation. You are writing a letter to complain to the manager of the hotel. In the letter:

• Complain about the quality of the food in the hotel restaurant
• Complain about the noise from the disco at night
• Explain that your room was not equipped as advertised in the holiday brochure
• Ask for compensation for your inconvenience.

THIS UNIT INCLUDES
Vocabulary ■ musical performers ■ artists and artistic activities ■ compound nou
■ word families: verbs and nouns ■ describing books
Grammar ■ participle clauses ■ determiners: *all, each, every, few, little*, etc. ■ *so a
such* ■ nominal subject clauses
Speaking ■ talking about the arts ■ describing a photo ■ discussion about music
festivals ■ stimulus discussion
Writing ■ a book review

10A   VOCABULARY AND LISTENING   Performers

I can talk about different types of music.

1 SPEAKING Look at the photos. What kind of music do you think these people are performing? Have you ever performed this kind of music?

2 🎧 3.24 Listen and number the musical performers in the order you hear them (1–10). Match five of them to the photos in exercise 1.

☐ a busker   ☐ a choir
☐ a DJ   ☐ a folk group
☐ a jazz band   ☐ an opera singer
☐ an orchestra   ☐ a rapper
☐ a rock band   ☐ a string quartet

3 🎧 3.24 VOCABULARY Check the meaning of the words and phrases below and complete the sentences. Then listen again and check.

Describing music aria beat chords chorus harmony
lyrics melody movement solo symphony

1 The opera singer began to sing an _____ .
2 The girl clapped at the end of the first _____ .
3 There were a hundred people in the choir, all singing in _____ .
4 Beethoven's Fifth _____ is a very famous piece of music.
5 The boy quite likes the clever _____ , but isn't keen on the music.
6 A drum _____ can go on for quite a long time, and can be a bit boring!
7 With modern jazz, there often isn't a strong _____ .
8 It's no good having a good voice if you play all the wrong _____ !
9 Dance music has a heavy _____ that makes people want to dance.
10 Live performers sometimes ask the the audience to join in with the _____ .

4 Which of the performers in exercise 2 are you likely to hear:

1 in a nightclub?   4 in a church or cathedral?
2 in an opera house?   5 in a concert hall?
3 in a stadium or a large   6 in a small music venue?
   arena?   7 outdoors?

5 SPEAKING Work in pairs. Do the speaking task below.

1 You want to take a British friend and his / her parents to a concert. Choose the concert in exercise 1 that is most appropriate and justify your choice.
2 Explain why you rejected the other choices.
3 Do you think it is better to hear live music or listen to a recording? Give reasons.
4 What qualities does a musician need in order to be a good performer? Give reasons.

⟫⟫ VOCABULARY BUILDER 10.1: PAGE 136 ⟪⟪

1 SPEAKING Look at the photograph. What does it show? How do you think it was taken?

2 Read the text. Check your ideas for exercise 1.

This picture, called *Boxing*, shows two men fighting on a skyscraper. The men, dressed in matching shorts and T-shirts, are very near the edge of the building.
The man wearing blue boxing gloves is hitting the other man, who is about to fall. This large picture, measuring 176 x 366cm, is one of a collection of photos currently exhibited by photographer Li Wei in Hong Kong. Li Wei, born in China in 1970, is well known for his unusual and gravity-defying photographs, produced without the use of computer software.

3 Read the *Learn this!* box. In which examples does the participle clause replace a non-defining relative clause? (For defining and non-defining relative clauses, see pages 25 and 27.)

LEARN THIS!

Participle clauses

1 We can use participle clauses to give more information about a noun. They can be described as shortened relative clauses (defining or non-defining).
*There's a man **making a call**. (= who is making a call)*
2 They contain either a present participle (*-ing* form) or past participle (*-ed*).
3 Clauses with a present participle replace an active verb. The verb they replace can be in any tense.
*She's wearing a necklace **belonging to her aunt**. (= which belonged to)*
4 Clauses with a past participle replace a passive verb in any tense.
*The match, **shown on TV this evening**, will be watched by millions. (= which will be shown on TV this evening)*

4 Underline all the participle clauses in the text in exercise 2. Answer these questions for each clause.

1 Does it replace a defining or non-defining relative clause?
2 Does it begin and end with a comma?

5 Rewrite the participle clauses in the text as relative clauses.

This picture, which is called 'Boxing' ...

>>> **GRAMMAR BUILDER 10.1: PAGE 125** <<<

6 Rewrite these sentences about *Boxing* using participle clauses to replace the underlined words.

1 The man <u>who is falling</u> from the building is the photographer, Li Wei.
2 The city <u>which stretches</u> into the distance is Beijing.
3 The photograph, <u>which was taken</u> in 2009, is part of a collection <u>which is called</u> *Beyond Gravity*.
4 Li Wei, <u>who was born</u> in Hubei, now lives in Beijing.
5 In 2006, Li Wei received an award for creativity, <u>which was presented</u> by the Getty Museum.

7 Look at the photo called *Li Wei falls to the Earth* and complete the phrases using the present or past participle of the verbs below.

bury   carry   chat   line   sit   wear

1 a road _____ with trees
2 a man _____ a blue T-shirt
3 a boy _____ on a wall
4 a man _____ upside down in the road
5 two men _____ to each other
6 a man _____ boxes on the back of his bicycle

8 SPEAKING Work in pairs. Describe *Li Wei falls to the Earth* to your partner. Include participle clauses from exercise 7.

> A man wearing a blue T-shirt has stopped and turned around. He's looking at ...

Music festivals

I can discuss music festivals.

1 🎧 3.25 Read the text. How many different festivals does it mention in total? Which one sounds most appealing to you? Why?

2 Are these sentences true or false?

1 Many British music fans go to European music festivals because the weather is better.
2 Travelling from the UK to the Rock Werchter is not difficult.
3 The Rock Werchter festival takes place in Brussels.
4 The Garden Festival is much bigger than the T-Mobile INmusic Festival.
5 Both festivals in Croatia take place near water.
6 A lot of Brits travel to Fiberfib for a taste of Spanish culture.

3 Complete the compound nouns with the words below. Find them in the text to see if they are written with a hyphen, as one word or as two.

acts   buses   Europe   goers   lovers   music   site   up

1 headline _____   4 music _____   7 line _____
2 dance _____   5 camp _____   8 shuttle _____
3 festival _____   6 mainland _____

>>> VOCABULARY BUILDER 10.2: PAGE 136 <<<

4 🎧 3.26 Listen to five people talking about music festivals. Match the speakers (1–5) with the opinions (a–g). There are two extra opinions that you do not need.

a The British climate isn't really suitable for open-air music festivals.
b Music festivals are the only way you can see several world-famous acts in one weekend.
c You're so far from the stage that you can't see anything – watching it on TV is better.
d Festivals always have a great atmosphere because everyone has the same interests.
e The sound system is never very good and most bands can't perform well live.
f The best thing isn't the music; it's eating, drinking and being with friends.
g There are too many people; it would be a horrible experience for me.

5 SPEAKING Discuss these questions in pairs.

1 Are there any music festivals in your country? Have you ever been to one?
2 What are the best and worst things about music festivals, in your opinion?
3 Which acts would you most like to see performing live at a music festival? Why?
4 What other kinds of festival interest you?

MUSIC AROUND EUROPE

British summers are not always well-suited to standing a field with thousands of other festival-goers, as fans of the Glastonbury Festival in south-west England have ofte discovered. So these days, thousands of music-lovers hea for mainland Europe for sunnier festival experiences. Her are some of the most popular destinations.

BELGIUM

Rock Werchter started in 1975 and always attracts big headlir acts, like Kings of Leon and Coldplay. The location in the cent of Belgium isn't exactly exotic, but it's a short journey from London to Brussels by train, and then on to Leuven where shuttle buses will take you to the site. The festival takes place in early July and lasts for four days.

CROATIA

The T-Mobile INmusic Festival in late June is a 20,000-capacit event beside Lake Jarun in the centre of Zagreb. One of the many festivals in the Balkans, it always has a strong line-up, including acts like Jamiroquai and Arcade Fire. Elsewhere in Croatia, there's a dance music festival called The Garden Festival in Petrčane in July. The site is a beautiful location overlooking the Adriatic Sea. It's a small festival, catering for just 2,000 clubbers, but with over 80 top DJs playing over two weekends.

SPAIN

In mid-July, Fiberfib is basically a big party by the beach in Benicassim, near Valencia. The town is usually popular with Spanish tourists – but this is one of the most popular festivals with Brits, so don't expect too much local culture. There's always a huge line-up of top acts. And there are excellent beaches about twenty minutes' walk from the campsite. But be warned – it reaches up to 40°C in the day, so the music plays from 6 p.m. – 8 a.m. and there's little chance of sleep. Finally, Sonar is a festival that takes place in Barcelona at the end of June. It attracts all the best artists and DJs from the dance music and techno scenes.

1 Look at the book cover. Then read the text and find out what happened to the author after he had finished writing the books.

NATURAL BORN WRITER

Stieg Larsson was a Swedish journalist who spent much of his time campaigning against right-wing extremism. Many Swedes were familiar with Larsson's work as a political activist, but outside Sweden, few people knew his name. He was a busy man who had little time for hobbies, but he did spend some time doing creative writing. Most evenings, he would spend a few hours at his desk, just to relax. He didn't need much sleep – only three or four hours every night. When Larsson had completed three novels, he sent them to a publisher, but died suddenly before any of them were published. Since his death, each book in what is referred to as the Millennium Trilogy has sold millions of copies. Larsson had no idea his books were going to be so successful and sadly he died before he could enjoy any of the money or fame.

2 Look at the determiners in red in the text and complete the table with ticks (✓).

Determiner	+ singular countable noun	+ plural noun	+ uncountable noun
every			
each			
no		✓	✓
any	✓	✓	✓
some		✓	
all		✓	✓
most			✓
much			
many			
few			
a few			
little			
a little			✓

3 Read the *Learn this!* box. Find two examples of determiner + *of* in the text in exercise 1.

Determiner + *of*
The determiners in the table can be followed by *of* in phrases like: *a few of his friends* and *much of the time*. However, we can't use *every* or *no* in these phrases. Instead, we use *every one* or *none*.
~~*Every of the windows was broken.*~~ ✗ *Every one of …*
~~*No of my friends were there.*~~ ✗ *None of my …*

⟫⟫⟫ GRAMMAR BUILDER 10.2: PAGE 125 ⟪⟪⟪

4 Complete the sentences with the determiners below.

all any each much no some

1 There wasn't _____ music in the film, just sound effects.
2 I haven't got _____ money – just €1!
3 _____ of his plays are written in French, others in English.
4 Unfortunately there are _____ tickets left for that festival.
5 _____ correct answer is worth one point.
6 _____ champagne is made in France.

LOOK OUT!

We use *few* and *little* (rather than *a few* and *a little*) when we want to emphasise the smallness of the number or quantity. It usually has a negative meaning. Compare:
Luckily, I've made a few friends at my new school.
Sadly, I've made few friends at my new school.

5 Read the *Look out!* box. Complete the sentences with *few, a few, little* or *a little*.

1 I'll ask my dad if we can go to the festival, but there's _____ chance he'll say yes.
2 Can you give me _____ time to think about it?
3 The mathematical problem is so complex that _____ people can understand it.
4 He's a very private person, and _____ information is known about his personal life.
5 I decided to spend _____ days with my grandparents.
6 The festival isn't well known. _____ famous acts play there.

6 Complete the sentences about your classmates with the phrases below. Try to guess the truth.

a few all many most none some

1 _____ of them can play an instrument.
2 _____ of them enjoy dancing.
3 _____ of them like opera.
4 _____ of them have been to a music festival.
5 _____ of them have sung in a choir.
6 _____ of them have written a novel.

7 SPEAKING Read your sentences from exercise 6 to the class. Find out if they are correct.

1 SPEAKING Work in pairs. Look at picture 2 and describe what is happening. Include participle clauses in your description (see page 95).

2 🎧 3.27 Read the texts quickly. Answer these questions.

1 What medical condition do both artists have?
2 What amazing talent do they share?

Alonzo Clemons

Alonzo Clemons is from Boulder, Colorado. According to Alonzo's mother, Evelyn, he was always trying to sculpt things as a baby, but she did not realise what he was doing. And then, he got hold of some modelling clay and she soon realised that he had a special talent. Before he could even feed himself or get dressed, he could make models of animals that were correct in every detail.

As Alonzo grew, his ability to sculpt increased rapidly, but he did not develop the other skills which children normally learn. Some doctors call people like Alonzo 'savants'. They have a developmental disability like autism, a condition which makes it hard for them to communicate or perform everyday tasks. But at the same time, they have a skill which they can do incredibly well. In some cases, that skill involves maths or memory; in other cases, music or painting. With Alonzo, it's sculpture.

It takes only 45 minutes for Alonzo to complete a small work. Recently, however, he has begun to do more ambitious projects. His most impressive work is called *Three Frolicking Foals*. It took Alonzo just three weeks to complete this life-size sculpture of three young horses. Like all of his work, they are anatomically correct in every detail.

In 1986, Alonzo exhibited his work for the first time. It was very popular and today, his work is on constant display at a gallery in Colorado, USA. Alonzo's special ability has helped him deal with his autism. He is now able to communicate better and lead a more independent life. He has a job and his own apartment, and he enjoys doing weightlifting at the gym. But sculpture is still his main passion.

3 Read the text again. Choose the correct answers.

1 Alonzo Clemons
   a learned how to sculpt from his mother.
   b could make detailed models at a very early age.
   c had a talent which his mother immediately recognised.
   d was very slow to learn how to put on his clothes.

2 'Savants' like Alonzo
   a all have fantastic memories.
   b can communicate well.
   c perform everyday tasks very quickly.
   d have learning difficulties.

3 When Richard's parents found a school for him,
   a his teachers sent him home.
   b his talent wasn't recognised for a long time.
   c he communicated with his teachers through his drawings.
   d he became interested in magic.

4 American people
   a didn't realise he had learning difficulties.
   b considered him as just an artist.
   c didn't consider him to be a true artist.
   d described him as their favourite artist.

4 Decide if the sentences are true or false for each artist.

		Clemons	Wawro
1	He was born in Britain.		
2	His parents discovered his rare talent.		
3	He had an interest in art from an early age.		
4	He became popular as soon as his works were exhibited.		
5	He couldn't communicate with people very well.		

5 **VOCABULARY** Complete the chart. Check your answers in the texts.

Verb	Noun
sculpt	1 _____
2 _____	drawing
paint	3 _____
illustrate	4 _____
5 _____	sketch
6 _____	exhibition

6 **SPEAKING** Work in pairs. Do the speaking task below.

You have the opportunity to go to an exhibition of either Alonzo Clemons' or Richard Wawro's works. Look at the pictures and photos. Which exhibition would you choose and why? Why are you rejecting the other option?

7 **SPEAKING** Which of these special talents and abilities would you most like to have and why?

1 The ability to do extremely difficult mathematical calculations in your head.
2 The ability to remember and recall huge numbers of dates, facts, numbers, etc.
3 The ability to draw or paint beautifully.
4 The ability to play a musical instrument to a very high standard.
5 The ability to learn a foreign language extremely quickly.

3

Richard Wawro

Tadeusz Wawro was an officer in the Polish Army who decided to settle in Scotland after the Second World War. He married a Scottish primary school teacher called Olive and together they started a family. Their son, Richard, was clearly unlike other children from an early age. His behaviour was extremely repetitive: he would spend hours playing the same note on the piano. He used to spend hours staring at the illustrations in books. Schools refused to teach him because he was difficult. In those days, little was known about autism, so Richard was simply described as being mentally disabled.

Richard's parents found a school for him when he was six, and his teacher there discovered his talent for drawing. 'What I saw was magic,' she recalls. 'I couldn't believe my eyes.' Richard hardly spoke; his drawings were a form of communication. He sketched pictures of his everyday life: his school bus, his breakfast, characters from the television. He always drew from memory, and the details were always perfectly accurate. He drew so much that his parents had difficulty providing enough paper!

In 1970, when Richard was eighteen, his works were exhibited for the first time in an art gallery. The exhibition was reported on a BBC news programme, and his career as an artist suddenly took off. Margaret Thatcher, who later became the British Prime Minister, described him as her favourite artist, and before long, he was travelling around the world. His favourite country to visit was the USA, because there he was treated as an artist, not an artist with learning difficulties.

4

1 🎧 3.28 **Look at the posters. Listen to Ellie and Alex discussing which of the four shows to see. What do they decide?**

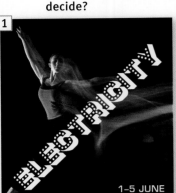

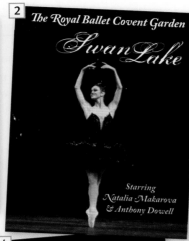

2 🎧 3.28 **Complete these sentences from the dialogue. Then listen again and check.**

1 It's not really _____ thing.
2 It just doesn't _____ to me.
3 I'm quite _____ it.
4 I think _____ be bored.
5 I wouldn't _____ I was a real fan.
6 That _____ more fun.
7 It should _____ really entertaining.

3 🎧 3.29 **PRONUNCIATION Add the sentences from exercise 2 to the lists below. Then listen, check and repeat, copying the intonation.**

Expressing enthusiasm
I'd really love to see it.
I love that kind of thing.

Expressing lack of enthusiasm
I'm not very keen on it.
I'm not particularly / really interested (in …).

4 SPEAKING **Work in pairs. Take turns to answer the speaking task below. Student A: Use posters 1 and 2 from exercise 1. Student B: Use posters 3 and 4. Try to include expressions from exercises 2 and 3.**

You are visiting your friend in the UK and she has offered to take you to a show. Which show would you choose and why? Why are you rejecting the other option?

EXAM STRATEGY

Remember to speak loudly and clearly. Try to maintain eye contact with the examiner.

5 **Work in pairs. Think about these questions and make notes of your ideas.**

1 What could be done to give more support to cultural activities like theatre, opera, ballet etc.?
2 How do cultural activities make a society better? Why do we need theatres, opera houses, concert halls, etc.?

6 🎧 3.30 **Listen to two students answering the questions in exercise 5. Which question is each speaker answering? Do they mention any of the ideas in your notes?**

LEARN THIS!

so* and *such
We can use *so* or *such* to emphasise an opinion:
1 *be + so + adjective:*
   It's so expensive!
2 *so + adverb:*
   They danced so brilliantly.
3 *such + adjective + plural noun / uncountable noun:*
   She's got such beautiful eyes / hair.
4 *such + a / an adjective + noun:*
   He's got such an amazing voice.

7 🎧 3.31 **Read the *Learn this!* box. Complete the sentences below with *so*, *such* or *such a(n)*. Listen and check.**

1 Opera houses can be _____ formal venues.
2 Opera-goers often look _____ posh!
3 It's _____ an expensive night out.
4 People work _____ hard these days.
5 Ballet is _____ old-fashioned.
6 Watching a play is _____ a different experience.
⟫⟫ GRAMMAR BUILDER 10.3: PAGE 126 ⟪⟪

8 SPEAKING **In pairs, ask and answer the questions in exercise 5, using your notes.**

I can write a review of a book.

1 Read the review. Are these sentences true or false?

1 The setting for the story is a beautiful lake.
2 Stanley shouldn't be in a detention centre.
3 The Warden has a secret reason for asking the boys to dig holes.

HOLES is a novel for teenagers. It was written by Louis Sachar and it was published in 1998. It's an adventure story about a group of boys at a detention centre in Texas. The detention centre is called Camp Green Lake and it's in the middle of a huge desert.

The main character is Stanley Yelnats, who has been sent to Camp Green Lake for a crime he didn't commit. Every day, the boys at the camp have to dig holes in the desert. They believe that the work is just punishment. What they don't realise is that the Warden at Camp Green Lake is secretly looking for treasure. One day, Stanley and his friend Zero run away. Everybody thinks they will die in the desert. I won't give the ending away! What I will say is that the book keeps your interest right to the final page.

I really enjoyed the book for a number of reasons. I identified with the character of Stanley, who always tries to help his friend. The setting is interesting and unusual. But what I liked most was the plot. It's a gripping story and you just can't put the book down. I would definitely recommend it.

2 How many phrases from the box can you find in the review?

Talking about stories
I identified with (*a character*)   It's the story of …
I liked the book because …   In the end, …
The main character is (*name*)   A film was made (*of the book*)
It was written by (*author*)   There's a twist at the end.
It's a (*type of story*)   I would definitely recommend it
It's set in (*place*)

3 Complete the text about *The Lord of the Rings*. Use the phrases from exercise 2.

The Lord of the Rings **is a fantasy story.** ¹_____
J. R. R. Tolkien. ²_____ an imaginary land called 'Middle Earth', and ³_____ a group of hobbits who have to destroy a magic ring. ⁴_____ called Frodo. ⁵_____ they succeed in destroying the ring. A few years ago ⁶_____ starring Orlando Bloom. It's a great book and ⁷_____!

Nominal subject clauses
We sometimes emphasise particular information in a sentence by putting it in a *What-* clause followed by *be*.
I really like adventure stories.
What I really like is *adventure stories.*
The ending made a big impression on me.
What made a big impression on me was *the ending.*

4 Read the *Learn this!* box. Find two sentences with nominal subject clauses in the review in exercise 1. Rewrite them as ordinary sentences.

5 Rewrite the sentences with nominal subject clauses starting with *What*.

1 All of the characters are looking for happiness.
2 The setting is really unusual.
3 I loved the twist at the end.
4 The main character really needs a holiday.
5 I really enjoy reading classic novels.
6 Stephen King is famous for writing thrillers.

>>> **GRAMMAR BUILDER 10.4: PAGE 126** <<<

6 Choose a book you know. Write notes under these headings. You can include any other important information.

General information	Story and characters
Title:	Where is it set?
Author:	Main characters:
Type of book:	What happens?
Your opinion	
Why did you like it? For example: It's funny / moving / exciting / gripping / interesting. It contains lots of interesting characters. I really wanted to know what was going to happen.	

>>> **VOCABULARY BUILDER 10.3: PAGE 136** <<<

7 Read the writing strategy below. Write a review of 200–250 words. Use your notes from exercise 6 and include phrases from exercise 2.

WRITING STRATEGY

Remember to use the present simple to summarise the plot of a story or film.

CHECK YOUR WORK

Have you:
- [ ] included the information in exercise 6?
- [ ] used phrases from exercise 2?
- [ ] checked your word count?

Unit 9

1 Complete each sentence with a noun and a preposition from the lists below.

nouns: bargain receipt sale stock till
prepositions: around back in off up

1 If you keep the _____, you can take those jeans _____ to the shop.
2 It took ages to save _____ for that jacket and now they're out of _____ !
3 There's £25 _____ this dress! It's an absolute _____ !
4 You can save a lot of money if you shop _____ and buy things in the _____ .
5 I wanted to pay _____ cash, but the shop assistant couldn't open the _____ !

Mark: _____ /5

2 Match the sentence halves and complete them with the correct verb.

1 She's going to the hairdresser's
2 He went to the garage
3 She's been to the optician's
4 They're at the photographer's
5 She went to the jeweller's

a to have his car _____ .
b to have her watch _____ .
c to have her hair _____ .
d to have her eyes _____ .
e to have their photo _____ .

Mark: _____ /5

3 Choose the correct tenses.

1 If you **have got** / **had got** up earlier this morning, you wouldn't have missed the bus.
2 We **wouldn't come** / **wouldn't have come** to the cinema if we'd known this film was on.
3 If I **would have** / **'d had** your phone number, I'd have called you.
4 They**'d have stayed** / **would stay** at the beach if it hadn't rained.
5 She wouldn't have got into trouble if she**'d have forgotten** / **hadn't forgotten** her homework.

Mark: _____ /5

4 Complete the dialogue with the words below.

can't be   could be   doubt   guess   looks

Debbie Look! What do you think that man is doing?
Jake   Well, I ¹_____ sure, but I ²_____ he's forgotten his house keys. I ³_____ that he's a burglar, Debbie!
Debbie Hmm. He certainly ⁴_____ like a burglar to me!
Jake   Or it ⁵_____ that he's checking the house for his neighbour.
Debbie I'm not so sure!

Mark: _____ /5

Total: _____ /20

Unit 10

5 Read the definitions and write the correct words.

1 Someone who plays music in the street. _____
2 Someone who plays music in a club for people to dance. _____
3 A large group of people who sing together. _____
4 Four people playing stringed instruments together. _____
5 A large group of musicians with a variety of instruments playing together. _____

Mark: _____ /5

6 Rewrite the sentences using participle clauses.

1 That's my neighbour **who is walking** his dog.
2 This watch, **which belonged** to my father, is worth a lot of money.
3 Listen to this song **which was written** by my teacher.
4 The bride, **who wore white**, walked down the aisle.
5 This is the DVD **which was given** to me for my birthday.

Mark: _____ /5

7 Correct the determiners in the sentences.

1 The film was terrible, so little people came to see it.
2 Hurry up! We've only got a few time left!
3 Most teenagers don't play many sport.
4 Don't ask me. I have any idea where he is.
5 No of the exam questions were easy.

Mark: _____ /5

8 Complete the dialogue with the phrases below.

doesn't appeal   kind of thing   particularly interested
really love   sounds

Boy   So, which acts do you want to see at the music festival? What about that new folk group? I love that ¹_____ .
Girl No, thanks. It just ²_____ to me. What about that jazz funk group? That ³_____ more fun.
Boy   I'm not ⁴_____ in that sort of thing. There must be something we both like!
Girl What about that singer-songwriter Bruno Mars? I'd ⁵_____ to see him.
Boy   OK. As long as you come to that rock group Sirius with me.

Mark: _____ /5

Total: _____ /20

Lead-in

1 Compare the photos. What kind of dance do you prefer watching? Are there any other kinds of dance that you enjoy doing or watching?

Listening

2 🎧 3.32 Listen to three short scenes. Explain in your own words why Anna is angry at the end of the third scene.

3 🎧 3.32 Listen again. Choose the correct answers.

1 The phone call between Zara and Libby ends at
   a three o'clock.
   b ten past three.
   c ten to three.
   d three minutes to ten.
2 How does Zara describe the relationship between Anna and Mike?
   a They don't see each other very often.
   b They're going out together.
   c They've split up.
   d They argue a lot, but they like each other.
3 Who is Zara expecting to receive a text message from after the rehearsal?
   a Libby.
   b Mike.
   c The director of the show.
   d Her dad.
4 What did Libby ask Mike when they spoke on the phone?
   a Whether he liked ballet.
   b Whether he wanted to meet up for a coffee.
   c Why he had phoned her.
   d Whether he had heard from Anna.

Speaking

4 Work in pairs. Why do you think Anna is angry? What do you think she should do? Compare your ideas with the class.

Reading

5 Read the emails. What was Libby's plan to help Anna and Mike get together? Did it work?

> ✉ **Inbox**
>
> Dear Libby
>
> It's a shame you couldn't make it to Liverpool for the weekend – especially as you'd got tickets for us to see *Romeo and Juliet*. It was so nice of you to surprise me. Did you have your car repaired? I hope it didn't cost too much.
>
> Anyway, I didn't waste your ticket – I invited Mike! We had a really great evening. He'd never been to a ballet before, but he enjoyed it, I think. The music is so romantic and the costumes were beautiful too (although I'm not sure Mike noticed those). We went for a drink after the show and to cut a long story short, he asked me out. He told me how much he liked me and that he wanted to see a lot more of me. I was quite surprised because I've never heard him talk about his feelings before. Maybe the romance of the music and the story had an effect on him. What do you think? Anyway, I said I needed time to think about it. Was that the wrong reply? I didn't want to seem too keen. Now I'm worried that I wasn't keen enough!
> love
> Anna

> ✉ **Inbox**
>
> Hi Anna
> Thanks for your email. I'm so pleased you enjoyed the ballet and went with Mike. And I'm sure the romance of *Romeo and Juliet* made a difference! In a way, it's lucky for you that my car broke down, isn't it? :-)
>
> By the way, you have to say YES! You're perfect for each other. That's my opinion anyway. Don't wait, phone him now.
> love
> Libby

6 Are these sentences true or false?

1 Anna gave Libby's ticket for *Romeo and Juliet* to Mike.
2 Mike told Anna that he liked the costumes.
3 Anna and Mike didn't go straight home after the show.
4 Anna knew that Mike was going to ask her out.
5 Anna said no when Mike asked her out.
6 Anna is not sure that she did the right thing.
7 Libby is sure Anna should say yes.

Writing

7 Imagine you are Mike. Write an email to a friend narrating the events of your night out with Anna. Include this information:

- which ballet you saw and your opinion of it
- what you did after the show
- your conversation with Anna and how she reacted
- how you felt.

Reading

1 `Get ready to READ` Work in pairs. Ask and answer the questions.

1 Do you often go to art galleries? Why? / Why not?
2 Do you like modern art? Why? / Why not?

2 Do the exam task.

READING exam task

Read the text. Five sentences have been removed from the text. Choose from sentences A–F the one that best fits each gap. There is one sentence that you do not need.

The huge gallery called the Turbine Hall at London's Tate Modern Art Museum is home to a new installation for the next few months. It looks as if the entire floor of the gallery has been covered with small grey pebbles, turning it into a vast beach. But they are not pebbles. **1 [ ]** And that is precisely what is there. A hundred million sunflower seeds have been spread out over the floor of this vast, industrial space. That in itself does not sound particularly artistic. **2 [ ]** Each seed was actually hand-made from porcelain by Chinese craftsmen and women. Sixteen hundred artisans, working every day for two and a half years, produced all these millions of tiny, unique works of art. Some of the artisans struggled to understand what they were making, but they were paid more than their usual daily wage and are now asking Ai Weiwei if they can be involved in his next project.

3 [ ] Not only are the seeds a common Chinese street snack, but they also represent the Chinese people. During the time of the Cultural Revolution, communist dictator Chairman Mao called his people 'sunflowers, always turning their faces to follow the sun'. The sun, of course, was the dictator Mao himself.

Unfortunately, a problem has arisen with this latest installation. **4 [ ]** However, it soon became apparent that this created a fine dust, which could be dangerous if people breathed in too much of it. **5 [ ]** Nonetheless, it is still impressive, and the gallery is expecting thousands of curious visitors.

A Initially, the public was allowed to walk over this sea of seeds and pick them up.
B The title of the installation by China's most famous living artist, Ai Weiwei, is *Sunflower Seeds*.
C According to the artist, the sunflowers mean more than one thing in Chinese culture.
D Now, visitors are only allowed to view the installation from the sides of the gallery.
E The exhibition has not been well received by the public.
F However, the amazing thing is that the seeds are not what they seem.

Speaking

3 `Get ready to SPEAK` Look at the photos. What kinds of art do they show? What adjectives would you use to describe them?

4 Do the exam task.

SPEAKING exam task

Look at the photos and talk about art, discussing the following questions.

1 How would you compare the four types of art shown in the pictures?
2 Who do various forms of art appeal to? What forms of art appeal to you? Give reasons.
3 Do you agree with the following statement? Give reasons.
   Art is less important in our lives than it used to be.

Listening

5 **Get ready to LISTEN** When you visit museums, do you ever go on guided tours or use an audio guide? Why? / Why not?

6 🎧 3.33 Do the exam task.

LISTENING exam task

Listen and mark the sentences true or false.

		T	F
1	The tour guide says Stonehenge is right next to them, on the left.		
2	The final structure was finished almost a thousand years ago.		
3	The group has already paid for the tickets.		
4	The car park and ticket office are across the road from the monument.		
5	Visitors are allowed to walk around as they wish.		

Use of English

7 Do the exam task.

USE OF ENGLISH exam task

Complete the text with the correct form of the words given.

Living in a foreign country can be an exciting and ¹_____ (reward) experience. It can also be a very challenging one. Many people are unprepared for the ²_____ (real) of living full-time in a different environment.

If you are planning to move to another country on a long-term basis, find out about the culture and religions and how much they play a part in everyday life. This type of research is particularly important in cultures where certain ³_____ (behave), habits or gestures have different meanings. For example, in many Eastern countries, you mustn't touch people's heads, not even patting the heads of small children. These are very ⁴_____ (offend) gestures, but easily done if you are not aware of this.

Culture shock has been officially ⁵_____ (identify) as a form of long-term psychological stress. ⁶_____ (typical), it can be split into a number of phases. The first is called the tourist or honeymoon stage, when the ⁷_____ (visit) is fascinated by their new home and it feels like a great adventure. The next stage is the ⁸_____ (reject) phase, when you feel homesick and can feel a sense of ⁹_____ (isolate). After that comes the conformist stage, when you accept the culture, and finally, there is the total assimilation stage. Now you can speak the language, have friends, and feel at home. Living in a foreign culture is a fascinating experience. Don't be afraid to try it. Just be ¹⁰_____ (prepare)!

Writing

8 **Get ready to WRITE** Put the expressions into the correct group.

although as because besides but for example
for instance furthermore however in conclusion
moreover on the one / other hand since so
to conclude to sum up what is more whereas

Contrasting	
Adding	
Giving an example	
Concluding	
Giving a reason	

9 Choose the correct words.

1 Travelling abroad is fun **however / although** it can be expensive.
2 If you live in a foreign country, it's sometimes difficult to make yourself understood. **Besides, / Whereas,** you have to spend time learning a new language.
3 You can sometimes earn more by moving abroad. **What is more, / On the other hand,** it can be difficult to find work.
4 You can make new friends if you live in another country. **Although / Moreover,** you can learn about a new culture.
5 You may be lonely at first, **for example / but** you'll soon make new friends.
6 You can't claim it's too expensive to travel **as / whereas** you can easily get a student travel card.
7 **On the other hand / To conclude,** I believe that spending time abroad is a good idea.

10 Do the exam task.

WRITING exam task

Write an essay (200–250 words) with the following title.

Do you agree that you learn more about a foreign country if you travel alone, rather than with other people?

Reading

1 **Get ready to READ** Work in pairs. Ask and answer the questions.

1 Have you ever been sailing?
2 Would you like to go on a sea voyage around the world? Why? / Why not?

2 Do the exam task.

READING exam task

Read the text. Choose the correct answers, A, B, C or D.

Naomi Power had just returned to New Zealand from a trip to Europe. During her time abroad, she'd had many interesting adventures, but had also met experienced racing sailor, Rob James. They had spent a lot of time together and developed a close bond. Rob had also invited Naomi on board his yacht and, as she'd never been on a yacht before, she happily accepted and Rob taught her to sail. It was the beginning of two special relationships – with Rob and with sailing.

Back in New Zealand, she was reading a magazine in her parents' living room, when she saw a headline: *French woman plans single-handed voyage around the world*. Naomi was immediately interested. She began to dream – what an adventure that would be!

Naomi started reading books such as Chay Blyth's *The Impossible Voyage* and became certain about two things: she wanted to spend the rest of her life with Rob, and she wanted to sail single-handed around the world.

Naomi flew back to England in March 1976, and she and Rob were married at the end of May. However, Naomi was a little worried about telling Rob that she wanted to sail around the world. To her surprise, Rob was very enthusiastic, though he tried to warn her about the dangers. They discussed the problems and risks, and thought of ways to prevent them. Then they began to think about where they could find a boat. They would also need a sponsor. 'You'll need at least £60,000 to buy and refit a boat,' Rob told her. 'Chay Blyth may help. He's got a lot of experience in finding sponsors.' But it was more difficult than they expected. Many people thought that Naomi was crazy to try to sail alone in the world's most difficult seas. However, Naomi did not lose hope. She knew that she had to be confident if she wanted other people to have confidence in her.

Then, one evening her luck changed. They were at Chay's house for dinner when one of the guests began to talk about sponsorship. He suggested it would be much easier to get a sponsor if Naomi took Chay's boat *Spirit of Cutty Sark*; she would only need about £10,000 to adapt the boat for single-handed sailing. Then a man named Quentin Wallop, who owned a yacht himself, agreed to sponsor her for £10,000 – and the challenge was on!

1 Naomi
  A sailed from France to New Zealand.
  B wanted her name to appear in magazines.
  C thought about travelling round the world when she met Rob.
  D had no sailing experience before her trip to Europe.
2 Before Naomi flew to England in 1976, she
  A made some decisions about her personal life.
  B thought her idea was completely unrealistic.
  C consulted Rob about all her plans.
  D contacted some famous sailors.
3 When Naomi told Rob about her plan, he was
  A amused.
  B irritated.
  C supportive.
  D frightened.
4 When planning the voyage, Naomi
  A didn't let any obstacles discourage her.
  B refused to listen to warnings about possible dangers.
  C got lots of encouragement from people.
  D had no trouble finding a sponsor.
5 Naomi received sponsorship
  A from the owner of *Spirit of Cutty Sark*.
  B to refit Chay's boat.
  C to cover all the travel expenses.
  D to buy a new boat.

Speaking

3 Do the exam task.

SPEAKING exam task

Compare and contrast the photos. Answer the questions.

1 What challenges are the people undertaking?
2 What physical and emotional qualities would you need to complete these types of challenges?
3 Why do you think people take on challenges like these?
4 Would you like to take on a challenge? Give reasons.

Listening

4 **Get ready to LISTEN** Complete the expressions connected with voting. Use a dictionary to look up the expressions you don't know.

candidate   counts   democracy   election   fed up   right
the Government   vote   worth

1 every vote _____
2 to be _____ with politicians
3 vote for a _____
4 _____ in an election
5 have the _____ to vote
6 to be _____ voting for
7 run in the _____
8 fight for _____
9 disagree with _____

5 Work in pairs. Take turns to describe the picture and answer the question. Use expressions from exercise 4.

Is it important to vote in elections? Why? / Why not?

6 🎧 3.34 Do the exam task.

LISTENING exam task

Listen and match the opinions (A–E) with the speakers (1–4). There is one opinion that you do not need.

Speaker 1	Speaker 2	Speaker 3	Speaker 4

A	You have the right to vote, so you should vote.
B	Every vote is equally important and can make a difference.
C	You should vote because people have suffered in the past to make it possible.
D	If you don't vote, you can't complain if you don't like things.
E	There is no point in voting until politicians improve.

Use of English

7 Do the exam task.

USE OF ENGLISH exam task

Complete the text with an appropriate word in each gap.

Oxfam

The name 'Oxfam' comes from the Oxford Committee for Famine Relief, which ¹_____ set up in Britain in 1942. It sent food to starving people in Europe during the Second World War. ²_____ the war, the group became known ³_____ 'Oxfam' and widened its objectives ⁴_____ include the relief of suffering due ⁵_____ wars or any other causes in ⁶_____ part of the world. In 1995 Oxfam joined up ⁷_____ independent non-government organisations in other countries to create Oxfam International. Their aim was to work together to ⁸_____ a greater impact in reducing global poverty and injustice. Oxfam International is now a world leader in the delivery ⁹_____ emergency relief. Furthermore, it organises long-term aid programmes in the poorest countries ¹⁰_____ the world.

Writing

8 **Get ready to WRITE** Complete the useful phrases with the words in the lists.

Giving an opinion

concerned   convinced   mind   see   seems

1 As I _____ it, ...
2 To my _____ , ...
3 I'm far from _____ that ...
4 As far as I'm _____ , ...
5 It _____ to me that ...

Presenting an argument

can   evident   hard   remember   worth

1 It's _____ to deny that ...
2 It _____ be argued that ...
3 It is _____ that ...
4 It is _____ bearing in mind that ...
5 We should _____ that ...

Presenting an opposing argument

argue   hand   said   say   spite

1 On the other _____ , ...
2 In _____ of this, ...
3 Having _____ that, ...
4 However, some people _____ that ...
5 That is not to _____ that ...

9 Do the exam task. Use some of the expressions in exercise 8.

WRITING exam task

The money that rich countries give to poorer countries does not really help them. Discuss.

Grammar Builder and Reference

1.1 Order of adjectives

The correct order of adjectives before a noun depends on their meaning.

	opinion	size	age	colour	origin	material / type / purpose	
a	lovely	big	old	blue	French	leather	bag
a	nice	tall	young		English		man

1 Put the words in the correct order to make sentences.

1 leather / at / miniskirt / Look / fabulous / that
   Look at that fabulous, leather miniskirt.
2 wearing / an / blouse / elegant / white / She's / lacy
3 shoes / high-heeled / wearing / ridiculous / She's
4 tight / socks / I hate / nylon
5 skirt / wearing / velvet / a / She's / spotty
6 stripy / green / like / your / tracksuit / I / baggy
7 a / That's / checked / Jacket / scruffy

1.2 Dynamic and state verbs

Dynamic verbs describe action. They can be used in simple and continuous forms.
I run ten kilometres every day.
I'm running in a race at the moment.

Verbs describing a state or situation are not usually used in continuous tenses.
I don't understand you. (state of mind)
(NOT – *I'm not understanding you.*)
This book belongs to me. (possession)
(NOT – *This book is belonging to me.*)
Common state verbs:

believe belong forget hate like love need prefer remember understand want

Be careful. Sometimes state verbs can be used with a 'dynamic' meaning and therefore we can use continuous tenses.
This cheese tastes nice. (feature describing the cheese)
I'm tasting cheese at the moment. (action)
There is a group of verbs that can be used as either state or dynamic verbs. These are some of them:

appear consider feel look think

When a verb describes an action we can use either the continuous or the simple form. However, when we are describing a state we must use the simple form.

	Dynamic verb	State verb
think	You think too much! What are you thinking about?	I think your skirt is too short.
feel	How do you feel? I'm feeling ill.	I feel that he should apologise.
look	If you look carefully you can just see the sea. What are you looking at?	That bed doesn't look very comfortable.
see	We see with our eyes. I'm seeing double!	I see what you mean.
smell	I often smell the flowers in the garden. The dog is smelling its food.	This cheese smells horrible!
taste	Taste the pasta and see if it needs more salt. He's tasting the wine, not drinking it.	The pizza tastes good.
appear	Harry always appears when food is ready. Jennifer Aniston is appearing in a play in London next week.	She appears to be in her mid-teens.

1 Choose the correct tense. Say whether the verb is dynamic or state.

1 **He thinks / He's thinking** it'll rain tomorrow.
2 **Mandy has / Mandy's having** breakfast.
3 **He appears / He's appearing** to be wearing a hat.
4 **I feel / I'm feeling** a bit silly in this suit.
5 **We consider / We're considering** moving abroad.
6 That burger **tastes / is tasting** disgusting!

2 Complete the sentences with the correct form of the dynamic and state verbs below.

belong know not like need not remember snow wait

1 'Why are you sitting there doing nothing?' 'I _____ for a film to start.'
2 _____ you _____ when Jason is arriving?
3 I enjoy listening to music, but I _____ dancing to it very much.
4 I _____ a new computer. The one I've got is really old and slow.
5 I've met her before, but I _____ her name.
6 It _____ and I haven't got a hat or gloves.
7 'Who _____ this DVD _____ to?' 'It's Margaret's.'

Grammar Builder and Reference

3 Complete the pairs of sentences with the present simple or present continuous form of the verbs.

1 *see*
  a I _____ George tonight. We're going to the cinema.
  b I _____ what you're trying to say, but I don't agree.

2 *taste*
  a This fish _____ really good. Is there any more?
  b 'What are you doing?' 'I _____ the sauce to check that it's got enough salt.'

3 *smell*
  a 'Put your shoes back on. Your feet _____ awful!'
  b 'The dog _____ my sock. It must smell good!'

4 *feel*
  a 'Your shirt _____ really smooth. Is it cotton?'
  b Mum _____ my brother's leg to make sure it isn't broken.

5 *look*
  a 'That hoody _____ cool. Where did you buy it?'
  b Liam is in the clothes shop over there. He _____ at the jackets.

1.3 Present tense contrast

We use the present simple to talk about:
- habits and routines.
  I usually get up at eight o'clock.
- a permanent situation or fact.
  Jack lives in London. It's his home town.
- timetables and schedules.
  The train leaves at 6.30 tomorrow morning.

Spelling: verb + third person singular
- We usually add –s to the verb:
  I start.   It starts.
- If the verb ends in –ch,–ss, –sh or –o, add –es to the verb:
  They teach.   She teaches.
  We don't teach.   He doesn't teach.
- If the verb ends in a consonant –y, we add –es and change –y to –i:
  They carry.   She carries.
  We don't carry.   He doesn't carry.

We use the present continuous to talk about:
- things that are happening now.
  We're watching a movie right now. Come over!
- annoying behaviour with *always*.
  He's always talking about himself.
- for arrangements in the near future.
  Sally and Tom are flying to Rome next Friday.

Spelling : verb + -ing form
- We add –ing form to most verbs:
  I wait.   She's waiting.

- If the verb ends in a consonant + –e we usually drop the –e and add –ing:
  They smile.   We're smiling.
- If the verb ends in a short, accented vowel and a consonant, we double the consonant:
  -m → -mming   -g → -gging   -p → -pping   -t → -tting
  You stop.   They're stopping.

1 Decide if the sentences are correct or not. Correct the sentences that are incorrect.

1 Is your dad usually wearing a suit to work?
2 I live with a family in Ireland for a month.
3 What are you reading at the moment?
4 The train is arriving this evening at six o'clock.
5 We don't go to the cinema this Friday night.
6 It's quite cold today. I take a coat.
7 She's a surgeon. She works in a hospital.
8 My brother is always borrowing my mobile! It's really irritating!

2 Complete the pairs of sentences with the present simple or present continuous form of the verbs in brackets.

1 **a** Matthew usually _____ jeans to school. (wear)
  b He _____ trousers today. (wear)
2 **a** I can't understand this film. What language _____ they _____ ? (speak)
  b I'm going to Italy on holiday, but I _____ Italian. (not speak)
3 **a** My sister _____ in London at the moment. (live)
  b My uncle _____ in Spain. He moved there 25 years ago. (live)
4 **a** I'm getting fed up with my little sister. She _____ ! (always interrupt)
  b He _____ when someone else is speaking. (never interrupt)
5 **a** What time _____ you _____ Kate this evening? (meet)
  b What time _____ the film _____ this evening? (start)
6 **a** My mum _____ to work. She usually goes by bus. (not walk)
  b Today the buses are on strike, so she _____ (walk) to work.

1.4 Verb patterns

Some verbs are followed by an infinitive.
John managed to finish his homework.

Other verbs are followed by the -ing form.
Sally fancied going away for the weekend.

Grammar Builder and Reference

verb + infinitive		verb + -ing form	
agree	mean	avoid	feel like
decide	pretend	can't face	imagine
expect	promise	can't help	insist on
fail	refuse	can't stand	keep
happen	seem	enjoy	spend (time)
hope	want	fancy	suggest
manage			

The negative in both cases is formed by adding *not* before the verb:
He decided not to go to the party.
Imagine not being able to see.

1 Complete the sentences with the correct form of the verbs in brackets.

1 Can you imagine _____ (not have) a fridge?
2 They agreed _____ (not stay) out late.
3 I feel like _____ (see) a film tonight.
4 Did you manage _____ (do) the shopping?
5 My parents refuse _____ (buy) me a laptop.
6 Harry can't face _____ (do) the washing today.
7 He suggested _____ (eat) at a new restaurant.
8 She pretended _____ (not see) him.
9 We avoid _____ (drive) to London in the rush hour.

1.5 Verbs that change their meaning

Some verbs can be followed by either the infinitive or the *-ing* form. In both cases the meaning of the verb is very similar.
I like to get up early. I like getting up early.
She continued to talk. She continued talking.

Some verbs change their meaning depending on whether they are followed by an infinitive or *-ing* form.
I remember living in Paris when I was young.
Meaning: this is a memory of something that happened in the past.

Did you remember to phone Jenny?
Meaning: this is an action that needs to be done – so you have to remember to do something.

I'll never forget swimming with all those sharks.
Meaning: this is a memory of an action.

Patrick forgot to go to football practice.
Meaning: this refers to an action that has not been done yet.

Please stop talking!
Meaning: end this action.

Karen stopped to ask for directions.
Meaning: stop in order to do something else.

We tried hitting it with a hammer, but we couldn't open it.
Meaning: attempt in order to solve a problem.

Sophie tried to save some money, but she spent it all.
Meaning: try hard to do something.

1 Complete the sentences with the infinitive or *-ing* form of the verbs in brackets.

1 Can you please stop _____ (whistle)? It's driving me mad!
2 On the way home we stopped _____ (buy) a paper.
3 'I can't reach the top shelf.' 'Why don't you try _____ (stand) on a chair?'
4 Please try not _____ (annoy) your brother.
5 Did you remember _____ (send) mum some flowers on Mothers' day?
6 I remember _____ (play) in that park when I was little.

2 Complete the sentences with the infinitive or *-ing* form of the verbs below. Which opinions do you agree with?

not be   lead   look   look   publish   understand

1 A lot of teenage girls enjoy _____ at pictures of models, and want _____ like them.
2 Most boys pretend _____ interested in fashion, but secretly they are.
3 I fail _____ why people are so interested in models.
4 I love reading about models. I often imagine _____ that kind of life.
5 Magazines should refuse _____ photographs of models who are too thin.

2.1 Past tense contrast

We use past tenses to talk about something which happened in the past.

- We use the past continuous to set the scene.
  The birds were singing in the trees that morning.
- We use the past simple to describe actions or events which happened immediately one after the other in the past.
  Joanna walked down the road, turned left, then saw the house for the first time.
- We use the past continuous to describe an action which was in progress when another action interrupted it. We use the past simple for the action that interrupted it.
  While we were staying at the campsite, somebody stole Fiona's camera.
- We use the past perfect to talk about an event which happened before another event in the past.
  I wasn't hungry because I had already eaten lunch.

Notice that with regular verbs the past simple and the past participle form of the past perfect is the same.
It crashed.   It had crashed.

However, with irregular verbs the past simple and the past participle form are often different.
I saw Peter.   He'd already seen me.

(There is a list of irregular *past simple* and *past participle* forms in the Workbook.)

Grammar Builder and Reference

1 Complete each sentence with the past simple and the past continuous form of the verbs in brackets.

1 James _____ (wait) for the bus when he _____ (see) his girlfriend with another boy.
2 Marcus _____ (break) his arm while he _____ (play) ice hockey.
3 We _____ (stop) playing tennis because it _____ (get) dark.
4 We _____ (have) dinner when my dad _____ (get) home.
5 The sun _____ (shine) so we _____ (decide) to go to the beach.
6 I _____ (listen) to my MP3 player, so I _____ (not hear) the doorbell.

2 Complete the sentences with the past simple and the past perfect form of the verbs in brackets.

1 I _couldn't_ (can) phone you because I _had left_ (leave) my phone at home.
2 Lucy _____ (run) all the way here, so she _____ (feel) exhausted.
3 My piano teacher _____ (get) angry because I _____ (not practise).
4 As soon as we _____ (finish) lunch, we _____ (go) into town.
5 By the time we _____ (arrive) at the cinema, the film _____ (start).
6 Mum _____ (shout) at me because I _____ (not tidy) the kitchen.
7 By midnight, Joanna still _____ (not phone), so I _____ (go) to bed.

3 Choose the best ending for each sentence: a or b.

1 I didn't have any money for the bus because I
  a spent it all.   b had spent it all.
2 It was a hot and sunny day, but a cool breeze
  a blew.   b was blowing.
3 When the phone rang, Lucy
  a answered it.   b was answering it.
4 I couldn't hear the film because the people in front of me
  a were making a lot of noise.
  b had made a lot of noise.
5 In the morning, we couldn't see our footprints in the snow because during the night it
  a was snowing again.   b had snowed again.
6 I had to use my brother's laptop because I
  a broke mine.   b had broken mine.

2.2 used to

We use *used to* + infinitive to describe past situations or habits that are different now.

I used to live abroad. (I lived there for a long time in the past, but I don't live there anymore.)
I used to work in a newspaper shop at weekends. (I worked regularly in the past, but I don't now.)

Affirmative	Negative	Interrogative
Sally used to live in Scotland.	Sally didn't use to live in England.	Did Sally use to live in Ireland?

1 Complete these facts with *used to* and the verbs in brackets.

1 The Toltecs from Mexico _____ (fight) with wooden swords so they didn't kill their enemies.
2 The Anglo Saxons _____ (kill) babies who were born on Friday.
3 Coca-Cola _____ (be) green.
4 Before 1687, clocks _____ (not have) two hands.
5 The *Mona Lisa*, now in the Louvre art gallery, _____ (hang) on Napoleon's bedroom wall.
6 Before 1820, Americans _____ (not eat) tomatoes because they thought they were poisonous.

2 Write the *used to* form of the verbs in brackets. Use the affirmative or negative, depending on the meaning.

1 We _didn't use to live_ (live) near the sea, but now we live on the coast.
2 I _____ (eat) unhealthy food, but now I eat a lot of crisps and chocolate.
3 This building _____ (be) a post office, but now it's an Internet café.
4 There _____ (be) a shopping centre in this town, but it closed last year.
5 I _____ (like) romantic comedies, but now I watch them all the time.
6 Our next door neighbours _____ (have) a BMW, but now they drive an electric car.
7 I _____ (do) my homework on time, but now I usually hand it in late.

3 Write questions and answers about Sam with *used to*.

	Now	10 years ago
1 have long hair?	Yes	No
2 wear glasses?	No	Yes
3 play the piano?	Yes	No
4 eat meat?	No	Yes

1 Did Sam use to have long hair?
No, he didn't.

4 Complete the sentences with *I used to* or *I'm used to*.

1 I lived in London for ten years, so _____ big cities.
2 I didn't like these glasses at first, but _____ them now.
3 I can speak Portuguese because _____ live in Brazil.
4 I'm disappointed with this exam result because _____ better marks.
5 I never go running now, but _____ .
6 The weather here is terrible, but _____ it.

2.3 Exclamatory sentences

We use exclamatory sentences beginning with *What …* or *How …* to react strongly to something.

We use *How …* with an adjective.
How strange!   How funny!

We use *What …* with a noun or an adjective followed by a noun.
What a meal!   What an incredible story!   What lovely clothes!

1 Choose the correct words.

1 My dad fell asleep in the middle of an interview!
   What / How funny!
2 I got lost in the centre of Tokyo.
   What / How a nightmare!
3 My uncle's house burned down in a fire.
   What / How terrible!
4 I keep getting text messages from somebody I don't know.
   What / How strange!
5 When I got home, there was a burglar in the kitchen.
   What / How a shock!
6 I failed all of my exams!
   What / How a disaster!
7 Why don't we have a party at the end of term?
   What / How a great idea!
8 My dad is going to buy me a new phone!
   What / How wonderful!

3.1 Defining relative clauses

Defining relative clauses come immediately after a noun and give vital information about that noun.
He's the doctor.
He's the doctor **who helped my grandmother**.

They can go in the middle or at the end of sentences. We do not use commas.
The man **who told me about this plate** was old.
I met the young woman **who cuts your hair**.

Defining relative pronouns are different depending on whether they refer to people, places, things or possessions.

Relative pronouns

who (that)	people
where	places
which (that)	things
whose	possessions

Who or *which* can refer to the subject or object of a sentence.

When they refer to the object, it is possible to omit *who* or *which*.

She's the girl **who** works here. (subject)
She's the girl **who** I met. (object)
She's the girl I saw on the bus. (object, omitting the pronoun)

We often use *that* instead of *which*. We can also use *that* instead of *who* in informal English.
Here's the book **that** you wanted.
Did you see the guy **that** kissed Mary?

1 Choose the correct words.

1 He's the police officer **who / whose** car was involved in an accident.
2 He works in the department **where / which** my aunt is in charge of.
3 That's the woman **whose / who** works a 60-hour week.
4 Jenny is the IT consultant **who / whose** fixed our computers.
5 She's the woman **who / which** applied for the cleaning job.
6 That's the building site **where / whose** my brother works.
7 Unskilled work is work **which / who** requires no qualifications.
8 India is the place **which / where** a lot of call centres are located.

2 Complete the sentences with relative clauses. Use the information below.

her company is really successful
~~my sister works there~~
the new hotel will be there
they make furniture
his job is to change texts from one language to another
they make microchips
they're researching climate change there

1 That's the theatre where my sister works .
2 She's the director _____ .
3 He works in a laboratory _____ .
4 That's the building site _____ .
5 Do you know any carpenters _____ ?
6 Tom works for an IT company _____ .
7 A translator is a person _____ .

Grammar Builder and Reference

3 Rewrite the two sentences as one sentence. Use *whose*.

1 That's the man. His name is Zack.
   That's the man whose name is Zack.
2 I met a girl. Her sister is in my class.
3 What's the name of the girl? Her cat died last week.
4 I know a boy. His mum works in the local supermarket.
5 There's a boy in my class. His first language is Italian.
6 Do you know anybody? Their parents are very rich.

3.2 Non-defining relative clauses

Non-defining relative clauses come immediately after a noun and give extra information about that noun.
Harrods is a famous department store.
Harrods, which is in Knightsbridge in London, is a famous department store.

Non-defining relative clauses give extra information which is not essential to the meaning of the main sentence.
The Times is a daily newspaper.
The Times, which is published in London, is a daily newspaper.

They can go in the middle or at the end of sentences, and start with a comma and end with a comma or full stop.
Abraham Lincoln, who was president of the United States in the nineteenth century, was shot whilst attending a play.
Kingston is the capital of Jamaica, which is an island in the Caribbean.

Non-defining relative pronouns are different depending on whether they refer to people, places, things or possessions.

Non-defining relative pronouns

who	people
where	places
which	things
whose	possessions

We cannot omit non-defining relative pronouns and we cannot replace *who* or *which* with *that*.

1 Combine the two simple sentences to make one complex sentence. Include a non-defining relative clause, either at the end or in the middle of the new sentence.

1 My sister works for British Airways. She's a flight attendant.
   My sister, who works for British Airways, is a flight attendant.
2 My aunt is a famous scientist. Her laboratory is at Cambridge University.
3 The head office of my dad's company is in Oslo. Oslo is in Norway.
4 Our accountant is retiring. I've known him for years.
5 I'm applying for a job in Glasgow. My cousin lives there.
6 A friend helped me to get this job. His mother is an IT consultant.

2 Invent relative clauses to complete the sentences. Use the questions to help you.

1 Steven Spielberg, who directed 'Schindler's List' , was born in the USA. (What did Spielberg direct?)
2 Italy, _____ , is in Central Europe. (What's Italy famous for?)
3 Champagne, _____ , is a very popular drink. (Where is champagne produced?)
4 Jennifer Aniston, _____ , starred in Friends. (Who is her ex-husband?)
5 10 Downing Street, _____ , is in the centre of London. (Who lives there?)
6 Madonna, _____ , was born in Michigan. (What does Madonna do?)

3 Complete each sentence with a different relative pronoun (*which*, *where*, *who* and *whose*). Then add commas if the clause is non-defining.

1 The man, ___who___ lives next door, is Tom's cousin.
2 This is Tod Garcia _____ comes from New York.
3 Is that the hotel _____ you stayed?
4 I like leisure centres _____ you can play squash.
5 Matthias _____ dad is German speaks four languages.
6 Who's the girl _____ sweatshirt you borrowed?
7 Where's the CD _____ I lent you?
8 My dad's car _____ he bought in 1995 has just broken down for the first time.

3.3 Question tags

We use question tags when we want someone to confirm something we are saying. A statement with a question tag often seems more polite than a direct question or plain statement.
You have experience working in a shop, don't you?

When the main verb is affirmative, the question tag is negative and vice versa.
You were at home, weren't you?
You weren't hungry, were you?

We use the verb *be*, auxiliary verbs (*do, have*) or modal verbs (*will, would*, etc.) depending on the tense of the verb in the statement.

Tense	Afirrmative	Interrogative
Present simple	You like cake,	don't you?
Present continuous	He's reading,	isn't he?
Past simple	She applied for the job,	didn't she?
Present perfect	He's left home,	hasn't he?
will	They'll be here soon,	won't they?
would	You'd like a coffee,	wouldn't you?

Grammar Builder and Reference

1 🎧 1.30 **PRONUNCIATION** Add question tags to the statements. Then listen, check and repeat.

1 You're hard-working and enthusiastic, _____?
2 He enjoyed the work, _____?
3 You've worked in a hotel before, _____?
4 The job involves dealing with customers, _____?
5 You wouldn't be able to start until May, _____?
6 Bar staff must do shift work, _____?
7 You won't tell anyone, _____?
8 You can drive, _____?

4.1 Past simple and present perfect contrast

We use the the past simple to talk about:
• completed events in the past.
  I visited my aunt last weekend.

We use the present perfect to talk about:
• how long current situations have existed.
  I've been at this school for six years.
• experiences which happened at an unstated time in the past (the exact time is not mentioned and is not important).
  My sister has met Brad Pitt.
• past events that are connected with the present.
  I've lost my watch. Have you seen it?
  Jane has already done her homework. Here it is.

We often use finished time expressions with the past simple (*yesterday, three months ago, last week, in 1999*), but unfinished time expressions with the present perfect (*for, since, already, just, yet*).
I went to Paris in 2006.
I haven't been to Paris yet.
She's been here since Tuesday.

We use *yet* and *already* with the present perfect when referring to the past. We use *already* with affirmative sentences. It goes before the past participle form or at the end of the sentence. We use *yet* in negative and interrogative sentences and it goes at the end of the sentence.
She's already left. / She's left already.
Have you eaten yet? No, I haven't eaten yet.

We use *just* to mean 'only', 'a second ago'. It is usually put before the past participle.
I've just finished my lunch. Have you just arrived?

We form the present perfect like this: *have / has* + past participle of the verb.

(There is a list of irregular past simple forms and past participle forms in the Workbook.)

1 Write the past participles of these verbs. Which ones are regular?

1 take	3 promise	5 write	7 finish
2 be	4 have	6 buy	8 mend

2 Complete the email with the present perfect of the verbs in exercise 1. Use the affirmative (✓) or negative (✗).

📧 **Inbox**

Hi Justin

I ¹_____ (✓) my history project at last! I ²_____ (✗) pages and pages – only about six pages, in fact. But it ³_____ (✓) a long time. I wonder if the teacher will like it. I ⁴_____ (✗) a great weekend. Too much work! In fact, I ⁵_____ (✓) at my desk all day today. Next weekend should be better. Dad ⁶_____ (✓) my bike, so I can use it again. And my brother Darren is talking about taking me to the music festival this year. He ⁷_____ (✗) the tickets yet, but he ⁸_____ (✓) to pay for mine!

3 Put the words in the correct order to make sentences with *just*, *already* and *yet*.

1 read / yet / haven't / I / book / that
2 brilliant / film / watched / just / I've / a
3 finished / they've / dinner / their / already
4 you / her / spoken / have / yet / to?
5 my / just / hospital / aunt / left / has

4 Complete the sentences using the past simple or present perfect form of the verb in brackets.

1 I feel better now that I _____ (have) a sleep.
2 My dad _____ (work) in a hospital for ten years between 1990 and 2000.
3 Manchester United are winning and Wayne Rooney _____ (score) twice.
4 _____ you _____ (lock) the door before you _____ (go) out?
5 Jenny isn't here; she _____ (leave) two minutes ago.
6 This town _____ (change) a lot since we _____ (move) here in 2004.
7 I _____ (never / meet) anybody as rude as you!

4.2 Present perfect continuous

We use the present perfect continuous to talk about:
• an action that began in the past and continues up to the present.
  I've been working for this company since 2002.
• an action which started in the past and lasted for some time. The result of the action is visible in the present.
  David has been playing tennis so he's really tired.

We form the present perfect continuous like this: *have / has + been + the -ing* form.

Grammar Builder and Reference

1 Complete the second sentence so that it means the same as the first. Use the present perfect continuous form of the verbs in brackets.

1 I got to the bus stop an hour ago and my bus hasn't arrived yet.
   I've been waiting for my bus for an hour. (wait)

2 I started guitar lessons years ago.
   _____ for years. (learn)

3 The rain started at midday and it hasn't stopped.
   _____ since midday. (rain)

4 We started this phone call an hour ago.
   _____ on the phone for an hour. (chat)

5 I started feeling ill on Saturday and I still feel ill.
   _____ since Saturday. (not feel well)

6 My dad fell asleep two hours ago and he hasn't woken up yet.
   _____ for two hours. (sleep)

4.3 Present perfect simple and present perfect continuous

We use the present perfect continuous to emphasise the duration of an action which started in the past. For finished actions we use the present perfect simple.

We have been living in London for twelve years. (We still live there now.)

They've lived in Moscow, Berlin and Madrid. (They don't necessarily live there any longer.)

How long is the most common time expression used with the present perfect continuous. *How often* or *how many / much* is usually used with the present perfect simple.

How long has she been sleeping?
How often have you worn that suit?
How many English lessons have you had?

When we use verbs describing a state or situation (e.g. *have, like, love, know*), we do not use the continuous form.

I've had an iPod for two years.

1 Complete one sentence in each pair with the present perfect simple and the other with the present perfect continuous.

1 *spend*
   a I can't afford that dress. I _____ all my money.
   b We _____ too much money recently – we should save more.

2 *have*
   a Americans _____ Thanksgiving dinners for hundreds of years.
   b I'm not hungry. I _____ my dinner.

3 *talk*
   a Look at the time! We _____ for hours!
   b I don't know Tom well, but we _____ on the phone once or twice.

4 *go out*
   a Ben and Sharon _____ a few times, but they didn't get on very well.
   b Shane and Karen _____ since the summer and are really in love.

2 Match 1–8 with replies (a–h). Then complete the replies with the present perfect continuous or present perfect simple form of the verbs in brackets.

1 Sorry I'm late.
2 Why is dad walking like that?
3 What's that funny smell in the kitchen?
4 You look really exhausted.
5 Why does Mum look so angry?
6 Some of these questions are very difficult.
7 Why are you looking so embarrassed?
8 Your sister's looking very healthy.

a I _____ (break) her laptop.
b I _____ (send) a text message to the wrong person!
c I _____ (wait) for ages!
d You _____ (do) the wrong exercise.
e I _____ (play) volleyball in the park.
f She _____ (eat) a lot of fruit and vegetables.
g Dad _____ (cook) again.
h He _____ (twist) his ankle.

5.1 Zero conditional

We use the zero conditional to talk about a result which follows a particular action.

If you click on that icon, it opens the email message.
If your hair gets wet, you feel cold.

We use the present simple to describe the action as well as the result.

Conditional clause	Result clause
If you **don't sleep** well, (present simple)	you **feel tired.** (present simple)

1 Use the prompts to make zero conditional sentences. Remember: the *if-* clause can come first or second.

1 most phones / not break / you / drop / them
2 you / push / this button / the light / come on
3 my dog / lie down / I / clap / my hands
4 cheese / melt / you / cook / it
5 you / turn around / lots of times / you / feel / sick
6 the alarm / ring / everybody / have to / leave

5.2 Speculating and predicting

We use modal verbs: *may, might, could* + base form to talk about events (situations) which could take place in the future.

I might go out for dinner tonight.

Grammar Builder and Reference

In negative sentences we use *may not* and *might not*, we do not use *could not*.
I might not go swimming next week.

We use *will* to predict. If we are not sure about our predictions we use *I think ...* or *probably*.
I think it will be nice tomorrow.

Predicting: first conditional

We use the first conditional to predict the result of a future action.
If global warming gets much worse, the climate will change.

We use the present simple to describe the action and *will* + base form to describe the result.

Conditional clause	Result clause
If scientists cure disease, (present simple)	people will live very long lives. (*will* + base form)

The conditional *if* clause can come before or after the main (result) clause.
Many people will have nowhere to live if the sea levels rise.

The modal verbs *may*, *might* and *could* can be used instead of *will* or *won't* in the result clause.
We may experience very hot summers in Europe if we don't do anything about global warming.

1 Write sentences using prompts and the expressions below. Choose the right expression depending on the probability.

will	→	will probably	→	could, may, might	→	may/ might not	→	probably won't	→	won't
100%		90%		70%		40%		10%		0%

1 it / snow / tomorrow (10% chance)
   It probably won't snow tomorrow.
2 I / pass / my exam (90% chance)
3 we / go on holiday / this summer (40% chance)
4 Cathy / say yes (0% chance)
5 my dad / buy me / a new bike (10% chance)
6 you / enjoy / this DVD (100% chance)
7 some friends / come round later (70% chance)

2 Complete the first conditional sentences with the correct form of the verbs below.

be   become   change   destroy   find   have   hit
live   program   not reduce   use

1 If the world's population _increases_ , our cities will ___be___ more crowded.
2 If a huge meteorite _____ the Earth it _____ everything.
3 If petrol _____ very expensive, people _____ their cars less.

4 If we _____ robots to do a lot of menial jobs, everybody _____ more time for hobbies and relaxation.
5 If we _____ carbon emissions, the world's climate _____ .
6 If scientists _____ cures for all major diseases, people _____ much longer.

5.3 Future perfect and future continuous

We use the future perfect for an action which will be finished before a stated future time.

NOW	hotel built	2025

By 2025, we will have built a hotel on the moon.

We use the future continuous for an action which will be in progress at a stated future time.

NOW		2030 living on moon

In 2030, we will be living on the moon.

We form the future perfect like this: *will* + *have* + past participle
By Friday afternoon, **we will have finished** all the exams.

(There is a list of irregular past simple forms and past participle forms in the Workbook.)

We form the future continuous like this: *will* + *be* + the *-ing* form
This time next month, I **will be sitting** on a beach.

1 Complete the sentences with the future perfect form of the verbs in brackets.

1 My exams are in March.
   By April I _will have finished_ my exams. (finish)
2 We're having dinner between 8 p.m. and 9 p.m. By 10 p.m., we _____ (have) dinner.
3 They're going away for a month on 1 March. By 7 April, they _____ (come) home.
4 I'm only staying in this house until the summer. By autumn, I _____ (move).
5 My dad is only planning to work to the age of 60. By the age of 63, he _____ (retire).
6 These flowers won't last more than a few days. By next week, they _____ (die).

2 Think about your own life one year from now. What will you have done? Tick (✓) or cross (✗) the things in the list. Then write sentences.

- finish this book ☐
- do some exams ☐
- buy a flat ☐
- get a job ☐
- have a birthday ☐
- leave school ☐
- start university ☐
- earn a lot of money ☐

A year from now, I will / won't have finished this book.

Grammar Builder and Reference

3 What will you be doing at these times? Complete the sentences with your own ideas. Use the future continuous.

1 At eight o'clock this evening, _____ .
2 At six o'clock tomorrow morning, _____ .
3 At nine o'clock tomorrow morning, _____ .
4 At midday next Saturday, _____ .
5 At midnight next Saturday, _____ .
6 At 11.59 p.m. on 31 December, _____ .

5.4 *will*, *going to*, *may / might*, present continuous and future continuous

We use *will* + base form for things we decide to do as we are speaking (instant decisions, offers, promises).
Bye John. I'll call you later.
That looks heavy. I'll help you carry it.

We use *going to* + infinitive or the future continuous for actions we have already decided to do in the near future (intentions).
I've already decided on Tom's birthday present. I'm going to get him a new mobile phone.
This time tomorrow, I'll be waiting for my exam to start.

If we are not sure whether something will happen or not we use *may* or *might*.

We use the present continuous for actions we have already arranged to do in the near future (plans).
We've booked the flight. We're flying to Barbados in February.

1 Choose the correct tense.

1 Liverpool **are playing / will play** Barcelona tomorrow. I bet **they'll lose / they're losing**!
2 I can't come to your barbecue next weekend. **I'll take / I'm taking** my driving test.
3 I love Lady Gaga. In fact, **I'll see / I'm seeing** her at a music festival next month.
4 **We'll go / We're going** to the Caribbean in November. Do you think the weather **is being / will be** good?
5 My parents **are going / will go** out tomorrow evening, so **we'll have / we're having** a party.
6 See you soon. **I'll send / I'm sending** you a text when I arrive.

5.5 Future time clauses

In future time clauses with *when*, *while*, *before*, *until*, *as soon as*, *the moment* and *after* which refer to the future, we use the present simple, not *will*.
I'll phone you **when** Peter arrives.
Sue will be doing her homework **while** we're at the party.
I'll go and get some popcorn **before** the film starts.
We won't make coffee **until** Fiona gets here.
They'll go home **as soon as** the match finishes.
Paula will kiss Tom **the moment** he walks through the door.
After school finishes, I'm going to go to the park.

1 Complete the sentences with *when* or *until*.

1 I won't speak to him _____ he apologises.
2 My dad wants to move abroad _____ he retires.
3 I'll phone you _____ I get home.
4 I probably won't get to the shops _____ it's too late.
5 Malaria will continue to kill millions _____ scientists find a cure.
6 I'm sure you'll remember him _____ you see him.

2 Complete the sentences with the correct form of the verbs in brackets.

1 I _____ you as soon as I _____ my results. (call / get)
2 I _____ the cat before I _____ the house. (feed / leave)
3 Jack _____ us when he _____ his plans. (tell / know)
4 I probably _____ home until I _____ 25. (not leave / be)
5 We _____ the lesson before Lucy _____ here. (start / get)
6 Ethan _____ his girlfriend while she _____ in Canada. (miss / be)

6.1 Reported speech (statements)

We use reported speech to report what someone has said without using their exact words.

When we change direct speech to reported speech, we usually change the verb form to go one tense back.
'Tom lives in Germany,' said Claire.
Claire said that Tom lived in Germany.

Direct speech	Reported speech
Present continuous ➔	Past continuous
'She's sleeping,' he said.	He said she was sleeping.
Past simple ➔	Past perfect
'He fell over,' he said.	He said he had fallen over.
Present perfect ➔	Past perfect
'We've won,' he said.	He said they had won.
can ➔	*could*
'She can swim,' he said.	He said she could swim.
will ➔	*would*
'They will be late,' he said.	He said they would be late.

- The pronouns often change.
  'I'm tired,' she said.
  She said she was tired. (*I* ➔ *he / she*)
  'We're upset,' they said.
  They said they were upset. (*we* ➔ *they*)
- Time expressions often change.
  'I saw Tom yesterday.'
  He said he had seen Tom the day before.

Grammar Builder and Reference

Direct speech	Reported speech
today	that day
tonight	that night
next week	the next week
yesterday	the day before
last month / year	the month / year before

1 Complete the reported speech with the correct verb forms.

1 'It's cold outside,' Helen said.
Helen said it _____ cold outside.
2 'I'm wearing a coat,' Jock said.
Jock said he _____ a coat.
3 'You're not wearing a hat,' Helen said.
Helen said he _____ a hat.
4 'I left it at home,' said Jock.
Jock said he _____ it at home.
5 'You can't go out without a hat,' said Helen.
Helen said he _____ without a hat.
6 'I won't be outside for long,' Jock said.
Jock said he _____ outside for long.

2 Rewrite the sentences in reported speech, using the correct time expressions.

1 'I was ill last week.' Agatha said _____ .
2 'I'm buying a new computer next weekend.' John said _____ .
3 'I can't go out for lunch today.' Anna said _____ .
4 'I'm not doing anything at the moment.' Tom said _____ .
5 'It will probably rain tomorrow.' I said _____ .
6 'We went to France for our holiday last year.' My grandparents said _____ .

3 Write these sentences in reported speech.

1 'I'm making pancakes for breakfast,' said Dad.
2 'I can't find my umbrella,' my sister said.
3 'We're moving to London,' my cousins said.
4 'I've seen *Batman Returns* five times!' said my brother.
5 'Chelsea played well, but lost,' said Rick.
6 'I'm taller than my brother,' said Maria.

4 Complete the sentences with *said* or *told*.

1 He _____ his girlfriend that he had rented a DVD.
2 She _____ him that she didn't like horror films.
3 He _____ that it wasn't a horror film, it was a thriller.
4 She _____ that some thrillers were very violent.
5 He _____ her that violent films were often exciting.
6 She _____ him that she didn't agree.
7 He _____ her that he would change it.

6.2 Reported speech (questions)

When we change direct questions to reported questions, the verb form often goes back one tense, pronouns change, and time expressions often change.
'Did you see the football match yesterday?'
She asked me if I had seen the football match the day before.

We usually use the reporting verb *ask* when reporting questions. In *yes / no* questions, we use the structure '(somebody) asked (me / him / them*, etc.) *if* ...'
'Did you go out?'
She asked me if I had gone out.

In *Wh-* questions, we use the structure (somebody) asked (me / him / them*, etc.) + question word (where, what, how*, etc.) ...
'Where did you go?'
She asked me where I had gone.

In reported questions the subject comes before the verb, and auxiliary verbs such as *do* or *did* are not used.
'What do you like?'
She asked me what I liked.

1 Complete the reported questions with the correct pronouns.

1 'What did you eat?' we asked our mum.
__We__ asked __her__ what __she__ had eaten.
2 'Why have you got my laptop?' Dad asked Sophie.
_____ asked _____ why _____ had his laptop.
3 'Did you forget about the barbecue?' we asked our friends.
_____ asked _____ if _____ had forgotten about the barbecue.
4 'Where have you been?' our friends asked us.
_____ asked _____ where _____ had been.
5 What time did you arrive home?' the policeman asked me.
_____ asked _____ what time _____ had arrived home.
6 'Did you finish your homework?' I asked Jack.
_____ asked if _____ had finished his homework.

2 Rewrite the sentences as reported questions.

1 'Are you listening?' the teacher asked her students.
2 'Why are you laughing?' I asked my sister.
3 'What did you do last night?' my best friend asked me.
4 'Can you speak Italian?' I asked my aunt.
5 'When will you get home?' my dad asked me.
6 'Is it raining?' my grandma asked.
7 'What's the time?' I asked my mum.
8 'How much money have we spent?' my friend asked me.

Grammar Builder and Reference

6.3 Speculating about the past

When we speculate about the past we use expressions like: *must have*, *could have*, *can't have*.

Must have is used when we are certain that something happened in the past.
The only place I haven't looked for my keys is the car. I **must have** left them there.

Can't have is used when we are certain that something did not happen in the past. This expression has the opposite meaning to *must have*.
I've checked the car – under the seats and everything. You **can't have** left your keys there.

Might have or *could have* are used when we aren't sure whether an event in the past happened or not.
Perhaps they're at home. I **could** / **might have** left my keys at home.

The phrases discussed above are formed like this: modal verb (*must*, *can't*, *might*, *could*) + *have* + past participle.

1 Complete the sentences with *must*, *might* or *can't*.
1 They _____ have gone home without telling us. I've got their train tickets!
2 I'm not sure where Sally is. She _____ have gone into town.
3 You _____ have seen the new Matt Damon film. It hasn't been released yet!
4 There's no bread. Somebody _____ have eaten it.
5 I sent Keith a text, but he _____ not have received it. He doesn't always carry his phone with him.
6 Susie _____ have been at school today. The teacher phoned and asked where she was.

2 Rewrite the sentences using *must have*, *might have* or *can't have*.
1 I'm sure Millie gave out the invitations.
Millie must have given out the invitations.
2 Perhaps Elizabeth went to the doctor's.
3 I'm sure Amelie didn't forget about the party.
4 Perhaps Tyler went on holiday.
5 I'm sure Archie missed the train.
6 Perhaps Alex fell off his bike.

6.4 Indirect questions

We make indirect questions with phrases like *Can you tell me ...?* *Do you know ...?* We use them to ask politely for information.
Excuse me. **Do you know** what time it is?

To make a *yes* / *no* question into an indirect question, we use *if*.
Could you tell me **if** the bus has left yet?

To change a question with the question word *wh-* to an indirect question we use the question word and change the form of the original question into a statement.
Would you mind telling me **where** the station is, please?

The word order and verb forms in indirect questions are the same as in a positive statement.
Do you know if **these jackets are in the sale?**

1 Rewrite the direct questions as indirect questions using the words in brackets.
1 How much is a single room? (Could you please let me know ...?)
Could you please let me know how much a single room is?
2 How many staff work here? (I'd be interested in knowing ...)
3 Is there Wi-Fi in the rooms? (I'd like to know ...)
4 Where's the hotel swimming pool? (I'd appreciate it if you could tell me ...)
5 When did my colleague leave? (I'd be interested in knowing ...)
6 Why did you take my passport? (Could you tell me ...?)
7 Is there another hotel near here? (I'd be grateful if you could tell me ...)

6.5 Verbs with two objects

Some verbs can be followed by both an indirect object (usually a person) as well as a direct object (usually a thing).

	[indirect object]	[direct object]
Peter gave	**Penelope**	**his keys**.

If we want the direct object to come first, we must put *to* or *for* before the indirect object.

	[direct object]	[indirect object]
Peter gave	**his keys**	to **Penelope**.
Peter cooked	**dinner**	for **Penelope**.

In English we avoid having a pronoun as a direct object at the end of the sentence.
Peter gave them to Sally.
(NOT – Peter gave Sally them)

1 Rewrite the sentences with the indirect object as a pronoun. Do not *use to* or *for*.
Mia's boyfriend made dinner for Mia last night.
Mia's boyfriend made her dinner last night.
1 Have you made a sandwich for me?
2 Tom's mum bought a new shirt for Tom.
3 Daisy owes £50 to her dad.
4 Beth's neighbour sold his car to Beth.
5 Patrick wrote a letter to his sister.
6 Scott sent a text message to Julie.
7 Dad booked a flight to Paris for us.
8 She showed her prize to her parents.
9 My uncle bought a new bike for me.
10 The hotel manager offered the best room to us.

Grammar Builder and Reference

7.1 Comparison (1)

The comparative and superlative of adjectives or adverbs with one syllable is formed by adding -er, and -est. We follow the same pattern with two-syllable adjectives that end in -y.

subject + verb	comparative form of adjective / adverb	object
John is	old (+ er) older	than Sue.
	slim (+ m + er) slimmer	
	busy (y + ier) busier	
John runs	fast + er faster	

subject + verb	superlative form of adjective / adverb
John is	(the) + old (+ est) the oldest
	(the) + slim (+ m + est) the slimmest
	(the) + busy (y + iest) the busiest
John runs	(the) + fast (+ est) the fastest

The comparative and superlative forms of adjectives or adverbs with two or more syllables are formed by adding *more* or *the most* before the adjectives or adverbs.

subject + verb	superlative form of adjective / adverb	object
John is	*more* + famous more famous	than Sue.
	more + popular more popular	
John talks	*more* + clearly more clearly	

subject + verb	superlative form of an adjective / adverb
John is	(the) + *most* + popular the most popular
John talks	(the) + *most* + clearly the most clearly

We can also form comparatives and superlatives of adjectives and adverbs with *less* and *the least*. *Less* is the opposite of *more*. *Least* is the opposite of *most*.

subject + verb	comparative form of adjective / adverb	object
Sue is	*less* + slim less slim	than John.
	less + famous less famous	
Sue talks	*less* + clearly less clearly	

subject + verb	superlative form of an adjective / adverb
Sue is	(the) + *least* + popular the least popular
Sue talks	(the) + *least* + clearly the least clearly

You need to learn the comparative and superlative form of irregular adjectives.

adjective	comparative	superlative
good	better	the best
bad	worse	the worst
far	further	the furthest

1 Use the prompts to make comparative sentences with *than*.
  1 Henry / passed his exams / easily / Philip.
  2 Ianthe / works / quickly / Emily.
  3 Joseph / drives / well / Zack.
  4 Andrea / sings / beautifully / Leah.
  5 Max / speaks / loudly / George.
  6 Victor / usually / arrives / late / Alice.

2 Complete the sentences with the superlative form of the adverbs in brackets.
  1 Geoff draws _____ (carefully).
  2 Andrew ran the 10 km race _____ (slowly).
  3 Jude always gets up _____ (early).
  4 Of all our class Matthew tries _____ (hard).
  5 Chris speaks French _____ (fluently) of all of us.
  6 Kate finishes her homework _____ (fast).

3 Rewrite the sentences using *less* or *the least*.
  1 Tracy and Pat are more intelligent than Emma. Emma is _____ of the three girls.
  2 Emma is more hard-working than Tracy. Tracy _____ Emma.
  3 Pat is more than popular Emma. Emma is _____ Pat.
  4 Ben and Isaac are more generous than Craig. Craig is _____ of the three boys.
  5 Craig is more confident than Isaac. Isaac is _____ Craig.
  6 Rome is less rainy than London or Paris. Rome is _____ of the three cities.

Grammar Builder and Reference

7.2 Comparison (2)

We often use the superlative form with the present perfect and *ever*.
It was the best holiday we've ever had.

Comparative adjectives and adverbs can be followed by either nouns or clauses.
Peter is taller than he used to be.

When we compare two things or people we can use *as ... as* to say that these things or people are the same.
Jill is as old as Julie.

To say that something becomes better, bigger or more expensive, etc. we use two comparative adjectives with *and* in between. Where we have a long adjective, we use *more and more* + base adjective or adverb.
It's getting more and more expensive to drive.

To express dependence of two elements in comparative form (e.g. *the longer I stay up, the more tired I will be tomorrow*) we use *the* + comparative adjective.
The more I see you, the more I like you.

1 **Put the words in the correct order to make comparative sentences.**

1 nearer / we did / than / to London / We live / before
2 was little / it was / as / His hair isn't / when he / long as
3 last month / That MP3 player / than / it / more expensive now/ was / is
4 ever / That's / I've / the best / seen / film
5 than / generous / used to / less / he / He's / be
6 used to / than / harder / work / you / You / now

2 **Complete the sentences with a double comparative.**

1 Jason is getting _thinner and thinner_ . (thin)
2 It's getting _____ to find a Job. (difficult)
3 Computers are getting _____ . (cheap)
4 Your French is getting _____ . (good)
5 Houses are becoming _____ . (expensive)
6 During the day it got _____ . (hot)

3 **Match the sentences halves.**

1 The more comfortable the bed, ...
2 The more he exercises, ...
3 The later it gets, ...
4 The more carefully you check your work, ...
5 The sunnier the weather, ...

a the fewer mistakes you make.
b the more tired I feel.
c the better I sleep.
d the more crowded the beach.
e the fitter he gets.

7.3 Second conditional

We use the second conditional to talk about situations that are unlikely or unreal. It can refer to the present or the future.
If I had a billion dollars, I'd live on a desert island.

We use the past simple in the *if* clause, and *would* + base form in the result clause.

Conditional clause	Result clause
If I had a billion dollars,	I would buy a castle.
(past simple)	(*would* + base form)

After *if* and *wish* we sometimes use *were* with *he* or *she*. Both *were* and *was* are correct. However, *were* is more appropriate in formal situations.
If I were you, I'd give the money to charity.
If he were older, he'd understand what I'm saying.

1 **Complete the second conditional sentences with the correct form of the verbs in brackets.**

1 I _____ (stop) seeing my boyfriend if he _____ (not get on) with my friends.
2 If my girlfriend _____ (go out) with another boy, I _____ (split up) with her.
3 If I _____ (fall out) with my boyfriend, I _____ (try) to make up.
4 I _____ (not chat up) a girl if I _____ (not fancy) her.
5 If I _____ (not be) so shy, I _____ (ask) her out.
6 I _____ (try) Internet dating if I _____ (have) a computer at home.
7 I _____ (not go out) with my best friend's brother if he _____ (ask) me.

7.4 *I wish, If only, I'd rather*

We use *I wish ...* or *If only ...* with the past simple to talk about situations we would like to change.
I wish it were summer.
If only I had a car.

We use *I wish ...* or *If only ...* + base form to say we would like somebody's behaviour to change.
I wish you wouldn't smoke.
I wish this machine would work.

We use *I'd rather* with a base form to express a preference.
'Do you want a cup of tea?' 'I'd rather have a coffee.'

We use *I'd rather* with the past simple to say that we want somebody's (or something's) behaviour to change.
I'd rather you didn't leave your bag there.

1 Write sentences with *I'd rather*.

1 I'm going to school tomorrow. (go shopping)
   I'm going to school tomorrow, but I'd rather go shopping.
2 We're having pizza tonight. (spaghetti)
3 Jason wants to watch a DVD. (listen to music)
4 I have to get up early tomorrow. (stay in bed)
5 We live in a flat. (house)

2 Write sentences with *I'd rather* to say you want these people's behaviour to be different. Use the words in brackets.

1 John wants to phone me after 10 p.m. (earlier)
   I'd rather John phoned me earlier.
2 Sarah wants to wear jeans. (skirt)
3 My brother keeps borrowing my bike. (use his own bike)
4 We haven't got much money left. (you / not spend it)
5 Kate wants to get a job when she leaves school. (go to university)

3 Complete the sentences about imaginary situations.

1 I haven't got a lot of money.
   If only I _had a lot of money_ .
2 Please don't open the window.
   I'd rather _____ open the window.
3 Please don't keep interrupting.
   I'd rather _____ interrupting.
4 I live in a small village.
   If only _____ in a big city.
5 I can't find my mobile phone!
   I wish I _____ my mobile phone!
6 We can't go to the beach because of the weather.
   If only _____ raining.
7 I can't stand it when you borrow things without asking.
   I wish _____ things without asking.

8.1 The passive

We make passive forms with the verb *be* + the past participle.

(There is a list of irregular past simple forms and past participle forms in the Workbook.)

Tense	Passive form
Present simple	Sweets **are made** of sugar.
Present continuous	A new supermarket **is being built**.
Past simple	Television **was invented** in 1926.
Present perfect	My car **has been repaired**.
Past perfect	The keys **had been lost** earlier.
Future with *will*	Your dress **will be cleaned** soon.

In passive constructions, we use *by* when we want to say who (or what) performed the action.
The jet engine was invented by Frank Whittle.

1 Complete the passive sentences.

1 The next Olympics __will be__ held in three months' time.
2 When I opened the fridge, I noticed that my chocolate bar _____ eaten.
3 How many jobs _____ lost since they introduced the new computer system?
4 Our house _____ burgled last night, but only a few things _____ taken.
5 Every year, hundreds of mobile phones _____ left in taxis.
6 Please keep the windows closed while your car _____ washed.

2 Complete the sentences using the passive form of the verbs below. Choose the correct tense.

kill   leave   publish   teach   use   follow

1 Her latest novel _____ next month.
2 The same currency _____ in about twenty European countries.
3 Alexander the Great _____ by Aristotle.
4 Last year, a CD containing top secret information _____ on a bus.
5 Over three hundred soldiers _____ by landmines since the conflict began last year.
6 Don't look now, but I think we _____ .

8.2 Indefinite pronouns

We form indefinite pronouns with *some-*, *any-* and *no-*.

people	someone / somebody
	anyone / anybody
	no one / nobody
places	somewhere
	anywhere
	nowhere
things	something
	anything
	nothing

We use pronouns with *some-* in affirmative sentences, and in offers and requests.
Somebody has eaten my lunch.
Can I do something to help?

We use pronouns with *any-* in negative sentences and in questions.
I haven't got anything to wear.
Did you meet anyone interesting?

We can also use pronouns with *any-* in affirmative sentences when we mean 'it doesn't matter who / what / where ...'.
Ask anybody round here and they'll help you.

We use pronouns with *no-* with affirmative verbs when the meaning is negative.

Nobody likes losing.

We use pronouns with *every-* in affirmative sentences and questions. They are followed by a verb in the third person singular.

Everybody wants to be successful.

Is everything ready?

1 Choose the correct words.

1 Why are you angry? I haven't done **anything / nothing** wrong.

2 There's **anybody / somebody** on the roof!

3 It's so simple, **anyone / someone** could do it.

4 **Anyone / No one** knows if aliens really exist.

5 Shall we start the meeting? **Everyone / Anyone** is here.

6 'What's the matter?' '**Anything / Nothing**. I'm fine.'

7 Have you seen my phone? I've looked **everywhere / nowhere**.

2 Use *some-*, *any-*, *every-*, and *no-* to complete the sentences in each group.

1 *-thing*

a Before you wash your trousers, check that there's _____ in the pockets.

b They lost _____ when their house burned down.

c I didn't buy _____ for lunch.

d My aunt has given me _____ to wear. It's beautiful.

2 *-where*

a Let's go _____ more private.

b There's _____ to sit on this train. It's really full!

c We never go _____ hot for our holidays.

d I hate going into town on Saturday _____ is so crowded.

3 *-body*

a Does _____ remember the way home?

b I think the shop is closed. There's _____ inside.

c I couldn't lift my bags onto the train on my own – _____ had to help me.

d Don't worry _____ makes mistakes sometimes.

8.3 Introductory *it*

We often use *it* at the beginning of sentences when we refer to time, weather, temperature, and distance.

It's seven o'clock.

It's Friday.

It took two days to travel from London to Australia.

It's sunny and it's 27 °C.

It's 100 km from here.

It is also used to avoid beginning a sentence with an infinitive or gerund (verb + *-ing*) or participle clause which would sound unnatural or very formal.

It's great being here. (= Being here is great.)

It's hard to say exactly what I mean. (= To say exactly what I mean is hard.)

It's a shame that she had to go home early. (= That she had to go home early is a shame.)

It doesn't matter where you go. (= Where you go doesn't matter.)

1 Match the sentences halves.

1 Is it far …

2 It took nearly an hour …

3 It has just started …

4 It's a shame …

5 Do you think it looks odd …

6 It seems impossible …

a to rain.

b to wear boots with shorts?

c to the nearest petrol station?

d to keep up with all the latest technology.

e to go home when you're having such fun.

f to drive five kilometres!

2 Rewrite the sentences to make them sound more natural using introductory *it*.

1 To do the housework took me over two hours.

It took me over two hours to do the housework.

2 What you wear for the party doesn't matter.

3 To bring an umbrella was a good idea.

4 To replace this watch is impossible.

5 That she passed her exams is great news.

6 To drive in this weather isn't sensible.

7 To walk to school takes ten minutes.

8 To swim in that river is dangerous.

9.1 have something done

We use the structure *have* + *something* + past participle to say that you arranged for somebody to do something for you. (You didn't do it yourself.)

I had my car cleaned last week.

You need to have your room redecorated.

We can also use this structure to talk about unpleasant events which have happened to us (which we didn't arrange).

I had my mobile phone stolen yesterday.

Grammar Builder and Reference

1 Complete the sentences with the correct form of the verb *have*.

1 I didn't repair my MP3 player. I ____had____ it repaired.
2 I haven't serviced my car. I _____ it serviced.
3 We aren't building a new house. We _____ a new house built.
4 I'm not going to clean the carpets. I'm going to _____ the carpets cleaned.
5 Did you cut down the tree or _____ you _____ it cut down?
6 We didn't make new curtains. We _____ them made.

2 Rewrite the sentences with the correct form of *have something done*. Don't change the tense.

1 Jessica hasn't restyled her hair.
Jessica _has had her hair restyled_ .
2 Harry won't remove his tattoo.
Harry _____ .
3 They didn't paint their house last year.
They _____ .
4 Sam isn't repairing his car.
Sam _____ .
5 Dave isn't going to install a new shower.
Dave _____ .
6 Sally didn't make the dress.
Sally _____ .
7 We're not going to build a new garage.
We _____ .

9.2 Reflexive pronouns

We use reflective pronouns when the object of the verb is the same as the subject.
He hurt himself.

Subject pronoun	Reflexive pronoun
I	myself
you	yourself
he	himself
she	herself
it	itself
we	ourselves
you	yourselves
they	themselves

We use reflective pronouns to put emphasis on the performer of the action.
They painted the bedroom themselves.

1 Write the correct reflexive pronouns.

1 Did Sally have her hair dyed?
No, she _dyed it herself_ .
2 Mum, did we have our house decorated?
No, we did it _____ .
3 Did your uncle have his flat cleaned?
No, he did it _____ .
4 Did you have your clothes ironed?
No, I ironed them _____ .
5 Do you have your nails painted?
No, I paint them _____ .
6 Did you and Mike have your bikes repaired?
No, we repaired them _____ .

2 Complete the sentences with the correct form of the verbs below and a reflexive pronoun.

burn   cut   help   hurt   talk   teach

1 Geoff is going to _____ _____ French.
2 '_____ _____ to more cake.' 'No, thanks.'
3 I _____ when I fell off my bike.
4 Mum _____ _____ while she was chopping the carrots.
5 'What did you say?' 'Nothing. I was _____ to _____ .'
6 The cooker's very hot. Be careful not to _____ _____ .

9.3 Third conditional

What would you have eaten last night if you'd had the choice?

I'd have eaten lasagne and garlic bread in my favourite restaurant. How about you?

The third conditional is formed by *if* + past perfect, *would have* + past participle.
If John **had arrived** earlier, he **would have seen** the start of the film.

We use the third conditional to speculate about the imaginary result of things which didn't happen.
If I'd driven faster, we would have arrived before six.

We often use it to express criticism or regret.
You would have passed if you hadn't been so lazy!
If I'd been more careful, I wouldn't have hurt myself.

We can also put the *if* clause after the clause describing the imaginary result.
I'd have invited you **if** I'd known you liked fancy dress parties.

The short form of both *had* and *would* is *'d*.
If I'd had more money, I'd have paid for you.

1 Write third conditional sentences. Start with the words in brackets.

1 The DVD player wasn't cheap. We didn't buy it. (If …)
  If the DVD player had been cheap, we would have bought it.
2 You couldn't afford the CD. You spent all your money on magazines. (If …)
3 We didn't buy the television. It wasn't in the sale. (We …)
4 Andy lost his receipt. He didn't get a refund. (If …)
5 Maisy didn't save her pocket money. She borrowed money from David. (Maisy …)
6 Philip didn't have a lot of money. He didn't lend Liam £10. (If …)

2 Use the prompts to write third conditional questions.

1 What / you / do / this morning / if / today / be / Sunday?
  What would you have done this morning if today had been Sunday?
2 What / you / eat / for breakfast / if / you / have / the choice?
3 Which country / you / visit / if / you / go away / last summer?
4 What / you / buy / last weekend / if / you / have / lots of money?
5 Which film / you / see / if / you / go / to the cinema / last night?
6 Who / you / visit / last night / if / you / have / the time?

3 Write answers to the questions in exercise 2.

1 *I'd have played computer games.*

10.1 Participle clauses

We use participle clauses to give more information about a noun. They can be described as shortened relative clauses (defining or non-defining).
*There's a woman **carrying a baby**.* (= who is carrying a baby)

They contain either a present participle (-*ing* form) or past participle.

• Participle clauses with a present participle (-*ing* form) replace an active verb. The verb they replace can be in any tense.
  *He worked in a shop **selling shoes**.* (= which sells shoes).
• Participle clauses with a past participle replace a passive verb. The verb they replace can be in any tense.
  *A valuable statuette, **made of gold**, will be sold tomorrow.* (= which was made of gold).

1 Rewrite the sentences replacing the relative clauses with participle clauses.

1 A painting which belongs to the Queen has been stolen.
2 These beautiful costumes, which have been worn by famous opera singers, are for sale.
3 The star of the show is an actor who is known by most people as a TV presenter.
4 It was difficult for people who were sitting at the back of the theatre to hear all the words.
5 I bought a copy of the novel that had been signed by the author.
6 This piece, which was written by my piano teacher, is one of my favourites.
7 The fast train, which leaves in five minutes, will get you to London in less than an hour.

10.2 Determiners

Each and *every* are followed by a singular countable noun. *Each* is used when all the people or things it refers to are seen individually. *Every* is used to refer to all the people or things.
Each egg is painted in different colours.
Every egg can be purchased for ten euros.

Few and *a few* are followed by a plural noun. *Few* has a negative meaning. *A few* has a neutral or positive meaning.
Few people came to the concert. It was very disappointing.
A few students stayed behind to help me.

Little and *a little* are followed by an uncountable noun. *Little* has a negative meaning. *A little* has a neutral or positive meaning.
People on this housing estate have little money and no future.
I have a little money – let's go out.

Many is followed by a countable noun. *Much* is followed by an uncountable noun.
There aren't many people here.
I haven't got much time to work.

All, *most*, *some*, *any*, *no* can be followed by either a countable or an uncountable noun.
Most people here have no free time at the weekend.
Some books are missing, but all the CDs are here.

We can use determiners with *of* before another determiner and a noun.
A few of my friends came to the party. (noun in plural)
All of the milk has been drunk. (uncountable noun)

When we use *no* and *every* with *of*, they change to *none*, and *every one*. We use a plural noun with *every one*.
Every one of the students passed the exam.

Grammar Builder and Reference

1 Choose the correct answers.

1 **Determiners with singular countable nouns**
The teacher gave **each** / **all** boy an exam paper.
'**No** / **Any** student should cheat in the exam,' she said.
'**Any** / **All** student caught cheating will be punished.'

2 **Determiners with plural nouns**
Few / **Little** people read poetry. We haven't got
much / **many** poetry books at home, but **each** / **most**
days I read **any** / **a few** poems.

3 **Determiners with uncountable nouns**
I didn't get **much** / **some** sleep last night. I drank
some / **a few** tea before bed, but **any** / **no** coffee.
I took a sleeping pill, but it was **little** / **few** help.

2 Choose the correct answers.

1 Nearly _____ ballet dancers retire in their thirties.
   a all   b all of   c every

2 Are you OK? You didn't eat _____ your lunch.
   a much   b most   c any of

3 There are _____ paintings in the exhibition,
   only photos.
   a none   b no   c any

4 The costumes are amazing. _____ of them was
   made by hand.
   a Each   b Every   c All

5 She threw _____ her sandwich on the ground for the
   birds to eat.
   a little   b a little   c a little of

6 The guests must have enjoyed the party, because
   _____ of them left before 2 a.m.
   a no   b none   c a little

10.3 *so* and *such*

We can use *so* or *such* to intensify the meaning of an adjective
or adverb.

be + so + adjective
I'm so happy!

so + adverb
They all ran so quickly.

such + adjective + noun in plural / uncountable noun
She's got such beautiful eyes / hair.

such + a / an + adjective + noun
She's got such an attractive face.

1 Complete the dialogue with *so* or *such*.

Jim	Do you fancy going to the cinema tonight?
Izzy	What time does the film start?
Jim	Nine o'clock.
Izzy	That's [1]_____ late! I need an early night. I'm exhausted.
Jim	Why are you [2]_____ tired?
Izzy	I went to Jack's party last night. I was having [3]_____ fun, I didn't want to leave!
Jim	But I don't really want to go to the cinema on my own. It's [4]_____ boring.
Izzy	Why don't you ask Emily?
Jim	I'm not sure she'd like this film. She's got [5]_____ good taste.
Izzy	But you thought I'd like it.
Jim	You like anything!
Izzy	Jim! You're [6]_____ rude.

10.4 Nominal subject clauses

We sometimes emphasise particular information in a sentence
by putting it in a *what* clause followed by the appropriate form
of the verb *be*.
We are looking for volunteers.
What we are looking for is volunteers.
I really like action films.
What I really like is action films.

1 Put the words in the correct order to make sentences.

1 a / need / I / What / is / laptop / new
2 saying / What / she's / is / missed / you / she
3 a / is / coffee / need / of / you / What / cup
4 a / they're / for / dancer / is / What / looking / good
5 spending / doing / they're / year / What / is / a / abroad

2 Complete the sentences with your own ideas. Then rewrite them starting with a *What*- clause.

1 I want _____ for Christmas.
   What I want for Christmas is …
2 I'd like to have _____ for dinner.
3 I enjoy _____ in my free time.
4 I usually wear _____ to school.
5 I'd like to _____ this summer.
6 I'm hoping to become a _____ .

Vocabulary Builder

1.1 Clothes

1 Label the clothes with the words below.

beanie   combat trousers   fleece   hoody   kagoul
leggings   miniskirt   platforms   polo shirt   roll-neck
sandals   v-neck

1 _____   2 _____   3 _____

4 _____   5 _____   6 _____

7 _____   8 _____   9 _____

10 _____   11 _____   12 _____

2 Match the pictures (1–12) in exercise 1 with the words (a–k) below.

a logo _2_   e laces ___   i strap ___
b drawstring ___ f sleeve ___   j zip ___
c cuff ___   g turn-ups ___   k button ___
d buckle ___   h collar ___

1.2 Compound adjectives

LOOK OUT!

A compound adjective is a single adjective made up of two or more words. These words are linked together with a hyphen to show that they are part of the same adjective.
short-sleeved   *blue-eyed*

1 Match each word in A with a word in B to make compound adjectives.

A	B	A	B
1 short	looking	6 sun	legged
2 broad	fitting	7 high	heeled
3 blue	shouldered	8 old	tanned
4 good	eyed	9 dark	fashioned
5 tight	haired	10 long	skinned

2 Complete the sentences with compound adjectives from exercise 1.

1 Soldiers in the army are normally short-haired .
2 That jacket is _____ . It must be at least twenty years old.
3 I don't like _____ jeans. I prefer them to be a bit baggy.
4 My brother is really _____ . All the girls in his class fancy him.
5 Don't wear _____ shoes to the nightclub. You can't dance in them.
6 People from Africa are usually _____ .
7 There's a _____ spider in the bath!
8 My brother has just spent two weeks lying on the beach in Spain. He's very _____ .
9 It's quite unusual for _____ people to have black hair.
10 A person with wide shoulders is _____ .

1.3 Adjective prefixes

1 Add the correct prefix: *un-*, *dis-*, *in-*, *im-*, *il-* or *ir-* to the words below.

1 ___ responsible   7 ___ believable
2 ___ mature   8 ___ credible
3 ___ tolerant   9 ___ friendly
4 ___ legal   10 ___ possible
5 ___ honest   11 ___ obedient
6 ___ literate   12 ___ rational

2 Rewrite the sentences using a prefix to give the adjectives the opposite meaning.

1 My mum's very patient.
My mum's very impatient.
2 My bedroom's quite tidy.
3 My writing's always legible.
4 My life is quite organised.
5 I eat at regular times.
6 I think I'm quite sensitive.
7 This chair is very comfortable.
8 This medical condition is reversible.

2.1 Noun formation from verbs and adjectives

The suffixes *-ment*, *-ion* and *-ness* are noun suffixes. We use *-ment* and *-ion* to form nouns from verbs, and we use *-ness* to form nouns from adjectives. The spelling sometimes changes.
disappoint (v)   *disappointment* (n)
hesitate (v)   *hesitation* (n)
happy (adj)   *happiness* (n)

Vocabulary Builder

1 Read the information in the *Learn this!* box. Use a suffix to form nouns from the verbs and adjectives below and write them in the correct column of the chart. Use a dictionary to help you if necessary.

confuse   depress   embarrass   enjoy   excite
irritate   kind   nervous   sad

-ment	-ion	-ness
1	1 confusion	1
2	2	2
3	3	3

2 Complete the sentences with nouns from the chart in exercise 1. More than one answer may be possible.

1 My dad, my brother and my sister all have first names beginning with 'D', which causes a lot of _____ when the post arrives.
2 After losing her job, she suffered from _____ for several years.
3 I'm not very good at tennis, but I get a lot of _____ from it.
4 Thank you for showing me such _____ . You were there when I needed you.
5 Imagine my _____ when I fell off my seat in the middle of the play!
6 I love going to football matches. You don't get the same _____ when you watch it on TV.

LOOK OUT!
Some related nouns and adjectives / verbs do not follow a simple pattern. Use a dictionary to help you learn these.

verb	adjective	noun
relieve	*relieved*	*relief*
shame	*ashamed*	*shame*
shock	*shocked*	*shock*

3 Read the *Look out!* box. Then use a dictionary to find the nouns related to these adjectives.

bored   guilty   jealous   pleased   proud   satisfied

2.2 -ed / -ing adjectives

> **LEARN THIS!**
> Adjectives ending in -*ed* usually describe how a person feels. A similar adjective ending in -*ing* describes what causes that feeling.
> *I was **bored** because the film was **boring**.*
> *This map is **confusing**. I'm **confused**.*

1 Choose the correct adjectives.

1 The match was really **excited / exciting**. Liverpool won in the last minute of the game.
2 I was really **shocked / shocking** to hear about your accident.
3 I can't get this new camcorder to work. The instructions are really **confused / confusing**.
4 I dropped all my books as I was going into class. It was very **embarrassing / embarrassed**!
5 Alistair is really **irritated / irritating**! He keeps talking when I'm trying to concentrate.
6 His parents were very **disappointed / disappointing** when they read his school report.

2.3 Phrasal verbs

> **LEARN THIS!**
> - Phrasal verbs consist of a verb and one or two prepositions. Some phrasal verbs are transitive, which means they are used with an object.
>   *We turned the music off.*
> - Other phrasal verbs are intransitive, which means they are used without an object.
>   *She stood up.*
> - Some phrasal verbs can be transitive or intransitive. Often, the meaning changes.
>   *The plane took off.   I took off my coat.*
> - Some phrasal verbs can have more than one meaning. The context will help you decide which meaning is correct or look in a dictionary.
>   *The protesters took on the police.* (= fought against)
>   *The restaurant took on a new waitress.* (= employed)

1 Use a dictionary to check the meaning of the phrasal verbs below. Then use each phrasal verb to complete two of the sentences (1–8). Use the past simple.

bring up   give away   put on   turn up

1 He was a millionaire, until he _____ most of his money to charity.
2 My grandparents were poor, but they _____ three healthy, happy children.
3 The teacher accidentally _____ the answer to the first question.
4 We _____ ten minutes late for the opera and they refused to let us in.
5 I _____ the TV when Lady Gaga started performing.
6 My brother was really embarrassed when I _____ the subject of his first girlfriend.
7 When I phoned my uncle, I _____ a different voice so that he wouldn't know it was me.
8 She stood up, _____ her hat and walked out.

Vocabulary Builder

3.1 Agent nouns

Agent nouns
We can use the following suffixes for people who do particular jobs or activities: *-er, -or, -ist, -ant, -ian.*
actor   journalist   manager
musician   shop assistant

1 Read the *Learn this!* box. Then complete the nouns below using suffixes. Use a dictionary to help you.

1 carpent___   12 optic___
2 archaeolog___   13 pharmac___
3 account___   14 fruit-pick___
4 child mind___   15 politic___
5 civil serv___   16 reception___
6 telesales operat___ 17 scient___
7 port___   18 social work___
8 electric___   19 software programm___
9 flight attend___   20 translat___
10 IT consult___   21 wait___
11 mathematic___   22 police inspect___

3.2 Useful phrases with *work*

work (verb)
1 *work* = function
   *This MP3 doesn't **work**. I think it's broken.*
2 *work out* = calculate; find the answer
   *I can't **work out** the answer to this sum.*
   *I can't **work out** why he did that.*
3 *work out* = train at the gym
   *Jason is very fit. He **works out** every morning.*
4 *work on* = try to improve
   *My son needs to **work on** his spelling. It's awful!*

work (noun)
1 *be out of work* = be unemployed
   *My dad's **out of work**. There aren't any jobs round here.*
2 *be off work* = not be at work because you are not well
   *My uncle's **off work** with a bad back.*
3 *get down to work* = start working
   *I've only got two hours to write this essay. I need to **get down to work**.*
4 *go back to work* = start work after a period away
   *She **went back to work** when her baby was a year old.*

1 Read the *Learn this!* box. Complete the sentences with a phrase with *work* in the appropriate form.

1 My mum decided not to _____ after she had had her first baby.
2 I dropped my mobile into a puddle of water and now it _____ .
3 Most industries have closed down in this area, so many people are _____ .
4 I quite like running or cycling to keep fit. But I hate _____ at the gym.
5 I can't _____ where that sound is coming from. Do you know?
6 Tom is _____ this week. He's got the flu.
7 Let's stop chatting and _____ . We've got a lot to do.
8 I can't really understand her. She needs to _____ her pronunciation.

3.3 Phrasal verbs: separable

1 Read the *Learn this!* box. Find two separable phrasal verbs in the fact file in exercise 4 on page 26.

Some transitive phrasal verbs are separable, which means there are two possible positions for the object.
*He took off **his jacket**.*
*He took **his jacket** off.*
However when the object is a pronoun, it always goes between the two parts of a separable phrasal verb.
*He took **it** off.*
He took off it.
Your dictionary will tell you if a phrasal verb is separable or not.

2 Rewrite the sentences putting the object in a different position.

1 My mum gave her job up last month.
   My mum gave up her job last month.
2 I'd like to set a business up when I leave school.
3 The company laid off twenty workers.
4 The manager decided to close the factory down.
5 Please fill in the application form.
6 The teacher gave out the exam papers.
7 Will you put away your things, please?
8 We worked the answers out by ourselves.

3 Rewrite the sentences replacing the underlined object with a pronoun.

1 My mum gave <u>her job</u> up last month.
   My mum gave it up last month.
2 The receptionist picked up <u>the phone</u>.
3 'Don't forget to put <u>the plates</u> away,' said the chef.
4 Don't forget to send <u>your application form</u> in.
5 The head waiter totalled up <u>the evening's takings</u>.
6 The secretary backed up <u>all the letters that she'd typed</u>.

3.4 Jobs and noun gender

1 Rewrite the sentences using a neutral word for each job.

1 The policeman arrested the shoplifter.
2 The air hostess served our food.
3 The manageress interviewed me for the job.
4 The chairman said the meeting would last half an hour.
5 Meryl Streep is one of the best actresses in Hollywood.
6 The spokeswoman explained the company's decision.

4.1 Inside the body

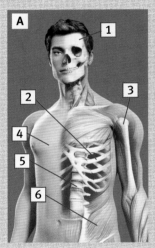 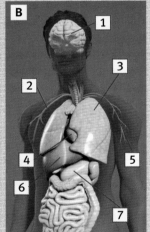

1 Match the parts of the body below with the pictures.

artery bone brain heart liver lungs muscle
ribs skin skull spine stomach vein

4.2 Food and nutrition

1 Choose the correct words in these sentences.

1 Lemonade contains a lot of **fibre / sugar**.
2 Bread, rice and pasta are forms of **carbohydrate / vitamins**.
3 Crisps and chips are usually high in **protein / salt**.
4 Brown rice contains more **fibre / sugar** than white rice.
5 Eating fresh fruit and vegetables provides you with **fat / vitamins**.

6 If you use more **calories / salt** than you eat, you lose weight.
7 Eggs, fish and meat all contain a lot of **carbohydrate / protein**.
8 Cheese, butter and cream contain a lot of **fat / sugar**.

4.3 Homonyms

1 Complete the definitions with the words below.

matter mind object show state treat trip turn

1 _____ :
   a short journey, there and back (n)
   to catch your foot and fall or nearly fall over (v)
2 _____ :
   a physical thing (n)
   to argue against something (v)
3 _____ :
   a performance (of a play, musical, etc.) (n)
   to bring somebody's attention to something (v)
4 _____ :
   something nice that makes a person feel good (n)
   to give medical attention to somebody (v)
5 _____ :
   your thoughts and memories (n)
   to feel unhappy about something (v)
6 _____ :
   the physical substance that things are made of (n)
   to be important (v)
7 _____ :
   a condition (usually temporary) (n)
   to say (a fact) (v)
8 _____ :
   the right time for you to do something (n)
   to move (something) round or over (v)

2 Complete each sentence using the same word twice. Choose from the homonyms below.

face fly land left park plant play study

1 We decided to _____ our car near the _____ .
2 Please _____ the audience and take your hands away from your _____ .
3 Which part did you _____ in the school _____ ?
4 The pilot had to _____ the plane on a thin piece of _____ near the lake.
5 He shut the door of his _____ and tried to _____ .
6 I want to _____ a tomato _____ in my garden.
7 I watched a _____ _____ in through the window.
8 She opened the door on the _____ and _____ the building.

Vocabulary Builder

4.4 Symptoms

1 Complete the chart with the correct phrases below.

a cough   backache   itchy   painful   shivery   sick

I'm feeling	
ill	light-headed
unwell	2 _____
1 _____	weak
dizzy	
I've got	
a headache	chest pains
earache	a stiff neck
stomach ache	4 _____
3 _____	a rash
a blocked nose	a pain in my [left side]
a runny nose	
My [thumb] is	
swollen	6 _____
5 _____	bruised
sore	numb

2 Complete the sentences with symptoms from the chart in exercise 1. Some of the sentences fit more than one symptom.

1 I'm feeling so _____ , I can't even carry my shopping bags home.
2 I've had _____ since I ate those prawns.
3 I've got _____ on my arm. Look, it's all red.
4 I can't smell anything. I've got _____ .
5 My right ankle is very _____ . Look, it's much bigger than the left one!
6 My shins are _____ after that football match. Look – they're black and blue!
7 I'm feeling _____ . Hold my arm, I'm going to fall over!
8 I can't turn my head to look at you. I've got _____ .
9 My back is _____ , can you scratch it for me?

5.1 Noun prefixes

<table>
<tr><td rowspan="7" style="writing-mode:vertical-rl">LEARN THIS!</td><td colspan="4">We can use the following prefixes to change the meaning of nouns.</td></tr>
<tr><td>mini-</td><td>small</td><td>co-</td><td>joint</td></tr>
<tr><td>multi-</td><td>more than one</td><td>pseudo-</td><td>not real or true</td></tr>
<tr><td>semi-</td><td>half</td><td>sub-</td><td>below</td></tr>
<tr><td>auto-</td><td>of or by yourself</td><td>ex-</td><td>former</td></tr>
<tr><td colspan="4">Your dictionary will tell you if you need to use a hyphen or if the noun and prefix are written as one word.</td></tr>
</table>

1 Read the *Learn this!* box and match the prefixes below with the nouns.

multi   mini   ex   auto   co   sub   semi   pseudo

1 biography
2 footballer
3 skirt
4 vitamins
5 zero
6 founder
7 science
8 conductor

2 Complete the sentences with the nouns in exercise 1.

1 My aunt only drinks water and takes _____ every day.
2 Pele is probably the most famous _____ in the world.
3 Mark Twain wrote an _____ that could only be published 100 years after his death.
4 Mark Zuckerberg is the _____ of Facebook.
5 Mountain climbers have to cope with _____ temperatures.
6 _____ first became fashionable in the 1960s.
7 Many people consider astrology to be a _____ .
8 Most _____ used in computers are made from silicon.

5.2 Verb + noun collocations

1 Complete the verb + noun collocations with the words below.

an announcement   the batteries   defeat   a fashion
help   patients   waste

1 reduce _____
2 treat _____
3 suffer _____
4 start _____
5 replace _____
6 provide _____
7 make _____

2 Complete the sentences with the verb + noun collocations from exercise 1. Use the correct verb form.

1 This remote control doesn't work. Maybe I should _____ .
2 Will Barcelona _____ at the hands of Chelsea?
3 You can _____ by reusing your plastic bags instead of throwing them away.
4 At PC Universe, we can _____ with setting up your computer.
5 One day, hospitals may refuse to _____ who don't give up smoking.
6 The company is going to _____ tomorrow about job losses.
7 Did Lady Gaga _____ for wearing shocking clothes?

Vocabulary Builder

6.1 Compound nouns (1)

1 Join the words in brackets to make compound nouns to complete the sentences. Use a dictionary to check if the compound nouns are written as one word or two.

Please put that _crisp packet_ in the _dustbin_ , not on the _flowerbed_ !
(bed bin crisp dust flower packet)

1 His _____ gave him a _____ as a _____ .
(birthday brush friend girl paint present)

2 Our _____ is playing _____ at the _____ next _____ .
(ball basket centre end history sports teacher week)

3 My _____ sits in his _____ playing _____ all day.
(bed computer games neighbour next-door room)

4 Can you go to the _____ and buy some _____ and some _____ , please?
(bags convenience jam store strawberry tea)

5 At this hotel, every room has an _____ on the _____ and a _____ in the _____ .
(alarm bath bedside clock room screen table TV)

6 The _____ in the _____ needs a new _____ .
(bulb desk lamp light living room)

2 Make three compound nouns for each of these words. Use a dictionary to help you.

1 sun _____ _____ _____
2 football _____ _____ _____
3 police _____ _____ _____
4 car _____ _____ _____
5 water _____ _____ _____
6 book _____ _____ _____

6.2 Easily confused words

Homophones
A homophone has the same pronunciation as another word, but a different spelling and meaning:
their and *there*, or *sea* and *see*.

1 Read the *Learn this!* box. Then find homophones of these words in 6.1 exercises 1 and 2.

1 flour _____   3 knew _____
2 weak _____   4 son _____

2 Circle the correct words.

1 I added too much **flour / flower** to the cake.
2 We went to Ireland by **plane / plain**.
3 Let's **meat / meet** in town at 5 o'clock.
4 **Bare / Bear** shoulders can easily get sunburnt in sunny weather.
5 Dad keeps all his wine in the **cellar / seller**.
6 I hope the cuts on my hands **heal / heel** quickly.
7 Children in some African countries have never known **peace / piece**.
8 This CD is a present. Can you **rap / wrap** it for me?
9 I don't want to spend the **hole / whole** day on the beach.
10 £200 for a pair of jeans? **You're / Your** joking!

6.3 Phrasal verbs: inseparable

Inseparable phrasal verbs
Some transitive phrasal verbs are inseparable. This means the object always goes after the particle, even if it is a pronoun.
I called on Katrina after school. OR
I called on her. NOT *I called her on after school.*
Common inseparable phrasal verbs include:
to do without (something)   to get in (a car, taxi, etc.)
to get on (a bus, train, etc.)   to get off (a bus, train, etc.)
to call for (something)   to stick to (a diet, etc.)
to count on (somebody / something)
to deal with (somebody / something)
to break into (a house, shop, etc.)

1 Complete each sentence with the correct form of an inseparable phrasal verb from the *Learn this!* box.

1 I hope I can _count on_ your votes at the next election.
2 Police are searching for the criminals who _____ our house.
3 I decided to go running every day, but it's hard to _____ that decision!
4 The racing drivers _____ their cars and drove off.
5 I couldn't afford to replace my phone, so I decided to _____ a phone altogether.
6 I _____ the bus too early and had to walk.
7 To be a good shop assistant, you must know how to _____ customers.
8 Some politicians have _____ a ban on fishing.

2 Rewrite the sentences in exercise 1 replacing the object of each phrasal verb with a suitable pronoun.

I hope I can count on them at the next the election.

Vocabulary Builder

7.1 Three-part phrasal verbs

Three-part phrasal verbs
Some phrasal verbs have more than two parts. These phrasal verbs are used with an object and they are inseparable.
run out of – *We've run out of milk.*
split up with – *Sam's split up with Becky.*

1 Read the *Learn this!* box. Complete the three-part phrasal verbs with the words below. Then match them to their meaning a–h.

down   on   on   out   out   out   up   up

1 get _____ with somebody
2 fall _____ with somebody
3 carry _____ with something
4 put _____ with somebody / something
5 look _____ on somebody
6 walk _____ on somebody
7 look _____ to somebody
8 go _____ with somebody

a be someone's girlfriend / boyfriend
b think you are better than somebody
c have a good relationship with somebody
d continue with something
e leave (your partner or family) suddenly
f have an argument with somebody
g tolerate somebody / something
h admire somebody

2 Complete the sentences with the correct form of the three-part phrasal verbs in exercise 1.

1 I _____ my grandfather because he fought for his country in the Second World War.
2 He _____ people just because they are less intelligent than him.
3 Mr Thompson _____ his wife and children and ran off with his secretary.
4 Jake _____ very well _____ Martha. They're always together.
5 I don't know how Sam _____ Felicity. She's so bad-tempered!
6 'When did Chris start _____ Hannah?' 'At Easter, I think.'
7 I'm going to _____ French next year, but I'm going to give up German.
8 Kate isn't speaking to David. I think she _____ him.

7.2 Idioms with *heart* and *head*

1 Match the idioms (1–10) with the meanings (a–j).

1 set your heart on something
2 lose heart
3 break somebody's heart
4 off by heart
5 take something to heart
6 head first
7 head over heels in love
8 laugh your head off
9 have a head for heights
10 a head start

a become discouraged
b be upset by something
c decide you want something very much
d from memory
e make somebody very sad
f be able to stand in high places without fear
g with your head before your body; too quickly
h laugh for a long time
i an advantage that you have before you start doing something
j deeply in love

2 Complete the sentences with idioms from exercise 1. Remember to change the pronouns where necessary.

1 I know a few poems _____ . I learned them when I was at primary school.
2 Josh got divorced and rushed _____ into a new relationship.
3 Don't _____ ! He was only joking when he said he didn't like your new hairstyle.
4 George is determined to be a doctor. He _____ going to medical school.
5 I _____ when John fell into the swimming pool. It was so funny!
6 We're losing 1–0 at half-time. But we mustn't _____ . I'm sure we'll score a goal in the second half.
7 I couldn't move when I reached the top of the tower. I just don't _____ .
8 Poor Karen! It _____ when Dan walked out on her.
9 She's got _____ when it comes to learning English because she spent a year in the USA.
10 They are _____ . They're completely inseparable.

Vocabulary Builder

8.1 Travel and transport

1 Complete the mind map with the words below. Some of the words can be used more than once.

nouns aisle cabin captain carriage driver
flight attendant luggage rack overhead lockers
platform runway tracks ticket inspector turbulence

verbs arrive board disembark land set sail take off

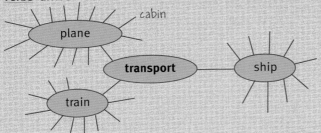

cabin

plane

transport

ship

train

2 Complete the sentences with words from exercise 1.

1 You need to put your bags in the _____ before the plane _____ .
2 The ship _____ at 11 p.m.
3 Passengers who _____ a train at a small station often need to buy their ticket from the _____ .
4 The _____ told the passengers he was going to fly higher to avoid some _____ .
5 It's very dangerous to walk across the _____ to the opposite _____ to get onto your train.
6 I asked the _____ if I could move to a seat next to the _____ .

8.2 Phrasal verbs: review

1 Find the phrasal verbs from the chart below in the text on page 76. Then complete the chart by writing a) or b) in each column. If necessary, check the sections on phrasal verbs on pages 129, 130, 133 and 134 of the Vocabulary Builder.

	a) transitive b) intransitive?	a) separable b) inseparable?	a) 2-part b) 3-part?
date back (line 1)			
set off (line 2)			
look up to (line 3)			
get about (line 7)			
come across (line 15)			
give up (line 19)			
end up (line 28)			

2 Complete the sentences with phrasal verbs from exercise 1. Use a suitable tense.

1 Are we nearly there yet? We _____ hours ago!
2 I'm sure we _____ some interesting people when we travel around Mexico next month.
3 We planned to camp, but we _____ staying in a hotel because the weather was so bad.
4 Some parts of this house _____ the fifteenth century.
5 In rural areas, it's often difficult to _____ without a car.
6 After waiting two hours for the bus, we _____ and went home.
7 I really _____ people who always go on environmentally friendly holidays.

8.3 Acronyms

1 🎧 3.07 **PRONUNCIATION** Read the *Learn this!* box. Listen and repeat all the acronyms. Do you know any more?

> **LEARN THIS!**
>
> 1 Acronyms are formed from the first letter of each word in a phrase.
> *USA* (United States of America) *UK* (United Kingdom)
> *CD* (compact disc) *GM* (genetically modified)
> *UFO* (unidentified flying object)
> 2 Usually, you pronounce an acronym by naming the letters. However, some acronyms are pronounced as words:
> *AIDS* (acquired immune deficiency syndrome)
> *NATO* (North Atlantic Treaty Organisation)
> *NASA* (National Aeronautics and Space Administration)
> *RAM* (random access memory)
> 3 A few acronyms are pronounced as a mixture of letters and words:
> *JPEG* *CD-ROM*

2 Complete the sentences with acronyms from the *Learn this!* box. Read the sentences aloud.

1 Some people refuse to buy food that contains _____ crops.
2 I've got 500 photos stored on my phone as _____ files.
3 We crossed the border from Mexico to the _____ near Monterrey.
4 My uncle claims that a _____ landed in his garden one night.
5 Scientists hope to develop new drugs to fight _____ .
6 _____ is planning to send a manned spacecraft to Mars before 2030.
7 My laptop only has 512 MB of _____ .
8 Ben Nevis, in Scotland, is the highest mountain in the _____ .

Vocabulary Builder

9.1 Banking

1 Check the meaning of the words below. Then use them to complete the text.

Banking   branch   cash machine   cheque book
current account   debit card   Internet banking   interest
PIN number   salary   savings account

I left school in July and got my first job. I immediately opened a ¹_____ and arranged for my ²_____ to be paid in every month. I also opened a ³_____ , which pays good ⁴_____ – about 5% a year. I chose a bank that has a ⁵_____ in my town but that also has ⁶_____ , as I'd like to manage the accounts online. I was given a ⁷_____ (though I don't think I'll write many cheques), and a ⁸_____ , which I can use to pay for things online or over the phone. I also received a four-digit ⁹_____ which I have to enter when I withdraw money from a ¹⁰_____ .

9.2 Advertising

1 Match the nouns and verbs below with the definitions. Use your dictionary to help you.

nouns   banner ad   billboard   brand   consumer   flyer
jingle   logo   pop-up ad   slogan   trailer

verbs   to launch   to promote   to purchase

1   a very large board used for advertising
2   short clips from a film or TV programme, used to advertise it
3   to buy
4   a person who buy things
5   a short piece of music used in an advert
6   a small piece of paper used for advertising
7   a product made by a particular company
8   a short phrase that is easy to remember, used for advertising
9   to make people aware of a product or service
10 an advert that opens in a new window when you visit a website
11 symbol or design used by a company to identify it
12 long, narrow advertisement on a website
13 to start selling a new product

9.3 Preposition + noun phrases

Preposition + noun phrases
Some nouns are used in expressions with a fixed preposition.
by cheque   in cash   on foot

1 Read the *Learn this!* box and complete the phrases with the prepositions below.

at   by   for   from   in   on   out of   under

1	_____	fun nothing a change	5	_____	first sight university (his) own expense
2	_____	chance mistake accident	6	_____	control (her) breath investigation
3	_____	holiday business purpose a diet	7	_____	touch luck work
4	_____	trouble a mess the end	8	_____	A to Z scratch memory

2 Complete the sentences with preposition + noun phrases from exercise 1. Use one phrase from each group.

1   Jason has been _____ . He's lost a lot of weight.
2   She told her friend the answer _____ so that the teacher couldn't hear.
3   I didn't mean to leave my bag at school. I did it _____ .
4   Toby's room is always _____ . He never tidies or cleans it.
5   My uncle has been _____ for three months. I hope he finds a job soon.
6   I lost all the notes I had made for my essay, so I'll have to start again _____ .
7   We usually go to France in the summer, but last year we went to Italy _____ .
8   Sue and Martin met at my party. It was love _____ . They've been going out ever since.

Vocabulary Builder

10.1 Artists and artistic activities

1 Complete the chart with the words below.

does draws fiction ~~gives~~ makes plays (verb)
plays (noun) poetry role screenplays sings stages
stars writes

Music	
A musician	plays an instrument.
	¹ gives a recital / a concert / a performance.
	performs / ² _____ a piece.
A composer	composes / ³ _____ music.
A singer	performs / ⁴ _____ a song / an aria.
A conductor	conducts an orchestra.

Visual arts	
An artist / A painter	paints a picture / a painting / a portrait.
	⁵ _____ a picture.
	⁶ _____ a sketch.
	creates a work (of art).
A sculptor	creates / ⁷ _____ / sculpts a work / a sculpture / a piece / a bust.

Literature	
A novelist	writes novels / ⁸ _____ .
A writer	writes novels / books / short stories.
A poet	writes poems / ⁹ _____ .
A playwright	writes ¹⁰ _____ / tragedies / comedies.
A scriptwriter	writes ¹¹ _____ (for films).

Drama and film	
An actor / actress	acts in / appears in / performs in / ¹² _____ in / has a ¹³ _____ in a play / a production / a film / a musical.
A director	directs a play / a production / a film / a musical.
A drama company	¹⁴ _____ / puts on / performs a play / a production / a musical.

10.2 Compound nouns (2)

1 Complete the compound nouns in the sentences with the nouns below. There are two nouns that you do not need.

camp dance goers festival headline line mainland
lover shuttle

1 We stayed at a great little _____ site near Venice.
2 Stevie Wonder was the _____ act at the Glastonbury Festival in 2010.
3 The roads leading to Glastonbury were jammed with festival _____ .
4 The _____ up at the Rock Werchter festival this year was amazing.
5 We caught a _____ bus from the station to the festival.
6 We're going to take our holiday on _____ Europe this year.
7 You don't have to be a music _____ to enjoy a music festival. There are lots of other things to see and do.

10.3 Describing books

1 Check the meaning of the adjectives below. Then match them with the aspects of a book which they describe.

colloquial detailed fast-moving likeable surprising
urban

plot	complex / ¹ _____ / believable / gripping
ending	satisfying / puzzling / moving / thrilling / ² _____
setting	familiar / unusual / futuristic / rural / ³ _____
descriptions	⁴ _____ / beautiful / fascinating / dull
characters	convincing / two-dimensional / ⁵ _____
dialogue	⁶ _____ / realistic / funny

2 Choose the correct adjectives.

1 I didn't identify with the characters because they were all so **convincing / two-dimensional**.
2 It was a gripping story, and the end was very **fast-moving / surprising**.
3 I enjoyed reading the **fascinating / dull** descriptions of ordinary life in the nineteenth century.
4 The author is in his fifties, and as a result, some of the dialogue between teenagers isn't very **realistic / funny**.
5 It wasn't clear at the end whether the hero had died or not. I really don't like **puzzling / thrilling** endings!